Fragments from Anti

B

Social Archaeology

General Editor
Ian Hodder, University of Cambridge

Advisory Editors
Margaret Conkey, University of California at Berkeley
Mark Leone, University of Maryland
Alain Schnapp, U.E.R. d'Art et d'Archéologie, Paris
Stephen Shennan, University of Southampton
Bruce Trigger, McGill University, Montreal

Published

FRAGMENTS FROM ANTIQUITY
An Archaeology of Social Life in Britain, 2900–1200 BC
John C. Barrett

ENGENDERING ARCHAEOLOGY
Edited by Joan M. Gero and Margaret W. Conkey

EXPLANATION IN ARCHAEOLOGY
Guy Gibbon

IRON-AGE SOCIETIES
Lotte Hedeager

THE DOMESTICATION OF EUROPE
Ian Hodder

THE ARCHAEOLOGY OF INEQUALITY
Edited by Randall H. McGuire and Robert Paynter

MATERIAL CULTURE AND MASS CONSUMPTION
Daniel Miller

READING MATERIAL CULTURE
Edited by Christopher Tilley

In Preparation

THE RISE OF MESO-AMERICA
Elizabeth Brumfiel

SOCIAL THEORY AND SOCIAL CHANGE
Christopher Gosden

AN ARCHAEOLOGY OF CAPITALISM
Matthew Johnson

THE ARCHAEOLOGY OF DEMOCRACY
Ian Morris

READING ARCHAEOLOGY
Christopher W. Tilley

FEMINIST ARCHAEOLOGY
Alison Wylie

Fragments from Antiquity

An Archaeology of Social Life in Britain,
2900–1200 BC

John C. Barrett

BLACKWELL
Oxford UK & Cambridge USA

Copyright © John C. Barrett 1994
The right of *John C. Barrett* to be identified as author
of this work has been asserted in accordance with the
Copyright, Designs and Patents Act 1988.

First published 1994

Blackwell Publishers
108 Cowley Road
Oxford OX4 1JF
UK

238 Main Street
Cambridge, Massachusetts 02142
USA

British Library Cataloguing in Publication Data
A CIP catalogue record for this book is available from the British Library.

Library of Congress Cataloging-in-Publication Data
Barrett, John C.
    Fragments from antiquity: an archaeology of social life in
Britain, 2900–1200 BC / John C. Barrett.
        p.   cm. – (Social archaeology)
    Includes bibliographical references and index.
    ISBN 0-631-18953-X (hb). – ISBN 0-631-18954-8 (pbk.)
    1. Man, Prehistoric – Great Britain.   2. Social archaeology – Great
Britain.   3. Great Britain – Antiquities.   I. Title.   II. Series.
GN805.B37 1993
936. 1 – dc20   92-45628
                                                                    CIP

Typeset in Gararmond on 11/13 pt by Best-Set Typesetters
Printed in Great Britain by T.J. Press (Padstow) Ltd., Padstow, Cornwall.

This book is printed on acid-free paper

To my father and the memory of my mother

Contents

Preface

It has taken me more than five years to write this book. During that period I have benefited from many discussions with friends, colleagues and students, and I am grateful to them all for the generosity which they have shown me, with both their time and their ideas.

A number of people have also commented upon earlier drafts of either all or parts of the text, and I am grateful to Barbara Bender, Richard Bradley, Ann Clark, Mark Edmonds, Shannon Fraser, Iain MacKenzie, Stephen Shennan and Bruce Trigger for their guidance.

Robin Boast, Roy Entwistle and Keith Ray allowed me to read their unpublished doctoral dissertations, while Alasdair Whittle made available his report on the excavations at Silbury Hill prior to its publication.

Roger Thomas helped with the photography and Lorraine McEwan produced all the line drawings. Ian Hodder's kindness and support as General Editor, and John Davey's enthusiasm and efficiency at Blackwell made the final stages of writing more pleasurable than I had assumed they could be.

This book has been written in the company of Kathy, Helen and Shona.

Glasgow, September 1992

Allant Travailler (Going to Work) by J. F. Millet. (Copyright: Hunterian Art Gallery, University of Glasgow)

Introduction

This book was in the final stages of preparation when I read about the discovery of the frozen and dehydrated corpse of a young man who died in the Alps some five thousand years ago. The degree of preservation is such that, to this day, we can still gaze into his face. The publicity which has surrounded the find is an indication of the way archaeological discoveries can surprise and excite us. The remarkable preservation is an obvious reason for this; skin, hair, clothing and wood have all survived, but the preservation gives us more than just a view of the unusual and the bizarre. Perhaps it also gives us a feeling of intimacy in our encounter with this one life, a recognizable human being who has strayed into our world with his possessions, from a journey overtaken by exhaustion and the closing in of the weather. Even his final thoughts seemed present for one mountaineering commentator who claimed that the traveller 'knew he would die'. This small tragedy can touch emotions in us all.

A characteristic of modern archaeological writing is to avoid such intimacies. We produce more generalized histories, not of 'people' but of 'processes', which place this or any other life in a larger context of economic and settlement systems, or in the mechanisms of social evolution. These layers of generalization have the effect of finally burying the individual, a move in archaeological writing which creates an unbridgeable distance between our own images of the past and the subjective and local intimacies of people's own lives as they were once lived. The move towards generalization seems to be the only realistic response for archaeology, given that our evidence is made up of residues whose regularities, as we understand them, appear to be the consequences of repeated and long-term processes and not the result of individual actions. Indeed, the strength of archaeology is often claimed to be its ability to write the histories of the long-term which subsume the momentary and idiosyncratic event.

Although this book is about a different part of Europe, it does cover the period during which our Alpine traveller died. It is also about the contrast which we recognize between such lives when seen as individual, subjective, local and fleeting, and the conditions which those lives once inhabited, described as the long-term processes characteristic of social and economic institutions. It appears that the contrast simply reflects the nature of our data, different scales of analysis revealing different cycles of historical time, ranging from the short-term histories of moments, events and individual lives, to the medium-term cycles of economic and political process and, finally, to the long-term, underlying currents of natural evolution and ecological change. How the archaeologist moves between these different temporal layers appears to be a methodological question; it concerns how different types of data are selected and deployed in different kinds of historical narrative. But it also raises questions about the structural and determinate relationships which operated across each of these layers of time. Sometimes the events of history appear as conjunctures which arose when deeper, underlying processes broke to the surface at moments of transformation. At other times we read of structural histories in which the structures operated as 'envelopes' containing, and largely determining, the form of the more superficial and shorter-term routines.[1] In either case the sense is maintained of an ultimate determinacy working from the bottom, deeper, structures up to the more superficial, momentary history of event and of individual life.

Such a model of history, with its geological metaphor of deep-seated, fundamental processes and of surface events, justifies current archaeological concerns with the general and the long-term over the particular, local and momentary. From this perspective, the death of a single mountain traveller around 3000 BC can do no more than exemplify the routines of a popula- tion whose activities were determined by *structures* of social and economic organization operating within some given environmental context. Notice how it is the archaeologist who 'unearths' these deeper, determinate struc- tures, which were already in place and which seem to have been operating behind the individual's motivations and desires.

The object of study that has emerged from this generalizing, or processual, approach to archaeology is the 'social totality'. This totality is described in terms of its fundamental organizing principles (its 'structure'). We employ various labels to identify the totality – *society* is perhaps that most com- monly used – and we distinguish between the organizing principles of differ- ent types of *social organization* or *social structure*. The aim of this book is to argue against working at this level of generality, against general models of society, and thus against the current archaeological consensus. At base it argues against the dichotomy which has been erected between life as lived in the immediate and the short term, and the history of long-term social institutions.

We must be careful about the significance of the point that is being made here. I am not arguing that we should choose between incompatible alternatives, rejecting a history of general processes for one of individual and particular moments. Nor is it my point to argue that both levels of historical analysis, the general and the particular, should exist side by side as a kind of dualism where the task of historical analysis is to shift its focus of attention between these 'levels', or to investigate how one 'level' determined or structured the other. Both approaches would preserve the dualism which is itself the problem, and both would also preserve the image of a linear causality operating between one level and another. My point is that it is the relationship *between* structure and event which must be rethought if we are going to understand how events, such as that ill-fated journey into the Alps, reworked the structural conditions which gave them their significance. Giddens has argued that this is to think in terms of a duality where certain orientated actions and events permeate deeply into the historical world as social structures.[2] We must consider the conditions which enabled certain events to reach out in this way to extend deeply though time and space. This requires that we recognize, in the fleeting and the momentary occurrences of human action, the expectation that those actions were appropriate and would be effective, that they made sense according to some recognizable order and logic in the world which they addressed and to which they also contributed. Structures are both the means by which socially recognizable actions are achieved, and their consequences.

One way in which the false dualism between a long-term 'structural' history and the short-term 'event' is often expressed is in terms of how we might think about the place of the individual's life within the history of any particular social formation. Brief in its duration, that life was lived according to desires, emotions and understandings, and according to convention. To what extent then is human agency either the expression of a free will, directed to optimizing rationally identified interests, or the product of determinate forces? Indeed, if we can talk about particular social formations without reference to the social agents who inhabited them, then do these lives matter at all?

We can begin to think our way out of this dilemma from an archaeological prespective. The individual life, as an object of archaeological research, is not generally taken to be concerned with the constitution of human agency as knowledgeable, creative and motivated. Instead it is an issue of research reduced simply to a methodological problem: to what extent can the material record trace the biography of an individual? This priority given to methodology arises because all archaeological enquiry normally proceeds by asking first, 'what actions in the past created the residues which I see before me today?', and second, 'what was it which determined the form and the organization of those actions?' Answers to the second question are taken as 'explanations' concerning the general determinates (either social or natural) which ultimately formed the 'archaeological record'. The answer to the methodological question of how we might recognize an individual's life is therefore predictable. We may recognize the hand of a single vase painter on a number of vessels, or we may observe the consequences of the actions and the policies instigated by some named individual whose name may even be inscribed upon the material record itself. The individual's life is regarded as recognizable in the record only as a repeated presence or as a biographical trace; the hand seen not on one vessel but on many, the monuments and the biography of some emperor, and so on. It is as if individuals had to be written into existence upon a material record for them to become archaeologically recoverable. Needless to say, for most areas of archaeological work, this repeated presencing of a single life simply cannot be recognized: we may find the debris from one flint-knapping event, for example, but we will never know if we were to meet the consequences of that same individual's actions elsewhere in another material context. We are also left with the problem of deciding how we are to situate the individual's biography within the more general processes; all too often we will regard the biography as the passive medium through which those processes had once operated. Clearly, the individual is not an analytically useful unit of archaeological study, and this much is indeed true.

In these rather trivial terms, individuals are taken as given, pre-existing the material consequences of their actions. The link between the action and its residue appears to be the object of archaeological enquiry. My case will be that we should abandon this whole approach and begin instead to investigate the more interesting questions concerning the ways in which lives were constituted as knowledgeable and motivated. This will demand an understanding of how, in any particular period, the lives of people were created by their engagement upon those material conditions which the archaeologist is also able to investigate. It is the *creation of people as subjects*, and not simply the creation of material things, which will be the object of our archaeological enquiry. This realignment in archaeological research will require us to accept that all human consciousness is contingent upon historical and material conditions, a position which further necessitates that we introduce the concept of *agency* into our analysis. Agency is the means of knowledgeable action, and is not reducible simply to the actions of the individual. Through agency, subjectivities (which in certain circumstances may have been expressed as the idea of the individual or as the idea of the community) are realized in practice.

This line of enquiry will secure yet another shift in our thinking because it will lead to a 'decentring', away from individuals as the authors of their conditions, to a consideration of agents as readers and interpreters, capable of drawing upon and acting upon those conditions. Expressed most simply, this means that agency is not something which lies behind the material residues of an 'archaeological record', to be recovered (literally 'dug out') by the archaeologist who explains that record as being a 'record of something' ('ideas', 'actions' etc.). Instead, agency lies in front of those conditions because it was the means of understanding and reworking them in an interpretive cycle, and it is this interpretive cycle which can be glimpsed through the archaeological analysis. In other words, we move away from asking 'what kinds of people made these conditions?', to an understanding of what the possibilities were of being human within those material and historical conditions. An archaeological engagement with the past now becomes an attempt to understand how, under given historical and material conditions, it may have been possible to speak and act in certain ways and not in others, and by so doing to have carried certain programmes of knowledge and expectation forward in time.

Despite the impression undoubtedly given by this very condensed introductory statement, this is not a book about archaeological theory. Certainly part of the purpose of this book is to follow through and clarify the above argument in some detail, but this will be done through an empirical study aimed at building a history of the period between about 2900 and 1200 BC in southern Britain. This is therefore a book about one of the most remarkable periods in European prehistory, when elaborate ceremonial practices emerged among some communities of subsistence agriculturalists of western Europe, and it considers how the place for such practices in the lives of those communities was gradually lost with the emergence of more intensive agricultural practices. The book concludes with the establishment of the agricultural landscapes of southern Britain at the end of the second millennium BC. Writing a history in the terms which have been outlined here (as an interpretation of how people might have understood their lives and the consequences their understandings may have had in their own actions) means that we must also stand back and consider how archaeologists claim to reach their own understandings of peoples who lived four thousand years ago. It is therefore essential for archaeologists to establish a degree of self-reflection, and this is what I have tried to develop as a secondary narrative in this book.

Both our own knowledge of the past and the knowledges developed by those others whom we study, draw in part upon the interpretation of a common materiality. These are the things which were once inhabited, worked upon and understood by others, fragments of which have survived today as a record of that past. This book will consider some of these fragmentary residues and it will examine the way different frames of reference have been brought to bear upon their interpretation. These different frames of reference include those which define the distant and objective views of the archaeologist as well as the local, intimate and subjective view of those whom we study. The first two chapters consider the material conditions which were reworked in two different areas of life at the end of the third millennium BC: ceremonial and mortuary rituals. We will examine how these conditions intervened in different regions of social practice and, in the third chapter, explore how images of a reality may have been created by these practices. The fourth chapter represents a critical evaluation of the way the current archaeological perspective changes that which it attempts to study; it looks in more detail at the way the archaeologist creates images of the past on the archaeologist's own terms. The fifth and sixth chapters deal with the transformation of the earlier ceremonial practices by the end of the second millennium BC, and with the formation of the agricultural landscapes of later prehistory. The fifth chapter considers mortuary rituals as a specific strategy contributing towards social transformation. The sixth chapter works across the entire period of this study to demonstrate how the various ritual and ceremonial practices were played out in the long-term transformations of social life. By this route I intend to chart the way those long-term structural conditions, which may characterize the fourth to late third millennia in western Europe, were created through the subjectivities of those who inhabited them. The seventh chapter considers the implications of the approaches which have been developed here for archaeological practices in general.

NOTE ON RADIOCARBON DATES

Calibrated (i.e. calendrical) dates are used throughout the text while the corresponding uncalibrated radiocarbon dates are cited in notes.

NOTES

1   Roland Fletcher has re-examined the way the *annaliste* tradition of thinking may be applied in archaeology (Fletcher 1992). As I read it, he argues for the examination of a nested hierarchy of carefully defined time-scales. The internal operation of each time-scale is neither reducible to nor overdetermined by another but is relatively autonomous. The relationship between each level within this hierarchy is one of a developing structural compatability or incompatability through time. We would appear still to be left with the problem of refining our understanding of the way in which processes, operating in each time-scale, are routinely structured in relation to each other.

2   Giddens's theory of structuration forms the basis for much of the argument contained in the rest of this book. For a general statement of this theory, see Giddens 1984.

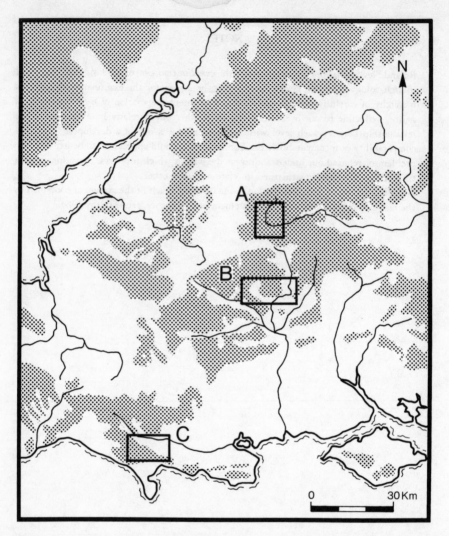

Figure 1.1 Map of southern Britain, showing those areas discussed in detail: the Avebury area (A) (see also figure 1.2); the Stonehenge area (B) (see also figure 2.1); and the Mount Pleasant area (C) (see also figure 4.3).

1

Processions of the Living . . .

The Archaeological Visitor

The great prehistoric earthwork of Avebury, carved out of the chalk downland of North Wiltshire, encloses within its 11.5 hectares the remains of three ancient stone circles and the houses of the modern village (figures 1.1, 1.2). Avenues of standing stones once reached out from two of the earthwork's four entrances. Over four and a half millennia separate us from those who built the earthwork, communities whose achievement John Aubrey, writing in the seventeenth century, suggested 'does as much exceed in greatness the so renowned Stonehenge, as a cathedral doeth a parish church'.

Today the monument is no more than a fragment of its original form, and the fragment was itself restored by Keiller between 1934 and 1939 following the systematic destruction, mainly during the eighteenth century, of the stones and the bank (figure 1.3). Keiller's excavations and restoration contribute most substantially to the monument which we see today.[1]

What are we to make of Avebury – the physical culmination of four and a half millennia of building, decay, destruction and restoration, a monument which is still only partially explored archaeologically? For any visitor, the stones, surrounded by a ditch originally cut almost 10 metres into the chalk, and a bank, now rising over 4 metres in its eroded form, must evoke a sense of wonder mixed with feelings of incomprehension. Is the reaction of the archaeologist any different, and if so, why?

We can recognize two different kinds of archaeological response to the monument. First, there is that of Keiller and others, who have provided a record of the monument as they saw it. The structural remains and the finds are described and stored as a museum archive, and a written report on the

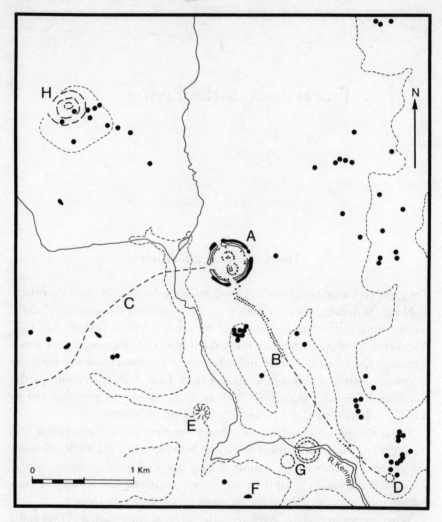

Figure 1.2   Map of the Avebury area showing: the Avebury enclosure (A); the Kennet Avenue (B); the line of the Beckhampton Avenue (C); the Sanctuary (D); Silbury Hill (E); the West Kennet long barrow (F); the West Kennet palisaded enclosures (G); and the Windmill Hill causewayed enclosure (H). Other long and round barrows are also shown.

material is presented to a wider readership. Some of the stones are reset to an approximation of their original position. The second and more general response has been to create a number of historical syntheses by writing a history of the past which places the remains at Avebury within the broader perspective of our current understanding of the mid to late third millennium BC.

Figure 1.3 Reconstructing Avebury. Keiller's workmen and one of the re-erected stones. (Copyright: RCHME)

It is important for the argument of this book that we examine how these archaeological responses differ from that of the visitor. The overall archaeological description of the monument, in terms of deposits and possible reconstructions, creates an archive of drawings, texts and photographs from which the most commonly abstracted synthesis is the plan. Monuments of comparable plan, or deposits and artefacts of comparable date, are often drawn together to define the material characteristics of the period in which they were created. Enclosures whose form is similar to that at Avebury and which are contemporary may be catalogued as if they represent a type fossil of the period.[2] Sequences of monuments and of artefacts may then take on the appearance of history, where each period of the past is represented by a different assemblage of material, and where the movement of history is represented by the movement from one artefact assemblage to another. Archaeology has tended to isolate the material residues of the past as the object of its study, and it is normal for archaeologists to refer to these material fragments as a *record* of the past.

The subjective encounters of visitors, on the other hand, occur as they enter the monument and as they move from one stone to another, or from the bank to the inner lip of the ditch. Only through a lengthy and repeated pre-ambulation by each visitor does the relationship between each element begin to emerge.

The visitors' encounter is therefore partial and erratic; they move around the monument from one place to the next, guided by paths, gates and by their own initiatives. In contrast, the archaeological perspective is holistic in as much as it stands outside an immediate and partial encounter with the monument. The visitors' movements within the monument also take time, whereas time is collapsed for the archaeological observer, because the various elements of the visitors' encounters are synthesized into a textual description of size and form; they are collapsed into the composition of a plan. The plan represents the monument observed at a single moment. What this archaeological objectivity achieves is to detach the observer from within the monument by creating an alternative frame of reference from which the totality of the site can be described. This objectivity is constructed at the expense of the practical engagement of occupying the architecture which it claims to describe, and it is constructed at the expense of time.[3] It is notable that the one moment and the one place where the loosely controlled and impressionistic account of the visitor and the rationality of archaeological objectivity come together at Avebury is at the plan of the henge which is displayed on information boards at various vantage points within the monument (figure 1.4). Here, depending upon their skill at reading such plans, each visitor can fix their own position within the overall scheme of the monument. However, the archaeologist, like John Aubrey, can emphasize the importance of a more detached perspective by reciting comparisons with other monuments, as if by comparing the size of Avebury with that of Stonehenge something significant has been revealed. But what is gained by such comparisons, other than a simple measure of the scale of each earthwork?

Figure 1.4 Visitors at Avebury. They orient themselves to examine a plan of Avebury displayed within the monument; it is an orientation which makes no reference to the architecture of the monument itself.

Understanding Avebury

The enclosure and the stone circles at Avebury were never originally planned, nor were they observed, as a single entity. A considerable amount of archaeological literature has struggled with the 'problem' of megalithic mathematics and astronomy by simply misunderstanding this point. The fallacy has been to convert regularity into a rule and thus to presuppose a planned intention.[4] It may indeed be possible to draw a series of geometric forms which 'best fit' the plan of the stones, but to arrive at this descriptive geometry does not imply that a generative geometry was used in the construction of the circles. The monument was not conceived as an entity, a plan in the mind of some autocratic chief. In discussing the causewayed enclosures of the fourth millennium, Evans has written of them as being ongoing projects which were never completed but simply abandoned; this is exactly the point I want to develop here (C. Evans 1988). Avebury is the physical remnant of a number of abandoned projects and not the culmination of a series of planned phases. These projects were undertaken at different locations within the landscape, and at these *locales* actions and exchanges between people created the material conditions which then helped, in turn, to sustain those particular human relations.

The construction of any tradition, the *habitus* of Bourdieu, involves a process of learning how to act, contributing to the creation of the biography of each participant (Bourdieu 1977: 78; 1984: 101; 1990: 42ff.). That learning is built out of a practical experience, and depends upon the senses of sight, sound, touch and smell. It is also grounded upon memories of the past and on expectations of the future. The immediate point of reference for a person's understanding of the world on which they act is their own body. The movement and orientation of the self in relation to others is the means of understanding one's place within a discourse and of gauging one's ability to act and to speak. The references made to position and to orientation are enhanced by the immediate topography and the architecture of the place; buildings enclose and channel the direction of movement and focus the attention of the eye. At certain places – in front of certain backdrops and behind certain screens – actions occur, words are spoken and others are left unsaid, creating the discourse of a social practice. As we observe the creation of an architecture out of the practical understandings of the place, so we see how certain actions and utterances were made possible.

Architectural fragments such as Avebury should allow us to think through the orientation of the practices which both created that architecture and which were staged within it. The monument should be viewed as a series of localized spaces, created as ongoing projects by builders who rarely glimpsed the totality of their creation. On Overton Hill, 2.3 kilometres to the south-east of Avebury, lies the Sanctuary, a complex of circular timber and stone settings which were ultimately linked to Avebury by the line of the Kennet Avenue. Burl has written that the Sanctuary 'is almost a chronicle of the history of stone rings in Wiltshire, their origin, their modifications, their destruction, their quiet mysteries' (1976: 317). Recorded in the eighteenth century by Stukeley, the site was rediscovered and excavated in the early twentieth century by Maude Cunnington. Schematic though her account is, it has been used both to establish a sequence of buildings on the hill and as the basis for various reconstructions of those buildings.[5] It is unnecessary to repeat the arguments here; they all assume that the stone settings, most notably two stone circles, are late in the history of the monument, and Piggott's underlying assumption that the earliest phase of the monument was also the smallest has received general acceptance. Uncertainty will always accompany a reading of Cunnington's account of her own work and of the stratigraphic details she recorded. However, our concern is with the practices which left little or no direct material trace on this site but which were structured by those enclosures. This allows us to circumvent some of the uncertainty of Cunnington's account. Instead of assigning the architectural remains to a series of building periods or events, as if this were an adequate representation of human history, let us view the physical remains as a palimpsest of modifications spanning several centuries at the end of the third millennium. Those modifications will have involved the reworking of principles which once sought to reveal an order amongst people and their actions.

Two themes were worked into the architectural fabric of the Sanctuary. One was enclosure, achieved by means of timber and stone circles. A cluster of such settings occupied an area some 20 metres in diameter, with a small open space some 4 metres in diameter at the centre. Ultimately this cluster was enclosed within a larger stone circle 40 m across. The second theme was to establish a line of access into these regions through a clearly demarcated entrance, and to continue that line across the interior with the use of additional focal points set on the inner periphery of the circles. These focal points were created by various forms of marker posts, stones and deposits.[6]

By drawing upon these two themes of movement and orientation, the occupants of this place would have enabled a complex disposition between themselves to have been established. Firstly there were those who were excluded from the interior of the circles, but who may have observed or listened to some part of the proceedings from outside. Secondly there arose distinctions among those who were able to enter the Sanctuary, created by where they stood and how they moved, and which used the access lines or focal points within the enclosures as places and moments of reference. Such places may have fixed certain actions and have enabled a certain sequence of those actions to have been established. The enclosures thus represented a series of stages upon which distinctions within a relatively isolated elect could have been repeatedly established over a number of centuries. The distinctions, enacted in the restricted area of this single place, could then have been stretched out over time and space, and thus placed on fuller view, by means of procession.

Processional activity did not begin with the construction of the stone rows of the Beckhampton and the Kennet Avenues, perhaps at the end of the third millennium; these rows are merely the physical manifestation of its existence. Today the stones leave a monumental trace across the landscape, marking out the line of the processions between one place and another. Again the distinctions between participants would have been maintained, for the processions would have moved through a landscape inhabited by those excluded from that activity, and amongst those who were included were those who led and those who followed.[7]

The view from Overton Hill could have covered almost the full line of the Kennet Avenue. It is only at a point within 50 metres of the southern entrance of the Avebury enclosure that the Avenue is hidden by the fall of the land.[8] It is at this point that the Avenue turns through a dog-leg (figure 1.5)

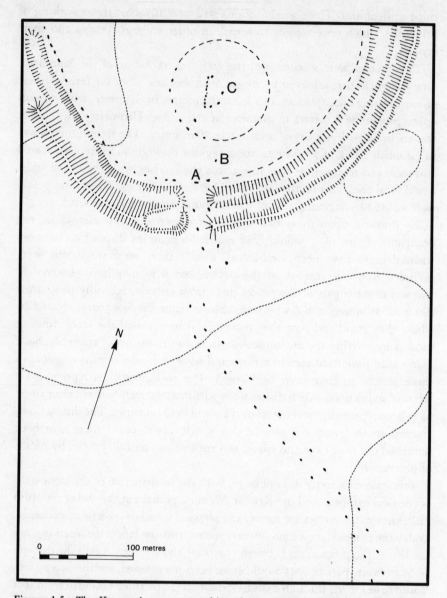

Figure 1.5 The Kennet Avenue approaching the southern entrance into Avebury. The Avenue turns through a 'dog-leg' before reaching the entrance causeway. Beyond the entrance stones (A) once stood the Ring-stone (B). The site of the Obelisk (C) is also marked. (After I. Smith 1965)

Figure 1.6   The approach to the southern entrance stones at Avebury.

and approaches the Avebury earthwork on a line running between the two massive entrance stones in the outer circle (figure 1.6). Once through this entrance the line of the Avenue is not continued by any stone settings, but in the area between the entrance and the southern internal circle once stood the Ring-stone, recorded by Stukeley and since destroyed. The diameter of the southern circle, as with its northern counterpart, is considerably larger than that of the outer circle of the Sanctuary and within it no evidence for any circular building survives.[9] Neither does any point on its surviving circumference appear to have been marked out, as at the Sanctuary, although a single isolated stone did once stand towards the southern edge of the circle. The circle was divided unequally by a 26-metre-long facade or screen of small standing stones. This ran north–south, terminating at stones set transversely at each end. West of this line, in the larger segment of the circle and near its centre, once stood the Obelisk which rose to a height of some 7 metres, the tallest recorded stone at Avebury.

Processions moving from one place to another, as from the Sanctuary to the southern circle at Avebury for example, will have established an order between the participants at the opening of the proceedings, and this could have been reaffirmed at their close. The facade may have acted as a backdrop, and in front of it lay a form of stage. Here stood those who, with the screen behind them, would have had their presence amplified by that simple device in the view of those who faced them. At Avebury itself the idea of such an amplifying mechanism might also explain something of the use of the massively constructed stone Cove (figure 1.7) situated at the centre of the northern stone circle.[10] But the southern facade might also, through other

Figure 1.7 The two surviving stones of the Cove in the northern circle at Avebury. The Cove faced east, and a third stone once stood to the right of this group.

uses, have acted as a screen, and by withdrawing behind it some would have entered into a 'back space' of potential secrecy or mystery separated from other observers. It is important to recognize that this 'regionalization' is not realized simply by the plan of the monument, but that it is created by the movement and by the orientation of the practitioners themselves. Those practitioners occupied different regions not only of space but also of time. To have moved between or around the stones of the screen would have brought together the two regions both for those who, as observers, simply stood and watched, and for those others whose own actions created the logic of the spatial and temporal division.

Architecture structures the possible dispositions employed between those who inhabit its spaces. It creates the physical conditions of a *locale* which are drawn upon by practices which, in turn, sustain their meanings by reference to the conditions which they occupy. Architecture is a material technology enabling the regionalization of a place to emerge through practice, creating different categories and moments of being. The fundamental reference is created between the architecture and the positions and orientations of the human body, and these references are used in the exchanges which take place between practitioners. These practices are not present in the void of the physical plan of a building. As Bourdieu has shown,[11] the implications of this slip through our fingers when we objectify space as physical form, but they can be recovered in a consideration of the possible interpretive strategies employed by the practitioners. Our questions have to be (however imperfect our answers): what kinds of discourse could have been sustained here; what could have been spoken and what left unsaid; what truths could have been discovered, and what were the implications for those who shared in them?

This discussion of Avebury has not involved a description of the totality of the monument and its archaeology, and like other visitors, and in common with those who originally inhabited it, our own perceptions have remained partial. We have moved somewhat uncertainly into the contexts of human practice and communicative discourse, claiming that these, rather than the simple description of material things, are topics for archaeological analysis. Discourse between people, the very act of talking, requires a practical competence of both language and context. To know when to speak, what to say and how to act requires an understanding of the immediate situation and the strategies of position, movement, posture and timing which are available to the interlocutor (cf. Giddens 1987; Goffman 1971). The archaeological evidence has been examined in an attempt to understand how a certain architecture could, as a context, have guided particular forms of discourse. Such discourse will have occupied both place and time. Being spatially defined and temporally episodic[12] in this way, discourse can be considered to occupy a *region* of time-space. People enter these regions orientated by those preunderstandings which enable them to recognize and to monitor their conditions and their roles as participants. The episodes of discourse and practice thus restructure the traditions which lay claim to them.

The architecture is itself created by similarly structured practices. It seems clear that the Sanctuary is the focus for a long sequence of building activity, although these buildings need not be the product of a planned design intended to meet the requirements of some future occupation. The same is undoubtedly true of the Avebury enclosure. The production of material conditions is recursively linked with the reproduction of the practical knowledge of knowing how to act. This is always more than reading a material 'text'; it moves beyond the text and involves the annotation and transcription of such texts. In this way practical knowledge is constructed through an engagement with material conditions. Architectural traditions and the traditions of practice contained by that architecture become two interlocked fields which exchange and transform a common set of symbolic resources. To explore this point in more detail we must now turn to Durrington Walls, another of the major henge enclosures in southern Britain but one which has been more extensively excavated than Avebury.

The Structuring of an Architectural Tradition

Durrington Walls lies 2.9 kilometres to the north-east of Stonehenge and was the first of the major henge monuments of southern Britain to be excavated on any scale after Keiller's work at Avebury.[13] The record of the structural remains uncovered in those excavations is detailed. The earthwork encloses some 14 hectares around a dry valley which drains to the south-east, towards the Wiltshire Avon. The excavations investigated a strip of land running roughly north to south through the interior of the enclosure and cutting through the south-eastern of the two entrances. The topography of the monument is dominated by the valley. The southernmost entrance lies towards the bottom of the valley and structural features immediately within that entrance were well preserved, being buried by an accumulation of hill-wash (figure 1.8).

In the lower reaches of the valley and across its axis, a line of timbers was erected forming a facade running south-west to north-east (figure 1.9). The plan of this structure is incomplete due to stream erosion and later activity. The facade could have run for a length of 37 metres, and in the centre there seems to have been an entrance where a single post stood slightly forward and downslope of the line. The diameter of the posts appears to have decreased from the centre outward, indicating a grading in their height. Upslope to the northwest, and 17 metres behind the entrance, stood a four-post setting 5 metres square enclosing a smaller inner circle of six posts. The posts of the square had been renewed and they were themselves enclosed within a small, and very irregular, timber circle. There is no stratigraphic evidence concerning the chronological relationship between the facade, four-post setting and circle, although the logic of the arrangement is for the four-post setting to have been the primary monument with a line of approach determined by the axis of the valley. The area around the four-post structure and circle, and between them and the facade, then saw the erection of an increasingly elaborate array of post settings, implying that they acted as the original points of reference for the subsequent structural history of the site. The history of all these buildings appears to have been lengthy and the posts were generally allowed to decay *in situ* rather than being dug out. Ultimately, the decayed timbers of the early four-post setting were replaced by a timber circle 10.8 metres in diameter, and a hearth overlay the position of one of the posts of the earlier innermost circle.

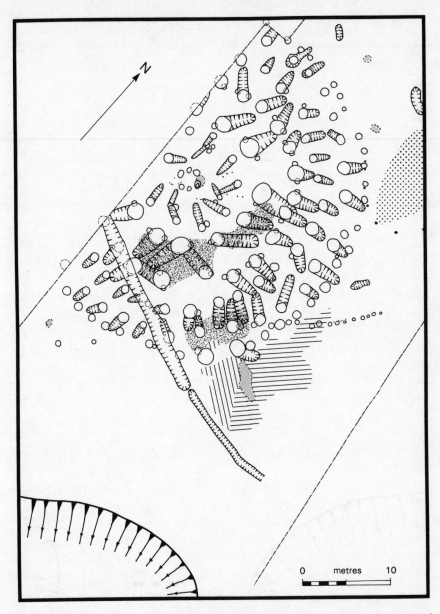

Figure 1.8 The palimpsest of excavated post-holes, surfaces and midden spreads which had survived on the site of the southern circle at Durrington Walls. (After Wainwright and Longworth 1971)

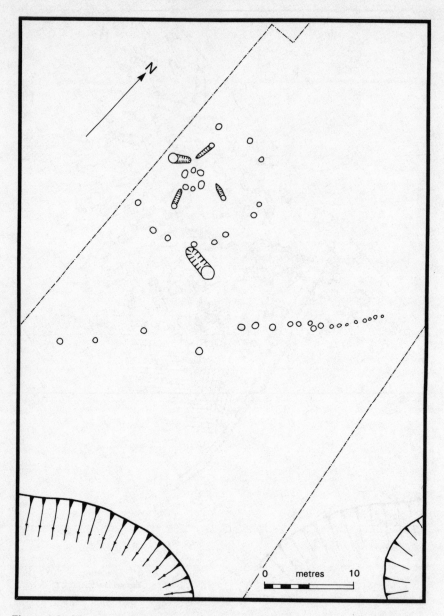

metres

0   10

Figure 1.9 The principal timber elements involved in the early stages of building on the site of the southern circle at Durrington Walls. Only the western ditch terminal has been excavated. (After Wainwright and Longworth 1971)

A post, erected between the central area originally demarcated by the four-post setting, and the line of the facade, became incorporated within a rough circle of posts which enclosed the entire central area.[14] The erection of that post predated the establishment of another, smaller circle around the central area. Ultimately additional post-rings extended far enough out to cut tangentially along the line of the now collapsed facade (figure 1.8). Two more massive entrance posts through the outer of these post-rings echoed the earlier entrance through the facade at this point, and there are indications that the posts were again graded down in height on either side of this later entrance. The constructional sequence of timbers in the area behind the entrance is obviously complex. This is most clearly indicated by the interleaving of the post-ramps (Wainwright and Longworth 1971: 34). Immediately beyond the entrance, to the south-east, lay a chalk platform and gravel floor, whilst areas of rammed chalk survived amongst the posts in the zone between the central area and the entrance.

There are two ways in which we could simplify this forest of constructional detail. Wainwright and Longworth (1971: 204ff.) and Musson (1971) suggest that the plan represents two phases of timber building, at least the second of which was roofed. Such an interpretation emphasizes the monumentality of the structure which also appears to represent a unified design. If we follow them in such an argument then, from the outset, the 'second phase' of building was planned and guided by the idealized concept of its final roofed form. This raises numerous problems, not least of which is understanding the conditions under which the invention or the instigation of this ideal plan could have occurred. There are no architectural antecedents for this style of building known in the fourth millennium.[15] The alternative is to recognize that this monumentality originated in neither the idea nor the plan, but rather in the practice and in the project. It existed and it was known only through the moments of its execution. The project was guided by relatively simple principles of spatial order and it was upon these that it worked itself out.

Once again, the referent against which this spatial order was constructed was the movement of the human body. The axis of the dry valley was cut by the original timber facade behind which stood a small building. It was through the steady embellishment of this *locale*, by encircling timber uprights, by the preservation of the line of the original facade as a boundary, and by the elaboration and primacy given to the zone lying between the central focus and the entrance, that the principles are most clearly recognizable in this lengthy and piecemeal programme of construction. It is not surprising that the various timber rings do not share common centres (Atkinson 1971), nor that the ideal scheme suggested by the excavator for a sequence of buildings from the centre out cannot be sustained in some of the stratigraphic detail which he himself had gathered, nor that the post-rings break up into clustered groups whose arcs align poorly upon the expected ideal of a circle. The building programme was not founded upon a pre-set plan. It was created more in the tradition of *bricolage* (Lévi-Strauss 1972: 16ff.), the reworking of the available resources by those with a competent and inventive understanding of particular orders of spatial practice. Through its empirical execution the project finally revealed a physical totality which would have increasingly restricted the way people could have operated within it. It is this final totality which has so bemused the archaeological observer, and which has resulted in the spurious reconstructions of a two-phased, roofed building.

Higher on the valley side the excavators unearthed the remains of a second building. The surfaces of the chalk were more exposed here and the remains had suffered greater erosion. In consequence, it is likely that evidence for some of the structural elements have been lost. None the less, we no longer need force the fragments which do remain to conform with the ideal of a second circular and roofed building. In its place we are left with those same simple elements concerned with the movement and the differentiation of people which we have previously recognized (figure 1.10). A double line of posts, probably defining an avenue, ran from the south up to a timber facade. Much of this is destroyed but originally the facade may have been 23 metres long with a central entrance, and the avenue's line is continued northwards beyond the facade by a few posts. Twenty metres to the north stood a large four-post setting, 5 metres square. This was enclosed by one timber circle and by arcs of other posts. Similar practices were being reworked in both places, rather than the same plan being copied.

The Organization of Labour

Both Avebury and Durrington Walls arose as monuments whose form was determined by the reworking of a common understanding. That understanding concerned rights of access, orientation and movement, which, under certain conditions, differentiated between the practitioners. A certain cultural expectation was thus worked out empirically through the processes of construction and use, but there is an apparent contrast, between the communal reserves of labour demanded by the programmes of construction, and the social distinctions which were made explicit through the spatial order of the monument. We will return to the implications of this contrast below; it is

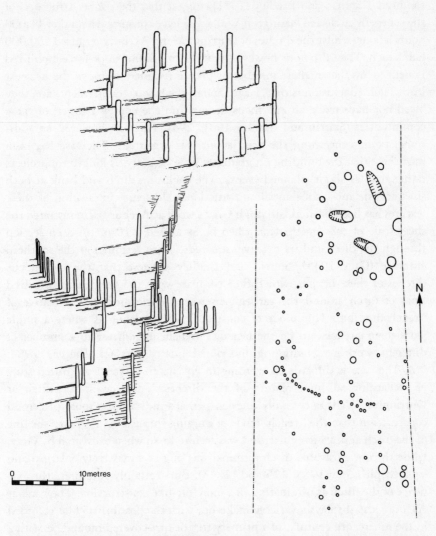

0   10metres

Figure 1.10   The northern circle at Durrington Walls. A plan of the post-holes (right) is accompanied by a possible reconstruction of the main timber elements. (Adapted from Musson, in Wainwright and Longworth 1971)

necessary here simply to consider the labour demanded by the construction of these monuments.

The total labour requirement may have been considerable, although the original labour estimates which Renfrew employed in his analysis of the monuments of the fourth and third millennia in Wessex are now known to be too high.[16] Startin and Bradley (1981) suggest that the timber structures of the southern circle at Durrington Walls will have consumed a total of 11,000 hours labour, whilst the ditches of Durrington and Avebury required 500,000 hours each. They also note, however, that the minimum work-force mobilized is defined by the smallest number of people required to move the heaviest load. Their conclusion is that, large though the labour requirements are, they 'need not have made an enormous demand on the energy budget' of these communities (Startin and Bradley 1981: 294). There is, however, an additional point concerning the way labour was organized. The case has been made here that the building programmes were executed as long-term projects rather than as single planned events. The enclosing ditch and bank at both sites are the most substantial constructional elements. Excavation of these features has been limited, although Gray's work at Avebury demonstrated the sheer scale of the construction when he excavated a 10-metre deep section through the ditch and its massive, squared eastern terminal at the southern entrance (Gray 1935). Startin and Bradley suggest that the continuous ditches of these henges, which they compare with the segmented or pitted lines of ditch around the earlier causewayed enclosures, are indicative of 'trench digging'. This mode of construction they define as where a single work-force cut forward on the face of a trench, in contrast to a number of different work-gangs digging individual quarry pits (cf. Bradley 1984: 76). The case is difficult to examine in any detail, given the limited scale of archaeological investigation of the ditches. The line of the ditch at Durrington Walls is certainly uneven, perhaps indicating a more piecemeal construction than the 'trench' mode of digging implies. At Avebury the line of the ditch appears irregular, and was seen to be so when excavated by Gray, while the one excavated ditch terminal was dug as a massively enlarged and squared pit (Gray 1935: 125 and pl. 43). Burl certainly interprets the evidence of the ditch as originating in a more pit-like construction. The bank at Avebury also displays a variable make-up, with the possibility, first recorded in the nineteenth century, of a primary turf or turf-covered mound beneath a later bank. Today the bank at Avebury is eroding into a mounded profile, which would indicate an internal, segmented structure, similar to that now known from a number of earthen long barrows, rather than one of a continuous mound.[17]

The issues here are complex. The labour requirements for these (and other near contemporary) monuments in Wessex are clearly greater than those demanded by the earthen long barrows and by most of the so-called causewayed enclosures of the late fifth and fourth millennium. It has been generally accepted that this difference in scale has implications for our understanding of the organization of the contemporary societies. In his original discussion of Stonehenge, for example, Atkinson argued that the monument was 'unlikely to have been the expression of the common will, but rather the fulfilment of a purpose imposed from above'. That dominant authority, in Atkinson's view, sustained a level of social integration that enabled the construction of a monument 'involving the displacement of so many hundreds of men from their homes for so long' (1979: 166). Clearly, in Atkinson's view, this dominant authority pre-existed, and thus facilitated, the mobilization of the work-force.

In his discussion of the period, Bradley places the monuments of the British late Neolithic in a more complex process of social evolution. On the one hand he emphasizes the traditional view that

> the building of sites like Durrington Walls marks a radical departure. The ditch alone may have required about 500,000 man hours. The detailed construction of these sites also differs from their, predecessors . . . The work may have taken place under closer direction and co-ordination. It is likely that the work force was larger and that it was engaged in construction over a much longer period. (Bradley 1984: 76)

However, while this sounds like an appeal to some pre-existing authority which had been capable of instigating and controlling the processes of production, Bradley also suggests that the monuments played some part in the creation of that authority. His argument is developed with reference to the work of John Cherry (cf. Bradley 1985: 4ff.; Cherry 1978). In attempting to establish some cross-cultural generalizations for 'the origins, spread and organisations of states', Cherry offered the example of Minoan Crete. Here, he argued, the dates for the founding of the peak sanctuaries 'indicate the contemporary and very sudden emergence of both the Cretan palace elite and a specific form of ritual activity'. The sanctuaries are presented as emerging with the early state, at a time 'when the social order was most fragile' (Cherry 1978: 429). The generalization, which is supported by Bradley, is that 'the *establishment* of a socially visible (though initially unstable) hierarchy necessitated more support . . . than did its subsequent *maintenance*' (ibid.). Bradley suggests by analogy that a process of political centralization is initially 'enforced through ritual and ceremonial rather than political coercion' (1984: 73). Large 'ritual centres', including those of late Neolithic Wessex, are regarded as having emerged at a time which 'may precede the emergence of identifiable elites in the archaeological record' (ibid.: 74).

Minoan sanctuaries are not directly comparable with the Wessex monuments in terms of either scale or function. However, the more contentious issue must concern the attempt to draw direct analogies between the case of an emergent state and that of Wessex in the late third millennium. Do forms of ritual display operate in the same way in all cases? What we require is a greater clarification in our understanding of the strategic deployment of ritual practice in the history of specific types of political authority. There is, for example, an obvious contradiction in explaining the construction of monuments by reference to a social hierarchy which, it is argued, also required those monuments to exist for it to become operational. This returns us to our own argument – by building Avebury and Durrington Walls new social realities were also constructed. These social realities did not lie behind the building of these monuments but emerged from their existence. It follows, then, that the mobilization of labour necessary for these undertakings must have arisen within earlier, and different, forms of political obligation.

Military coercion and the bureaucratic monitoring of a population are the forms of political domination which we would normally associate with a centralized state, and which we would therefore also expect to encounter operating with a specific territorial jurisdiction. We would have to accept these modes of domination as precisely the forms of institutionalized power necessary, if we are to envisage either Avebury or Durrington Walls being built according to a single plan and with a rapid, almost catastrophic, mobilization of labour. Centralized bureaucracies and military authorities are institutions which would have sustained the forms of *authoritative* and *intensive* power required to execute a preformulated strategy on this scale through a highly organized and tightly controlled operation.[18] This is the very point which Atkinson recognized in discussing the form of authority which he believed had operated behind the construction of Stonehenge. It is also the point in MacKie's (1977) model of theocratic astronomer priests which he applies to this period. Such cases should only be accepted if such forms of institutionalized authority can be traced as emergent prior to the periods of monumental construction. It does not appear that they can.

The alternative, as argued here, demands that the processes of constructing Avebury and Durrington extended over several centuries. These building projects objectified and transformed traditional expectations concerning the spatial and temporal ordering of people and practices. Such cultural expectations were reworked in the building of the enclosures, avenues and facades, and resulted in the architectural settings which would, by their very scale, have transformed the ceremonial and ritual practices undertaken within them. What we must attempt to understand is the way the established obligations of communal labour, embedded within traditional and routine practices of subsistence production, came to be orientated towards other, ceremonial and ritual, practices which were specific to the locales concerned. We will return to this issue in later chapters.

Making an Elite: Silbury Hill

There are two general issues which can be isolated in an attempt to summarize the substantive argument of this first chapter. First, the issue of temporality. The monuments so far discussed created architectural settings where differences in the orientation and positioning of the participants distinguished between them, in the ceremonies which, from time to time, took place there. This was more than a simple distribution of people across the various spaces of the monument. For the distinctions to have operated, and for them to have been seen and to have been understood, it was necessary for people to *move* between these regions; to enter and leave each other's presence, to observe passively or to act, to lead processions or to follow. The practice of social life is thus lived out through time; it is performed. It was this practical performance which reproduced certain forms of social authority, but those who stood at the head of this system of authority did so partly through their use of these monuments. Thus, those who headed the processions, or who faced out from the Cove at Avebury, or indeed from the inner facade-like setting of the trilithons at Stonehenge, will have held the focus of the many. That elite did not simply initiate the building of Avebury, Durrington or Stonehenge but was, instead, created out of the realization of these projects.

This brings us to our second theme, best expressed in terms of the contrast between the communal labour of construction, and the elite practices operating in the setting of these monuments. The former drew upon reserves of knowledge and co-operation which routinely operated in the widespread and diverse practices of subsistence activities. This extensive and co-operative effort also managed to create staged settings which only certain individuals could, under specific circumstances, come to occupy. Silbury Hill expresses this contrast well.

Silbury lies a little over 1 kilometre to the south of Avebury (figure 1.2). Rising to a height of 40 metres and with a base covering 2.1 hectares, it represents the largest artificial prehistoric mound in Europe (figure 1.11). The labour requirement for the entire mound is calculated at 3 million hours. Our understanding of Silbury depends upon early excavations, which include the digging of two tunnels into the mound, and the interim account of

Figure 1.11   Silbury Hill from the Kennet valley. The excavations of the Kennet palisaded
sites can be seen in the foreground.

excavations in the late 1960s which reopened one of those tunnels (Atkinson
1968, 1969, 1970; Malone 1989: 95ff.; Whittle forthcoming). Atkinson
argues that although a structural sequence can be identified, the mound is
none the less the product of a continuous building programme. The full evidence for this is not yet available, although Malone has observed that 'perhaps
the various phases of the site took decades, if not centuries to complete'
(1989: 99).

Silbury began with a small fenced enclosure, some 20 metres in diameter,
which was built on a slight promontory in the bottom of the Kennet valley.
Within this enclosure a composite mound of clay, turf and quarried soils was
constructed, resulting in a possible drum-like platform standing some 4.5
metres high. No central deposit has ever been found beneath this platform,
although the central area was extensively disturbed by earlier excavators. A
radiocarbon date from unburnt hazel and plant roots in this mound suggests
a constructional date in the second quarter of the third millennium, and
insect remains indicate that it was constructed in late summer.[19]

This primary mound was then enclosed within a series of successive
enlargements built from chalk quarried from the hillside and from two quarry
ditches. The earlier of these ditches is buried within the final mound, and its
unweathered state is one of the features which Atkinson took as indicative of
a single building operation. The mound is made up of a number of chalk
dumps revetted by chalk blocks, with the final structure rising to a flat
platform, 30.5 metres in diameter.

All accounts of Silbury emphasize the obvious, the scale of construction,
whilst often commenting upon the mystery of its purpose:

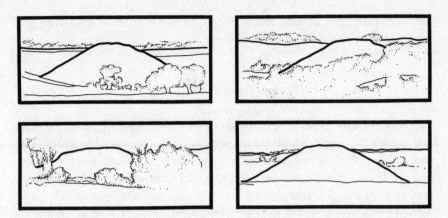

Figure 1.12 Four views of Silbury Hill (Devereux 1991) showing how the platform projects above the skyline. The views are from (top left and clockwise) East Kennet long barrow, the Sanctuary, West Kennet long barrow and Beckhampton long barrow.

> Excavations, theories, and intuitive speculation have all failed to pro-
> duce definitive answers for the function of Silbury, and it seems more
> than likely that there will never be any archaeological breakthrough
> which can tell us why the site was built. However, researches carried out
> to date have afforded a good deal of information about how the site was
> built and with what material and manpower. (Malone 1989: 95)

The irony is between the scale of a communal building operation and its
unknown purpose. However, if we place Silbury within the context of our
own consideration of the Avebury region, then something of the mystery
dissolves. Perhaps the simplest thing to do is to accept Silbury for what it is,
an elevated platform. Not only is that platform, which seems to rise above the
distant horizon when viewed from many places in the surrounding country-
side, widely visible (figure 1.12), but so are those who stand upon it.[20]
Admittedly the view is restricted from some areas, including from Avebury
itself, although Malone's assertion (1989: 99) that the platform 'cannot be
seen from within the Avebury circles' is simply untrue. However, within
Avebury more immediate focal points attract the attention; it is only in the
wider landscape that Silbury becomes a significant point of reference, particularly in moving along the Kennet Avenue. Once again, the labour of
construction, extensively organized and competent in its skills, contributed
towards the possibility of a ceremonial presencing of an elite. That possibility
allowed for moments when a relatively few people were, quite literally,

elevated and placed beyond reach, but in full view of those who had given them the means to occupy that position.

The Question of Objectivity

Categories of data (types of find, site or artefact assemblage), catalogues, plans and written descriptions – all these comprise the conventional language of an archaeology which is concerned with the collation, comparison and synthesis of large bodies of information. Such linguistic conventions objectify (make real) an archaeological record as a material phenomenon belonging to our own world.[21] Whilst the visitor may wander around Avebury with an increasing feeling of incomprehension regarding the monument and its place in the past, the archaeological frame of reference establishes a security regarding our ability to describe the present. Archaeologists may aim to study the past, but their first step is to describe material residues as they appear to exist in our present-day world.

Most archaeologists have difficulty in recognizing this static 'record' as the result of their own prejudiced encounter with the material evidence. The definition of the record is regarded as unproblematic, and the foremost task of archaeology is supposedly to establish the facts concerning the material evidence from which history may, one day, be written. However, the creation of such a record has important implications for the way in which any history can be written with reference to it. Obviously archaeologists must link their observations about these static material things to the dynamics of the past. If we wish to discuss some particular historical process, we must demonstrate how that process is represented in the present-day material residues; failure in this will clearly limit the scope of archaeological interpretation.

Discovering a past, which none of us will ever see directly, by reference to present-day material remains is always likely to be a contentious procedure. Some have argued, for example, that the link between past 'social processes' and their material residues is so ambiguous that archaeologists can never use those residues to make any secure statement about the processes from which they originate. The argument is that we simply cannot work back from the present 'record' to the extinct mechanisms which generated it.[22] This objection would effectively place the study of ancient society beyond the scope of archaeology. It would relegate all statements on these matters to the realm of unverifiable speculation. Such pessimism regarding the necessary limitations of archaeological analysis should be refuted quite simply: all human material production is social, therefore the archaeologist confronts the products of past

societies by simply examining that material, even allowing that the relationship between social practices and their material conditions is complex (cf.
Bradley 1984: 1–5). Building an understanding of the situated relationship
between social practice and material conditions is not an option, it is *the*
intellectual demand of archaeology. Just what is required for a 'social archaeology' to be viable is one of the main themes of this book, and in writing it
I will follow, somewhat critically, the attempts of others to establish this
more optimistic view of what archaeology can achieve.

Our perceptions of the past and the way we describe the present-day record
are intimately connected. Our thinking about the past cannot be bracketed
from our conceptualization of the available evidence. Renfrew, for example,
has directed a considerable amount of energy towards arguing the case that all
societies can be thought of as systems of human organization, where the
structures of such organizations (i.e. the social structure) will always be
mapped diagnostically by the spatial characteristics of their material
residues.[23] Sequences of such residues can therefore represent the passing of
time between one kind of social organization and another. The presentation of
the evidence as a static record presupposes a particular relationship between
material production and social reproduction and, as I hope to demonstrate, it
has a significantly limiting effect on the kinds of history we are likely to write.
Most importantly, the view of the past as a sequence of stable systems of social
organization, interspersed by horizons of change, is increasingly recognized as
an inadequate understanding of how social dynamics operate. In it we are
offered little opportunity to examine how change may have emerged from
longer periods of stability; indeed the periods of supposed stability themselves almost deny the passing of time. History becomes limited to questions
of *change*, although an understanding of exactly what has changed is sometimes less than clear. This restricted concept of history arises directly from the
current operational definition of an 'archaeological record'. The recurrent
association of particular types of artefact and monument, conceptualized as a
static record of past unchanging conditions, means that only changes in the
form, style and organization of the material can mark intervening horizons of
social transformation and the passing of time. The three ages of stone, bronze
and iron is an obvious example of this stop–go history. The problem which
emerges from this discussion concerns the issue of time, in particular, the
absence of the routine passing of time from the concept of an 'archaeological
record'.

We began this chapter with the difference between the visitor's understanding of Avebury and that of the archaeologist. This difference is created
out of the particular encounters each establishes with the material remains.

Characteristically, the visitor's encounter involves walking through the monument; observations are ordered spatially and temporally. There is little regularity in the organization of this time-space frame of reference, however, and the observations of each visitor may appear confused and incompatible one with another. Each visitor is also likely to notice a considerable amount of structural detail at various moments of their individual and subjective perambulation. On the other hand, the monument, or particular parts of it, are described purely in terms of spatial relationships by the archaeologist. That description, a holistic representation, is contained within a text or a plan. The temporal element of the visitor's encounter within the monument is replaced by the landscape view available to an external observer. The site is seen as if at one moment, and the history of the site is represented as a sequence of such moments. This view, established from a point outside the material conditions under study, creates the image of an 'objective' record.[24] Critically, however, the material record has become external not only to the observer but also to those historical processes which the archaeologist is interested in studying. The monument is inhabited by neither the archaeologist nor by those who built and who used it.

Contemporary archaeology has made great play upon the need to establish generalizations which characterize particular types of historical process (the term 'processual archaeology' has come to be applied to these approaches), rather than linking the material record with specific historical events. The event is significant only in as far as it is one of a class of similar events. From this generalizing perspective considerable amounts of superfluous detail appear to be contained in the material record recovered by the archaeologist. In the case of Avebury, the general processes of social evolution are sometimes taken to be indicated simply by the size of the monument, leading to comparisons being made between it and the other large Wessex henges, and relating the general data of scale to total workload estimates and the organization of labour required for overall construction. Avebury is assigned to a class of large sites, the construction and function of which can only be understood in terms of general organizational processes. Details, such as the arrangement of a particular stone setting, appear as superfluous information, recording only the specific characteristics of building events at a particular site. The current understanding of an archaeological record therefore removes the temporality of an encounter with the evidence and also results in generating a sizeable body of unusable detail among the carefully (and expensively) recorded data of archaeological observations (Shanks and Tilley 1987a: 54ff.).

What I have tried to do is to question the existing differences between the archaeologist and the visitor by inviting archaeologists to become visitors to the monuments they are attempting to understand. I intend this to involve a consideration of what it meant to occupy these places. This does not mean that archaeologists need abandon explicitly ordered frames of reference from which to work upon their evidence, and from which to create histories which can be assessed by other observers. The writing of history does not simply become the product of a personal empathy with the place, although it is creative and it does require us to recover a temporality within our data. The approach which we will develop throughout this study will also preserve, indeed extend, an understanding of general processes, but it will be an understanding which will incorporate more of the observational details of our data than is usual at present. In effect this book is an appeal to rethink the nature, and the consequences, of current archaeological objectivity, to explore the different ways in which we may revisit our evidence and to think again about the archaeological writing of history. As it moves beyond a mere description of the material, what is it that the writing is attempting to create?

Current orthodoxy is that our writing may aim to identify different types of *social totality* which produced the various material residues which archaeologists recover. Unfortunately for this orthodoxy, it has become increasingly obvious that such 'societies', conceived of as single, bounded entities characterized by, or reducible to, some essential organizational properties, never existed. As a consequence Shanks and Tilley state that a series of 'unavoidable questions' now confront the practice of archaeology. They ask (1987a: 27):

1   How is social reality created and structured?
2   What is the place of material culture ... within social reality?
3   How is social reality related to time; how and why does social reality change?
4   What is the meaning and form of gaining knowledge of past social reality?

Our answers to the first three questions will determine our answer to the fourth because it is through the former that we will build the necessary, self-critical awareness required to deal with the latter. The initial premise I wish to develop, and which is the central theme of this book, is that archaeologists must conceptualize their material evidence, not as an external trace or record of a type of society, but as the medium of social practice. The argument, as it has been developed above, moves us away from dealing with the material evidence as if it were some externalized and objective record of a past process, and leads to the recognition that the material was implicated in the creation of past human subjectivities. The object of archaeological analysis should be to understand how those subjectivities could have been constituted out of a human agency which worked upon the material conditions it inhabited. People know the world they inhabit, and they rework that knowledge through their active engagement with that world – they move out and inhabit it. This situates our analysis of the past in a frame of reference which is more local and particular than is normally employed, simply because we are now concerned with the day-to-day maintenance of traditional practice by people rather than with the long-term existence of some abstract 'social system'. This does not mean that we should turn our backs upon the long-term view of history, nor should we ignore the broad geographical scale over which social institutions were reproduced. Our approach to such matters must be an enquiry into the conditions which enabled such institutions both to come into being and to be sustained, and at issue here is our use of the term *structure*.

Structures are most frequently taken to be a kind of 'envelope' which limit and constrain the actions of people. They may be geographical and ecological constraints or, as Braudel put it: 'the fairly fixed . . . relationships between realities and social masses'.[25] However, the view that structures emerge as the geographical and technical conditions, or as the social institutions, which constrain the individual agent cannot be maintained in this unrefined form.[26] Throughout Braudel's writings we find structural conditions operating internally to the practices of human agency. In the way that E. P. Thompson has written of class, being neither a structure nor a category but being 'something which in fact happens . . . in human relationships',[27] so do structures actively enable human subjects to come into being as inventive and purposeful agents. When Giddens defines structures as the sets of rules and resources which are implicated in the institutional articulation of social systems, he means that structures cannot be treated as *things* which have certain natural properties and which operate externally upon agency. Instead they emerge as the 'pre-understandings' which orientate the human subject, enabling that subject to act knowledgeably and effectively.[28] Tradition becomes a necessary condition of agency, where such traditions are the structural conditions reproduced, monitored and re-evaluated in actions and in speech. Agents now emerge as being increasingly competent in the practicalities of their lives, whilst they are still defined by the structures of obligation and authority which they acknowledge and reproduce. Institutions are reproduced over extended regions of time-space, as traditional prejudices structure a common understanding of conditions and enable specific actions to be effective and routinely accepted.[29]

Material culture is part of the structuring medium; it both orientates, and is the product of, actions and discourse. In the recently developed model of material culture as text (Moore 1986), this recursive process is seen to be akin to a continuous cycle of authorship–reader–annotator–author–...The social agent both creates and reads, from a culturally situated (i.e. prejudiced) position, the texts which they and others have created and are about to create. The archaeological evidence thus has the appearance of a heavily annotated text. But historical analysis is more than a simple re-reading of the surviving fragments – it is an attempt to understand those recurrent practices of authorship and annotation which extended beyond each text and which were the living-out of history.

NOTES

1   Keiller's excavations were published after his death (I. Smith 1965). Gray surveyed the monument and made cuttings into the bank and ditch (Gray 1935). A more recent survey of the earthworks and stones and a reassessment of earlier work, particularly the surveys of Aubrey and Stukely, is given by Ucko et al. 1991, although see also Burl 1992. For recent excavations in the immediate environs of Avebury: Whittle 1991.

2   The Avebury enclosure is normally classified as a 'henge', although the size of such enclosures varies considerably. The currently employed definition of henges remains that established by Atkinson (in Atkinson, Piggott and Sanders 1951). For the most recent catalogue of this type of enclosure: Harding and Lee 1987.

3   For a critique of objectivity being constructed at the expense of an understanding of practice: Bourdieu 1977 and 1990.

4   The point repeats that of Bourdieu 1977 and 1990. Most of the work on 'neolithic astronomy' arises from the field survey of monuments resulting in the plan of stone settings within a particular topography. These are the description of the consequences of human actions and not an understanding of the modes of engagement which gave rise to those consequences; effects are presented as their cause.

5   For the excavation of the Sanctuary: Cunnington 1932. For the reconstruction of the Sanctuary buildings: Piggott 1940; Musson 1971; Burl 1976: 318.

6   Using Cunnington's original 1932 nomenclature for the Sanctuary, two entrance posts (B33 and B34) and two stones (1 and 41), which were on the outer stone circle and set radially to the arc of that circle, marked the points at which the double line of stones belonging to the Kennet Avenue cut the arc of the circular enclosure and so, presumably, defined the entrance. Once inside the enclosure various focal points on the circumference of that enclosure were provided by such devices as a 'facade' of two paired posts flanking a single stone (H1–5) and a grave set at the foot of stone C12 which also corresponded with the position of a single post D5 set within a ring of otherwise double posts. Fleming (1973) discusses the techniques used in other stone circles by which focusing devices were constructed on one part of the circumference.

7   For a discussion of the way processions operate as a means of distributing people according to rank and precedence, see Graves 1989.

8   Cunnington (1932: 303) noted the extent to which the Avenue was visible from the Sanctuary.

9   The diameter of the southern circle was some 100 metres, that of the northern circle some 98 metres.

10 The Cove in the northern circle was a setting of three massive stones which enclosed an area (effectively a deep facade) opening to the north-east. Similar structures elsewhere have been discussed by Burl who argues that they were designed to act 'as a focus' (1988: 10).

11 Bourdieu writes, with reference to a very different context: 'the house, for example, is globally defined as female, damp, etc., when considered from the outside, from the male point of view, i.e. in opposition to the external world, but it can be divided into a male-female part and a female-female part when it ceases to be seen by reference to a universe of practice coextensive with *the* universe, and is treated instead as a universe (of practice and discourse) in its own right, which for women it indeed is, especially in the winter' (Bourdieu 1977: 110).

12 'To characterize an aspect of social life as an episode is to regard it as a number of acts or even events having a specifiable beginning and end, thus involving a particular sequence' (Giddens 1984: 244). For an attempt to develop the idea of social practice regionalized into 'fields' of time-space see Barrett 1988a.

13 Wainwright and Longworth 1971. Evidence for additional timber buildings within Durrington Walls has been recovered by geophysical prospection: RCHME 1979, fig. 110.

14 This is circle 2D in Wainwright and Longworth 1971, fig. 14. The account given here deliberately makes no attempt to accommodate the sequence of circular buildings which was proposed by the excavator.

15 This lack of an architectural antecedent was noted by Piggott who first suggested that large circular roofed buildings existed in the late Neolithic, based upon a reinterpretation of the Sanctuary (Piggott 1940).

16 Renfrew's original model for neolithic Wessex (1973), and which we will consider in ch. 7, drew heavily upon seeing the sequence of monuments in the region as representing a sequence of increasing labour demands (and thus an indication of an increasing organizational ability to mobilize that labour). The labour estimates partly derived from the work of Atkinson (1961), and these estimates have now been challenged (Startin and Bradley 1981).

17 I am grateful to Roger Thomas who has also observed this point and has discussed it with me. For comments on the Avebury evidence: Burl 1976: 61 and 171; I. Smith 1965: 194. For long mound construction: Kinnes 1992: 71ff.

18 The definition and operation of such forms of power as *authoritative* and *extensive* are suggested by Mann 1986: 6ff.

19 The details of, and the problems in interpreting, the radiocarbon sequence are discussed by Whittle, forthcoming.

20 The subtlety of the positioning of the Silbury mound is discussed by Devereux (1991), although we need not accept his suggestions of 'sight-lines' implying a primarily astronomical purpose for the mound.

21 The argument that it is self-evidently true that archaeologists only study modern-day material and static residues has been made on numerous occasions over several years by Lewis Binford (e.g. Binford 1977).

22 For these relatively pessimistic views of the limit of archaeological 'inference' see M. A. Smith 1955 and Leach 1973.

23 Renfrew 1977. For the general development of Renfrew's work see Renfrew 1984.

24 Cosgrove 1984 for the landscape objectified to an external observer.

25 Braudel 1980: 31. Throughout his writing Braudel develops the idea of 'structures' as limiting and constraining conditions operating upon human actions, although his materialist history obviously also accepts that these physical, structural conditions are also enabling.

26 Giddens 1984: 174ff. Giddens's work is of central importance for the arguments which will be developed throughout this book.

27 Thompson 1968: 9. For critical reviews of Thompson's treatment of 'agency' and 'structure' see Anderson 1980 and Giddens 1987: 203ff.

28 The idea of agency as carrying forward expectations into experience has been widely discussed. An understanding of agency must involve an engagement with the 'horizon' of expectations from which the agent attempts to interpret the world: cf. Gadamer 1975, and see also Heckman 1986 and Warnke 1987.

29 'The most deeply embedded structural properties, implicated in the reproduction of social totalities, I call *structural principles*. Those practices which have the greatest time-space extension within such totalities can be referred to as *institutions*' (Giddens 1984: 17).

2

. . . And of the Dead

The Communal and the Individual

The sheer size of the Avebury earthwork will prompt reflection upon the scale of the undertaking involved in its construction. The labour of those who toiled to cut the ditch and raise the bank, or who hauled the stones up into place, is now commemorated by the monument. This commemoration of a *communal* labour may be contrasted with an apparent identification of the *individual*, encountered amongst the 'single grave' burials which, in southern Britain, date to the beginning of the second millennium. Bradley (1984: 74) suggests that 'the development of large ritual centres may precede the emergence of identifiable elites in the archaeological record. Communal monuments hide the individual hand; single burials reveal it.' In a similar vein Shennan (1982: 156) has written that

> the . . . appearance of rich individual burials in the archaeological record of many parts of Europe in the Early Bronze Age was the result of the rise of an ideology which sought to legitimate social differentiation, not by hiding it, but by representing it as natural and immutable through the use of material culture in the form of prestige items and ritual symbols which constantly reiterated the message.

Both authors use the different categories of archaeological evidence to propose the operation of two very different kinds of social strategy. One strategy hid, whilst the other made explicit, the existence of rank and status amongst the living. This contrast is also evoked with reference to the way time enters into the processes of social evolution. On the one hand the ideology of the community *preceded* that of the individual, whilst on the other the ideology of the individual was *constantly reiterated*.

The large enclosures of Wessex were obviously constructed through communal effort, and we have considered how that labour was organized by a common understanding of social and spatial order. That architecture was also enabling because it represented a set of spatial referents across which people and actions could be distributed and against which they were understood. As an example of this we have examined the ways an audience's attention would have been focused by creating a stage upon which certain people and actions were displayed.

So far the scale of our analysis has been local; the regionalization of activity within the monument has been our concern rather than the totality of the monument. Ultimately we are concerned with the position and orientation of the participant. Only in this way does it become possible to grasp how architecture orders time-space as a medium to distinguish between actions and people. Out of this arose the authority of those who could act for others who could only observe. Thus were prior claims of legitimacy reinforced and extended. Surely, it was in these monuments that the message was 'constantly reiterated', and this message would not have been hidden even though the monuments had required the labour of the majority to build them.

Let us now turn to the other chronological question which is posed by Bradley, the possibility that the ritual centres may have preceded the emergence of identifiable elites. This question raises issues beyond the simple dating of a sequence of monuments and concerns the relationship between the period of monument construction and the longer-term histories of the social formations which the monuments helped to sustain. It is in the very nature of archaeology, where stratigraphic observations are the primary source of information for assessing the date of any building, that the acts of construction which disturb the ground are those which dominate our understanding of a monument's chronology. Artefacts and radiocarbon determinations derived from primary deposits do not, however, define the chronology of a building's use. Certainly the life-span of the timbers at Durrington Walls will have been limited by natural decay to, perhaps, a century, but we have no clear understanding of either how long after initial construction the enclosure, and structures within it, continued in use, or how that use may have changed through time.[1] Three radiocarbon dates from the primary levels of the Durrington enclosure ditch fall around 2500 BC, and material from the packing of one post-hole in the southern circle produced three dates within the third quarter of the third millennium (i.e. 2500–2250 BC).[2] Sixty metres to the south, and overlooking the main enclosure, lay another building, again

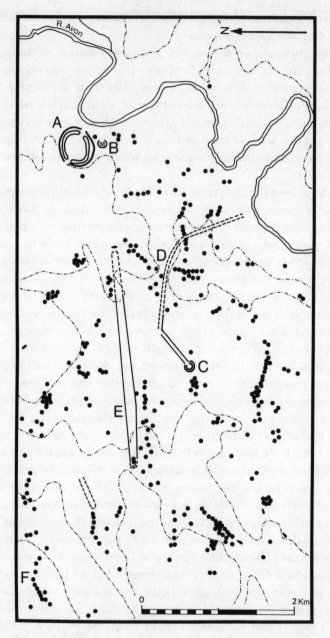

Figure 2.1 Map of Salisbury Plain showing: Durrington Walls (A); Woodhenge (B); Stonehenge (C); the Stonehenge Avenue crossing King Barrow Ridge (D); the Stonehenge Cursus (E); and the Shrewton Barrow Cemetery (F).

made up of multiple rings of standing posts, which this time was enclosed by a bank and ditch.[3] Here, at Woodhenge, radiocarbon dates indicate that the primary ditch silts were forming during the last half of the third millennium.[4]

On the basis of all these dates, the building project around Durrington could have been restricted to the centuries of the third quarter of the third millennium. There is, however, a further complication concerning the interpretation of Stonehenge. Stonehenge lies within 3 kilometres of Durrington (figure 2.1), a distance of little more than that between Avebury and the Sanctuary.

By the last centuries of the third millennium, one of the most remarkable stone-built structures of the ancient world had been erected on a low spur above the dry valley of Stonehenge Bottom. Erected in an earlier enclosure, and probably on the site of an earlier timber building, Stonehenge of today is the result of a complex sequence of building modifications.[5] The monument was approached from the east along an Avenue of two banks and ditches; these run straight for the half kilometre from Stonehenge Bottom.[6] Visually, Stonehenge dominates this approach (figure 2.2). Set centrally within the Avenue, but just outside the entrance of the earthwork enclosure, were two portal stones. These may have stood about 2 metres apart, and only one of these stones, the Heel Stone, now survives (figure 2.3).[7] The entrance gap of the original earthwork had been realigned onto the Avenue by throwing bank material into the south-easterly ditch terminal. Immediately inside this entrance stood another pair of portal stones, of which the only survivor is the fallen Slaughter Stone.

From within the entrance, and indeed from along most of the approaching Avenue, the stone circle appears as a screen of standing stones originally linked by an unbroken line of lintels (figure 2.4). Enclosed behind this screen is a second, free-standing ring of smaller Bluestones within which stood an inner horseshoe arrangement of trilithons (figures 2.5 and 2.6). These trilithons were also accompanied by an arc of Bluestones. The five trilithons are pairs of standing stones, each pair carrying a single, massive lintel. In overall height the trilithons were taller than the stones of the outer ring, and the westernmost trilithon, at the head of the horseshoe, was the tallest of them all. The surviving trilithons can still be seen rising above the outer screen of the stone circle as the monument is approached from outside. Entry from the Avenue into the centre of Stonehenge would seem to have involved passing between two sets of portal stones (and possibly around two further standing stones), between stones of the outer continuous ring and through the inner Bluestone circle, before arriving at the relatively small area defined by the

Figure 2.2 Approaching Stonehenge along the Avenue from Stonehenge Bottom.

Figure 2.3 The entrance to the earthwork enclosure at Stonehenge. The Heel Stone in the foreground was the left (southerly) member of a pair of stones. Behind this the outer circle of sarsens and lintels can be seen, above which projects the surviving members of the inner horseshoe arrangement of trilithons.

Figure 2.4 Stonehenge, with the outer screen of standing stones which was once linked by an unbroken line of lintels.

Figure 2.5 The interior of Stonehenge with the southerly arm of the free-standing trilithon horseshoe. The horseshoe arrangement of smaller Bluestones stands in front of these massive sarsen stones.

trilithons and the Bluestone horseshoe. This inner arrangement effectively represents a deep facade, built on an altogether grander design than the Cove at Avebury. The western apex of the Stonehenge facade was further enhanced by the positioning of the now fallen Altar Stone. Having entered this enclosed space, and by turning around to face the east, the view would have been

Figure 2.6 The surviving upright of the tallest and westernmost trilithon at Stonehenge. The fallen stones of this trilithon are in the foreground.

Figure 2.7 The view from the centre of Stonehenge eastwards. The Heel Stone stands in the distance; the circle of smaller Bluestones stands in front of the sarsen circle.

framed by the stones of the outer ring and by the portal stones beyond (figure 2.7). The midsummer sunrise may have appeared to strike between these stones. The processional avenue, screen and facade are all features familiar from our earlier discussion of Avebury and Durrington. Stonehenge is surely the greatest surviving example of this type of ceremonial architecture, uniting an east–west axis of bodily movement with the movement of the sun and the passing of the seasons (figure 2.8).

Sometime towards the middle of the second millennium a double ring of pits was dug around the outside of the stone circle,[8] and an indication of a further modification to the monument comes from the Avenue. This was extended from Stonehenge Bottom eastwards, crossing King Barrow Ridge where it skirts to the north of a line of bronze age burial mounds (the New King Barrows). The Avenue then swings south, passing between two pre-existing round barrows. Radiocarbon dates would confirm that this extension of the Avenue belongs to the second millennium.[9]

Too much cannot be made of the few radiocarbon dates we have from Durrington, Woodhenge and Stonehenge; we are obviously dealing with a high degree of chronological uncertainty. However, these monuments cannot be treated as autonomous sites whose histories of use can be determined simply by the dates for their construction. They are places within a landscape, and the totality of that landscape might have been realized through the kinds of ceremonial and ritual processions which we have envisaged at Avebury and which are implied by the Stonehenge Avenue. Such practices, if they occurred, will have regularly reworked the available physical resources by linking together places whose histories will have extended beyond the immediate periods of construction to embrace, and to be transformed by, the natural decay of the buildings. The Stonehenge Avenue literally reaches out from the third into the second millennium, implying that the displays of procession were maintained well into the period in which we find the occurrence of single grave inhumations. The line which the modified Avenue follows also implies that its use now made reference to those burials.

Mortuary Rituals

For more than a century, British archaeologists have discussed the implications of the seemingly obvious contrast between the communal treatment of human skeletal remains, enountered in many neolithic mortuary monuments, which generally predate the great enclosures and belong to the fourth millennium BC, and the 'single grave' traditions of the second millennium and the

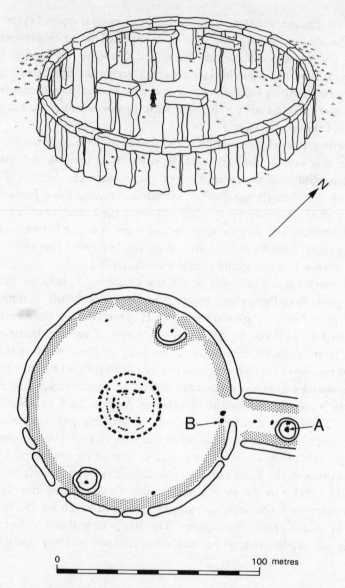

Figure 2.8 Schematic reconstruction of the sarsen circle and inner trilithon arrangement of Stonehenge, excluding the Bluestones and the Altar Stone (after F. Le Brun), not to scale with a plan of the restored stone arrangements at Stonehenge showing the Heel Stone (A) and Slaughter Stone (B). (After Burl 1976; Pitts 1982; RCHME 1979)

early Bronze Age.[10] Before the advent of radiocarbon dating, the accepted chronologies for the Neolithic and early Bronze Age were very short; for example, when Piggott published his *Neolithic Cultures of the British Isles* in 1954 he was able to confine the history of the entire British Neolithic to within 500 years. Consequently, what we now recognize to have been long-term transformations were effectively collapsed into brief and seemingly dramatic chronological horizons, and one such horizon appeared to mark the change in the way the dead were treated. Radiocarbon has now lengthened our chronology for the Neolithic and Bronze Age. The former now covers at least two millennia, and it is clear that the changes in mortuary practices were the culmination of much longer-term processes.

It is generally accepted that the development of 'single grave' burial by the end of the third millennium does represent a significant shift in the nature of indigenous social practices, displaying a previously unattested emphasis upon the status of the individual. The argument could now withstand rather closer scrutiny in the light of our analysis of the ceremonial enclosures. Given that an elaborate means for making explicit the differences between the living already existed in the late neolithic ceremonies of Wessex, should we necessarily accept Shennan's suggestion that the changes in mortuary rituals signified the rise of an ideology concerned with the immutable qualities of social rank? Surely one form of such an ideology was already in place?

The view that the mortuary traditions of the Neolithic should be characterized as 'communal' arises from the numerous excavations of earthen and stone mortuary mounds in northern and western Europe. Many of these contained reserved areas which might hold the mixed remains of a number of individuals.[11] Two traditions of monument building have been defined on the basis of the building materials used. Within megalithic tombs we find stone-built chambers, whereas turf and timber were the main building materials in the non-megalithic tradition. In both, the reserved areas were normally enclosed in a mound of stone, turf or soil, or of rubble derived from surrounding quarry ditches. Most studies assume that these monuments were the tombs of communities who practised a form of communal burial rite, and once this view was adopted archaeologists were happy to accept that a common set of beliefs motivated this rite. This has encouraged generalizations to be made about such beliefs on the basis of observations on the fragmentary remains of a variety of different monuments. The net effect has been for archaeology to create the synthesized totality which is known as the 'neolithic burial tradition'.[12] This archaeological synthesis took its most elaborate form with the invention of the 'megalithic missionaries': that elect group of itinerants who supposedly spread the idea of communal burial around the Atlantic seaboard of Europe.[13] Cultural archaeology was able to sustain this entire edifice by treating each local variation in the form of individual monuments as the transformation of an architectural and funerary tradition which had mutated from a definite and founding point of origin.

Although the assumptions which lay behind cultural archaeology have been dismantled, we will still find archaeologists engaged in the endless comparison of structural features between one monument and another. To what end? No single creed of beliefs need have determined the treatment of the dead, so none need be sought each time a new tomb is excavated. When Piggott discussed the plan of the megalithic structure at West Kennet he made the analogy with a Christian church, claiming that the architecture satisfied the requirements of 'prescribed liturgical and ceremonial perform-ances' (1962: 61). The analogy is surely misleading, imposing as it does a means of religious practice, which we will only encounter amongst 'religions of the Book' with their written laws and creeds, upon the oral traditions of the Neolithic.[14]

There never was a single body of beliefs which characterized 'neolithic religion'. If such had existed then we might wonder why so many neolithic communities did not build tombs, or why so many tombs were either empty or contained few bodies whilst others contained many. The variety of practices attested by these monuments cannot be explained as the expression of a single, underlying cultural idea. Certainly the monuments may have repre-sented a core or dominant body of symbolism which, whilst being widely recognized, was none the less deployed to carry forward many possible tradi-tions of knowledge.[15]

Funerals, of which burial is one strategy, involve the removal of a corpse from among the living and its disposal, a process which might also ensure the departure of the spirit or ghost which would otherwise haunt the community. The living are also changed by such rituals. It is from them that the mourners are selected, perhaps through their affinal relationship to the deceased, and their duties will focus upon the treatment and disposal of the corpse. By their actions in officiating at the funeral, they will ensure that certain of the duties and statuses of the deceased are relocated within the living community. Funerary rites therefore control both the transition of death and the reproduc-tion of the obligations and statuses of the living. The latter has tended to be overlooked in archaeological studies which focus almost entirely upon the treatment of the corpse, taking that treatment to be indicative of the de-ceased's status. An alternative is to recognize the dual transformation achieved by funerary rites, namely the transition from life to death and the re-establishment of the ideal totality of the living community. Funerals do not simply look back upon the life of the deceased but also enable the participants to look forwards to the remaking of the community.

Although excavators normally assume that the recovery of human remains attests to the fact of a burial, there are other strategies which operate with reference to the human corpse and which will result in similar archaeological deposits. The circulation of human material, demanded perhaps at those moments when ancestors were required to intervene amongst the living, is one example. Even when the presence of ancestors seemed all-pervasive in people's day-to-day lives, we might still expect a particular place to be selected where they could be approached and to which sacrifice was directed. Indeed, it would not be surprising if such foci were also to contain the physical remains of those ancestors, available perhaps for display on occasions associated with ancestral rites. These rituals would have re-inscribed relations between the living with new meanings, because of the clear identification they established of those who could initiate, and direct, such proceedings through their control of the ancestral remains.

The physical remains of the corpse now becomes a medium through which different, if closely related, strategies might have operated. By distinguishing between funerals, in particular burial, and ancestral rites we are in a rather better position to untangle the complexity of the archaeological evidence. Funeral rites control the transformation of death itself and relocate certain statuses and obligations among the living. Ancestral rites allow an approach to be made, by the living, to those who are already dead. The relationship between the two is obviously complex; funeral rites can create ancestral resources, and the ancestral domain may have been prepared to receive the dead at times of burial. We must be more careful in considering the technologies by which these relationships between the living and the dead were structured, because it was through these technologies that the living transformed the material conditions which defined their own existence.[16]

Let us now return to the apparent contrast between the 'communal' burial tradition of the Neolithic and the 'single grave' traditions which arose at the end of the third millennium. Funeral rites obviously existed in all periods; they secured a cultural separation between life and death, and defined the passage travelled from one state to the other. Such rites will have focused upon the treatment and the transformation of the corpse, in which the period of liminality (the actual transition from 'life' to 'death') will have played a particularly significant part.[17] The organization of these rites will have varied enormously, and this variation must largely determine what has survived archaeologically. Obviously burial within an earth-dug grave is one funerary rite which secures a high degree of archaeological visibility, in contrast for example to cremation and the subsequent scattering of the ashes. The organization of the funeral will have contributed to the way the relationship between life and death was understood by the participants. The relationship was structured spatially as the corpse was carried into death, a journey which may have terminated at the grave, or at the funerary pyre, or elsewhere. Each socially recognized death will have initiated the period during which that path had to be followed, an activity which, each time it was repeated, had the potential of inscribing a spatial orientation between life:death upon the remembered landscape. When both were practised, funerary and ancestral rites would have required some common focus. The dead may have been transferred to an ancestral tomb or to a burial ground where the correct moment of deposition may itself have been judged in terms of the state of the corpse. By negotiating, in this way, the length of the liminal period it would have been possible for the moment of the final committal to be fixed by reference to a more routine cycle of ancestral celebrations.

Time and place could be used to construct the cultural values of life:death in such a way that certain values (such as the presence of the ancestors) appeared to structure other activities (such as burial). The dominant cultural value would have also found expression in language where ideas of inheritance and ancestral intervention were expressed. Any particular use of these cultural resources will have had obvious implications for the organization of future funerary and ancestral rites. The third millennium appears not so much to mark a shift from 'communal' to 'single grave' burial as a more complex transformation whereby different mortuary rites (funerary and ancestral) were situated in the contemporary landscape by different forms of monumental referent (the 'tomb' or the 'single grave').

Monuments and the Ancestral Presence

Neolithic mortuary mounds did not spring fully formed into the world of the fourth millennium because the communities suddenly discovered their need for collective burial. The monuments, and those which succeeded them, arose as a manifestation of projects structured by the ways people understood the transformation from life to death and by the ways in which that understanding engaged with the physical realities of their contemporary, acculturated world. Again it is the duality which operated between the participants' expectations of how they should act and the physical consequences of their actions which is important. The dead were carried into a world which was ready to receive them, a pre-existing order which structured the initial process of deposition. Once completed, the burial deposit would facilitate the possibility of future ancestral veneration. As Kinnes has commented, it is hardly surprising that megalithic monuments can be described as of 'multiperiod' construction (Kinnes 1975; cf. Corcoran 1972). They were an architecture which witnessed constant use and reworking, only some of which will have left any archaeological trace. Multiperiod monuments are not a sequence of monument types as if constructed by placing one monument upon another. They arose as the consequences of reworking certain categories of space and architectural form. It was by the practical use of these categories that the possible relationships between life and death, and indeed the very concepts themselves, and between the living and ancestors were brought into existence.

Something of this reworking can be illustrated by reference to a single monument, although the example is drawn from beyond our immediate area of study. Excavation beneath the megalithic cairn at Gwernvale, in Glamorgan, South Wales, revealed lengthy periods of pre-cairn activity (Britnell and Savory 1984; cf. Barrett 1988b: 34ff.). The traces of timber structures and artefacts indicate that some of those who had participated in those activities did so by positioning themselves to face a natural monolith. The path of approach they took towards that monolith ultimately defined the line of the major axis of the cairn, and the monolith became incorporated within the cairn as the 'blind' facade. Lateral chambers in the cairn opened to the north and to the south. These physical remains are the material scars which were inscribed upon this place by practices whose histories were contingent upon the available architectural resources, people's ability to interpret them and then to act upon those interpretations. They were part of the means by which it became possible to speak of, and refer to, the ancestors. These interpretative procedures, the reading of material conditions, might well have displayed a discontinuous history. We have no reason for assuming that a single and consistent meaning was derived from the re-reading of these texts.[18] Rather, we need to remain sensitive to the way each architectural embellishment will have transformed the physical conditions of future action. Gwernvale is a product of one such series of interpretative strategies which eventually accommodated the rites of human burial at that locale. J. Thomas (1988a) has argued that the laterally-chambered cairns of south-west Britain, of which Gwernvale is one, offered the architectural resources necessary for the funeral process that transformed and reduced the corpse into de-fleshed remains. At the same time these monuments could have become an increasingly important focus for ancestral veneration.[19] If we should not expect a single creed of belief to have been played out in these actions, then we similarly need not seek a single pattern of activity concomitant with the rigid application of such beliefs. We delude ourselves by trying to fix our own understanding of the monument by the application of such functional categories as *tomb*. Should we not try instead to envisage the possible significances placed upon death as it intervened in those other practices executed at such monuments? That certain dominant meanings emerged, and that these were carried forward over a period of time thus structuring the institutionalized practices of the living community, seems clear.

What are the implications of the megalithic and non-megalithic architecture which developed in at least some parts of western Europe during the fifth and fourth millennia? In most cases the monuments enclosed, indeed often sealed, areas or chambers reserved for human remains. In the case of megalithic chambers, it is quite possible that these could have been reopened to facilitate the removal of ancestral remains and the incorporation of additional material as part of a funerary ritual. By way of contrast, the non-megalithic architecture irretrievably enclosed the human material within a mound after a fairly short-lived period of activity. With no future access to that material possible, other than through re-excavation, there are certainly no archaeological grounds for believing that these mounds acted as cemeteries, accommodating the repeated deposition of human remains. The monumental conditions which were being built – long or round mounds, some with distinct facades and forecourts – created a focus for activities whose execution might have made some reference to the ancestral remains stored or sealed within the mounds.

Archaeological traces of burial are, for most of the fourth and third millennia, only poorly represented amongst surviving archaeological deposits. Some burial may have taken place in the megalithic monuments, but burial need not have been a regular practice at these sites. In areas of non-megalithic architecture, burial rites are even more difficult to identify. Whatever funerary rites were practised they did not commonly involve burial in graves, and if deposition of the corpse took place at locations where earthwork monuments had been constructed, then it did so in such a way that left little archaeological trace.

Up to this point we have been concerned with the relationship between mortuary rites, which incorporate both funerary and ancestral rites, and mortuary monuments. We must now recognize that funerary and ancestral rites need only have been one part of a broad spectrum of activities which contributed towards this programme of monument building. Monuments of superficially similar form, such as long mounds, may have been built by drawing upon a much wider variety of symbolic resources, and it need come as no surprise to encounter long mounds which contained no human remains at all. Our archaeological expectation that things of similar form were necessarily of similar function is simply misguided. The way labour obligations were directed would have been expressed through a cluster of symbolic resources; it is these which we should aim to investigate, and not assume the primacy of one particular resource (such as the mortuary rite). By the time the non-megalithic mounds were in place, they did not function as tombs, but they were among the most dramatic features of the Neolithic and Bronze Age upland landscapes. Their continued significance may at times have been fleeting, acknowledged in those momentary actions or in stories by which people made reference to them.

Let us return then, armed with these fairly general observations, to a reconsideration of the monuments around Avebury.

The Avebury Region

Some burials belonging to the fourth millennium are attested in the region. On the high ground to the north-west of Avebury lies the earlier, causewayed enclosure of Windmill Hill. This is demarcated by three rings of interrupted ditch, accompanied by banks on the inner edge of each ditch. What chronological evidence there is indicates that the enclosure was built in the second half of the fourth millennium. Two infant burials were recovered by Keiller, both from the lower ditch fillings. There was little evidence in either case of dug graves, and the bodies, flexed and resting on their right sides, may simply have been placed in the ditches and then covered by soil and rubble (I. Smith 1965: 136). More recently, a third burial of an adult male has been recovered from beneath the outer bank (Whittle 1990a). These burials contrast with other human skeletal material which was scattered throughout the enclosure ditch fills, including fragmentary bones and skull fragments from three juveniles, and the skull and long-bone fragments of at least four adults. In publishing the excavations of the megalithic monument at West Kennet, Piggott established the idea that skeletal material was periodically removed from the chambers. Smith argued that the Windmill Hill skeletal fragments resulted from the similar use of human bone as 'fetishes or as mementos' (I. Smith 1965: 137; cf. Piggott 1962: 68; Brothwell 1961). Windmill Hill and West Kennet (we shall return to the latter site) both raise the methodological problem of distinguishing between the archaeological remains of burial and the remnants of those acts which were concerned with the continuing veneration of human remains. Obviously both kinds of activity may also have taken place at a number of locations within the landscape which need not be specifically associated with the building of any particular earthwork.

On the slopes above the head of the Kennet valley lie the remains of a number of long mounds, the type of monument traditionally associated with neolithic mortuary activity. Three such mounds have been extensively excavated, those of Horslip (Windmill Hill), Beckhampton Road and South Street (Ashbee, Smith and Evans 1979). In none of these can it be demonstrated that mortuary rites were an essential element of the process of mound-building. Pre-mound evidence indicates a lengthy history of land use and environmental changes which include clearance, cultivation and grazing at South Street, and open pasture below the Horslip mound. Each mound obviously lay within the patchwork of a subsistence landscape, and their siting was presumably determined by the regionalization of human activities across that landscape. Each was a place of specific congregation, whose significance was predetermined by the nature of the activities which had long taken place there, but which have left us such insubstantial traces. These traces include a line of intercutting pits and scatter of artefacts from beneath the Horslip mound, and traces of burning, stake-holes and a scatter of flint flakes situated close to a field edge beneath the South Street mound. Small clusters of stake-holes and areas of burning clearly predated the Beckhampton mound by some years, but three ox-skulls had been placed on the ground surface demarcating the axis of the mound immediately prior to its construction.

These traces are the slight, and apparently inconsequential, remains of the meetings and exchanges between people who by these acts of inscription remembered the significance of each place. Of course the mounds are not 'single phase monuments' (cf. Ashbee, Smith and Evans 1979: 17) which had, fortuitously, sealed these earlier remains. Construction was contingent upon the way people occupied the landscape, giving the areas of pasture above the valleys a more local and specific significance.[20] It was the presence and the actions of certain people here at particular times of the year which defined the significance of these places, the creation of a cultural geography in terms of time and place. Elsewhere some regionalization of the landscape may have been structured by reference to mortuary rites, with the construction of embanked enclosures to contain the human remains. However, at Horslip, Beckhampton Road and South Street we find no explicit reference to the dead. The building of the Beckhampton and South Street mounds involved the construction of a series of fenced bays into which were dumped deposits of sarsen, turf and chalk rubble. The Beckhampton mound was further revetted by chalk and turf and the South Street long mound was fronted by a solid mass of chalk rubble. The flanking ditches, whence much of the building material came, were abandoned once the mounds were in place. These places had been materially transformed and they were recalled in future references by virtue of the earthworks which had been erected over them. They may not have contained human remains; what the future inhabitants of this landscape will have understood by these monuments is another question.

If the relationship between mortuary rituals and the significance of certain places in the neolithic landscape appears at most ambiguous, then there were other places where mortuary rites were drawn more explicitly into the building of a monument. The megalithic mound of West Kennet is one such example. It is one of a small number of megalithic mounds in the Avebury area (figure 1.2) and the only example to have seen modern excavation.[21] The mound lies along the contour of a false crest above the Avon, and less than 1.5 kilometres to the west of the neighbouring megalithic mound of East Kennet. Excavations, originally by Thurnam and later by Piggott, have concentrated almost entirely upon the stone chambers in the eastern end of the mound and as a consequence we know little about the history of the mound itself. Circumstantial evidence does suggest that the mound is the product of a complex constructional sequence in which the stone chambers were not necessarily primary but may have been set within a pre-existing mound. Again we must also guard against assuming that the significance of the place was originally defined with reference to mortuary rites. Nevertheless, by the time the chambers had been erected and the dead and ancestors invited to reside here, mortuary rites were one of the central concerns of those who visited the site. The date of construction of the chambers is unclear, there being no radiocarbon dates for material from the stone holes, although the ceramic evidence would certainly indicate that they were standing by the mid fourth millennium.

The megalithic structure takes the form of a central passage out of which opens two pairs of lateral and one western chamber. The passage itself was entered through a curving facade of stones which were slightly graded in height towards the central opening, and which formed the backdrop to a small staged forecourt area to the front of the monument. Thurnam excavated the western chamber, going in through the roof, and a length of the passage leading eastward from it. Piggott removed the fills of the remaining four chambers and the rest of the passage and unravelled the later architectural history of the forecourt.

In its original form the megalithic structure offered a complex series of operational choices to those who entered. Let us, for the sake of argument, maintain a distinction between those whom convention allowed to move between the forecourt stage and the chambers, and those who could only observe. The common theme of the megalithic and timber architecture which we have outlined in the first chapter is maintained here; a facade in front of which lies a stage upon which the orientation of the participants distinguished between those who faced towards the facade and those who faced out from it (figure 2.9). It was the latter who were able, by their own actions, to bracket a period of activity which linked the front-space of the stage with the back-space of the chambers. This period commenced when the initiates turned away and moved into the area hidden within the body of the mound, and it was terminated as they re-emerged. The contrast was clearly drawn between the bodily movement of these participants and the fixed, and relatively passive, gaze of the observers. The movement of the initiate was, however, circumscribed by the form of the passage and chambers. In plan the chambers seem to represent the neat oppositional logic between front:back and left:right[22] but, as a region through which a person might move, that subjective experience cannot be so easily described. A series of choices existed, either to move directly through to the back (western) chamber, or to turn left or right into the side chambers before reaching the western chamber, or to enter these side chambers last upon return from the deepest reaches of the western chamber. Whilst this western chamber may appear as the point of reference about which movement in and then out of the tomb was constructed, the simple spatial geometry of the side chambers could be reordered by the choices made concerning temporal priority. Spatial relationships cannot be described as fixed once we recognize that their ordering is realized by a sequential movement through time. This is of critical importance when we come to consider the deposits recovered from these chambers because the ability to monitor and to reinvent a spatial ordering between the chambers will always have been possible for those who gained access to them.

The monument orientated each participant and called upon them to recognize the distinctions which existed between them. For those who moved between the forecourt and the chambers and for those who watched, the monument represented a container of resources accessible only to the former. The material on the floor of the side chambers which were excavated by Piggott, and from the western chamber excavated by Thurnam, comprises a substantial deposit of human bone with the addition of one cremation from the north-east chamber. The bone deposits were concentrated towards the rear of each side chamber lying, so Piggott records, on a turf line. How such a turf had survived the building of the stone chambers or any intensive activity within the chambers is unclear. However, those who gained access to these deposits may have added to them, or withdrawn bones for display outside the tomb, or they may have consulted and reordered the material they found.

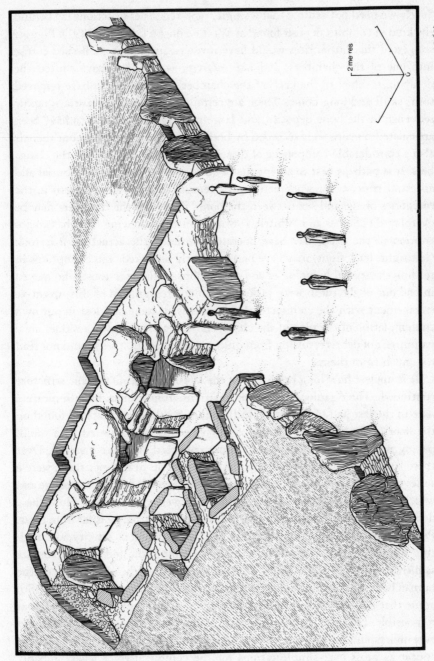

Figure 2.9 The West Kennet long barrow. An isometric view of the chambers and forecourt. (After S. Piggott 1962)

Surely we need not assume that a single, repeated series of actions lay behind the kind of complex deposit found at West Kennet (cf. Barrett 1991). Piggott suggested that burial rites would have involved introducing a fleshed corpse into one of the chambers, and later activity would then have shifted the decaying residual to the back of the chamber and might also have removed some skull and long bones. There are certainly indications of a stratigraphic sequence in the bone deposits, and large parts of what appear to have been articulated remains were recorded by both Piggott and Thurnam, but there is also a considerable component of disarticulated bone scattered in the chambers. It is perhaps best to accept that a quite complex interplay of burial and ancestral rites was at work here, and attempts to establish a pattern in the categories of age and sex between the bones in each of the chambers may be overplayed (Thomas and Whittle 1986). Whilst not denying that the categorization of the dead may have operated spatially, the actual form it took (left:right, back:front) may have been regularly reworked, and the options in reading the spatial homologies and oppositions available to those who moved in and out of the tomb were varied. Again our recognition of this inventive engagement with the architectural resources is all too easily lost in our own contemplation of the plan of the chambers. The archaeological residues are a palimpsest of debris resulting from quite varied strategies; we should not read too much from them.

It is unclear how long these uses of the West Kennet megalithic structure continued. Three radiocarbon determinations from human bone indicate a date in the last half of the fourth millennium for the bone material found on the floor of the chamber.[23] Some of the bone had been covered by a rough paving which was derived, in part, from collapsed chamber material. Over these layers, and apparently filling the chambers up to the roof slabs, were a series of artefact-rich 'blocking' deposits which extended into the passage and which Thurnam also recorded as filling the western chamber. How these deposits had been introduced into the chambers and passage is far from clear. Piggott regarded them as the product of a single period of activity, although this would imply a considerable period of time indicated by the artefact sequence (perhaps 1,500 years or more) separating the deposition of the human bone and the final filling of the chambers. Thomas and Whittle (1986) argue that a more gradual process, perhaps a series of intermittent acts, was responsible. However, it seems unlikely, perhaps unnecessary, that we should ever understand the processes of infilling in any detail; all current suggestions appear as gross over-simplifications for the complexities of what probably took place. It is possible that intermittent access into the interior of the tomb occurred over a very long period. All we can do is to recognize that the ultimate effect of that activity was to close up the chambers and to convert the hollow structure into a form of solid sculpture where entry would only have been possible by excavation. Thus, in the fourth millennium the participants could have staged one form of practice, where initiates moved between the front stage and the back-space of the chambers, but by the beginning of the second millennium such practices were no longer possible. The back-space areas had long since been closed off, and the stage itself was also redesigned. A more massive and continuous facade now ran across the eastern face of the mound (figure 2.10). Activity in front of this facade would still have been orientated with respect to it, but direct movement between this region and the back-space of the chambers had long since become impossible. Any entry into the chambers would then have involved pulling aside the capstones and excavation down into the deposits. That such entries were made might be indicated by the beaker pottery high in, but not at the top of, the fill in the north-west chamber. If burial rites had involved the transportation of the corpse into these chambers then the last time such rites may have been practised was over a millennium before the final sealing of the tomb. There is a clear and lengthy chronological break between any burial deposits being made here and the 'single grave' traditions of the late third millennium.

Funerary rites become recognizable in the archaeology of the late third and early second millennia because at least some of the dead were now put into earth-dug graves. Whether these burials represent the establishment of an ideology which explicitly recognized individual status is another matter. The burial tradition had the effect of marking out specific locations in the land-scape by acts which were directly connected with the termination of a funerary ritual. Generally these locations seem to have been chosen to be away from the major enclosures, although they did occasionally involve reuse of earlier long mounds. The nature of each grave deposit and its archaeological residues was determined by the overall structure of the funerary rite. If funerary rituals secure a cultural transition between life and death, then the corpse is the obvious symbolic medium through which much of that ritual is likely to be structured. Its isolation, preparation and dressing may have marked the beginning of the funerary ritual, whilst the liminal phase could have been lengthy and involved not only the transportation of the corpse but also its storage and its decay. The ritual period usually closes with the stabilization of these liminal transformations and with the final acts of dis-posal which include the lighting of a funerary pyre or the placing of the cadaver in its grave. Throughout the process the mourners are defined through their relationship to the corpse. They may prepare, tend and carry it and they officiate at the graveside; further, as I have stressed above, the burial

Figure 2.10 The West Kennet long barrow with the later sarsen facade standing across, and blocking, the entrance.

becomes a rite of transition for them, involving their isolation from the rest of the community, an isolation which may end with the final deposition of the corpse, but which may also be marked after this by other means such as particular forms of dress.

Acts which closed a particular path between life and death were amongst those which also began the return of the mourners to their wider community. In the case of the inhumation rituals of the early second millennium, those final acts focused around a grave which had been, quite literally, carved into a particular place on the landscape. We will return to consider the full implications of this funerary practice in chapter 5; for the time being we can simply take an example by way of illustration.

On a spur of high ground just over 4 km to the south-west of Avebury and beyond the end of the Beckhampton Avenue something of the last stages of an inhumation ritual can be recognized (figure 2.11). Here, at Hemp Knoll, a coffin was brought to the graveside. It contained the corpse of a 35- to 45-year-old male. The body was tightly bound in a 'foetal' position; it was decorated with a bone toggle, possibly suspended from the waist, and a piece of polished greenstone traditionally identified as an archer's bracer was attached to one arm. A beaker had also been put in the coffin, at the feet of the corpse. When the coffin was lowered into the grave the body lay facing east. As the chalk rubble was piled back into the grave an antler pick and an ox-hide were thrown into the fill and it seems quite reasonable to accept the suggestion that the ox-hide represented 'some sort of cloak' (Robertson-MacKay 1980: 148). Perhaps this 'cloak' was the garb associated with one of the officiates at the burial and, if this is so, then the grave-fill captured not only the moment when the corpse was securely removed from amongst the living, but also the moment when the mourners could have cast off their role and begun their return to the community. Although the deposits overlying the grave were much eroded, it seems likely that the grave was marked by a low chalk mound which was later enlarged by a further capping of turf and chalk and surrounded by a ditch. The burial of a child on the old ground surface immediately preceded the building of this mound.

What was new about the single grave inhumation ritual was not that it reflected either a new type of social formation, or the ideology of that formation, but that the funerary rituals appear to have been reordered in such a way as to fix the end of each individual ritual at a specific and permanently marked location in the landscape. It was at these places that the dead were defined and from which the living carried forward the obligations which they had inherited from that death. Inhumation graves of the early second millennium often appear rich because of their associated artefacts; it is this which has led to the suggestion that they are the graves of an emergent social elite. However, such grave assemblages will include the residues of decoration and dress derived from the corpse, artefacts placed beside the corpse such as the beaker, and artefacts specifically associated with mourning and abandoned at the end of the ritual. It is the role of the *grave* as a container of deposition at the close of the funerary ritual which has ensured that so much material survives archaeologically. By contrast, for example, in the case of cremations it is the funerary pyre which fulfills the function of closing the funerary process and the resulting archaeological deposits are consequently 'impoverished'.[24] These artefact assemblages are not so much an indicator of a newly established elite as the fortuitous outcome of a reordered funerary ritual.

A number of writers have argued that the earliest inhumation rituals of the late Neolithic represented a direct challenge to the ritualized authority which had traditionally derived from the control of the ceremonial centres. This challenge operated, so it is argued, through the appropriation of a new and exotic range of symbolic resources which were included in some of the grave deposits.[25] There are two issues here. The first is the assumption that the artefacts contained in beaker and later grave assemblages were in fact exotics,

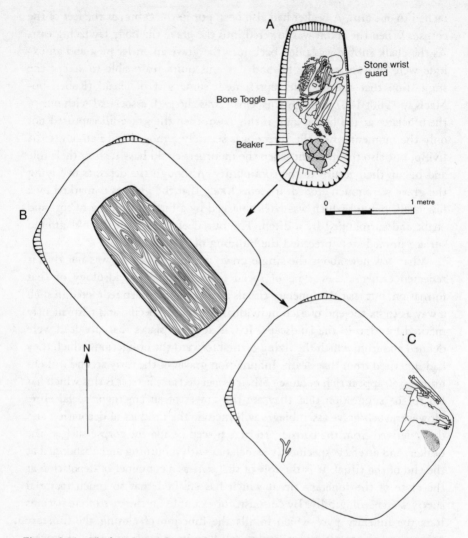

Figure 2.11 The burial procedure at Hemp Knoll. The corpse and associated artefacts were placed in a coffin (A) which may then have been covered and lowered into the grave (B). As the grave was backfilled an antler pick, ox-hide and some charcoal were also deposited (C). (After Robertson-MacKay 1980)

something which we will consider in detail in chapter 4; the second issue concerns the actual mechanism by which the burial rituals could ever have been able to launch such a sustained challenge against traditional forms of authority. The argument put forward on the latter issue depends upon an acceptance that the burial rituals involved the public sacrifice of materials which were procured through restricted and probably competitive exchange networks. By using these items in this way they were converted into a form of 'symbolic capital', the sacrifice of which emphasized both the success of those involved and the failure of those excluded by their inability to procure the necessary ritual paraphernalia.[26] Could the control and the consumption of such artefacts at the funeral offer any such challenge to the traditional structures of authority? It would be difficult to see how, simply in terms of scale. The material accompanying the corpse at Hemp Knoll, or the beaker, knife-dagger and shaft-hole axe from the grave at East Kennet (Kinnes 1985: A8) are all quite small artefacts. The Hemp Knoll material was placed in the coffin, perhaps at an early stage of the ritual process. In any case it is difficult to imagine who else saw this assemblage, other than those who were attending directly upon the preparation of the corpse. This was the very group who had already defined themselves partly through the use of those particular objects, and partly through the order of the funeral procession itself. The more public display of the funerary ritual took place not so much through the medium of the artefacts placed around the body, but rather through the funeral cortege. What was being claimed in these rituals may have been a form of social identity, marginal to other more dominant forms of political control but which need not have operated as a direct challenge to those dominant political structures.

The marginality of these single grave burial practices is implicit in the location chosen for the graves. Funerary processions seem to have terminated away from the enclosure at Durrington.[27] The grave of a child was placed within the inner timber setting of Woodhenge,[28] and the burial of an adult male had been performed in a grave cut into the bottom of the ditch. Such burials were clearly secondary to the enclosures they inhabited. In the case of Avebury, those burials which occur in association with the monument do so at the Sanctuary and along the line of the Kennet Avenue, and not within the circles themselves. In the Sanctuary the grave of an adolescent was dug against one of the stone-holes of the inner ring; the corpse was tightly crouched and facing east, and by its legs lay a beaker (Cunnington 1932: 313). In the Avenue, graves had been dug at the foot of four of the stones so far excavated, two of which seem to have been dug soon after the stones had been erected, and in no case did the graves predate the erection of the stone.

Conclusion: Images of the Community and the Individual

We began with a contrast, between the *idea* of the community and the *idea* of an individual distinction in status. Does such a contrast adequately describe the form of the historical transformation which occurred at the end of the third millennium? The enclosures, mortuary deposits and burials are the material conditions by which knowing subjectivities were carried forward in time. The social project is always created out of the way people are able to stand before others and to speak and to act with the authority of those who expect to carry forward their utterances because they are understood and are effective. For this to occur, such utterances must conform with the pre-expectations of those who listen. They must maintain some degree of control over a common body of symbolic resources and have some hold on particular traditions of knowledge.

The changing material conditions were used by humans who had memories and expectations about themselves, others and the world which they inhabited, and they spoke and acted with reference to these available physical resources. Different resources could enable different ways of talking and different traditions of understanding to come into being and, as we will see in the next chapter, they allowed the possibility of metaphysical values to be realized, for example in the way ancestors were presenced through the medium of the megalithic and non-megalithic monuments. No neat sequence of social types emerges; rather we find the complex overlaying of experiences and understandings which acted upon and created the human subject. Communal burial traditions were not replaced by single grave traditions at the end of the third and the beginning of the second millennium. Instead, ancestral resources had occasionally been mobilized during the fourth and early third millennium, perhaps for relatively short periods of time, by strategies which marked out and which gave certain places a monumental form. By the early second millennium burial rites started to operate in a somewhat similar way through the use of the individual grave as a fixed point within the landscape. Burial rituals were instigated by the death of an individual, and the corpse acted as the central symbolic medium for the transmission of that ritual. The inherent concern with the rights and obligations inherited by surviving kin was not something new. What was new was the way the burial reworked the landscape, leaving a different kind of material trace. If these burial practices did allow for competition in social status then, in whatever way that competition may have operated, be it in the nature of the funeral feasts or the grandeur of the procession or in the claim to a particular place in the burial ground, it is unlikely that such displays could have surpassed in scale the elaborate processional displays which were well established in and around the henge complexes of southern Britain. These displays may well have continued into the opening centuries of the second millennium.

Ancestral, ceremonial and funerary rituals created images of a moral and political order which were read and understood from the perspective of other and more diverse experiences. The significance of those images lay in the way they were read and thus addressed those other, absent experiences. The latter part of the third millennium seems to have witnessed a shift away from the mediation of ancestors, as a metaphysical basis of social order, towards living intermediaries. The emergence of this ritualized elite at this time may have paved the way for subsequent changes in the funerary rituals. Transformations occurred not because different and seemingly conflicting ideological images were available but because the experiences and expectations through which those images were recognized were themselves able to change. Consequently it is to the relationship between day-to-day experience and the ritualized imagery that we must now turn our attention.

NOTES

1 Pottery sherds were recovered from the weathering cones in the upper levels of some of the post-holes; Richards and Thomas (1984: 214) suggest that these derived from vessels which had originally been stacked at the foot of the standing posts. Notice, however, should also be taken of the cairn which was built over the top of one of the post pits after the post had decayed (Wainwright and Longworth 1971: fig. 119 no. 32).

2 The dates from the enclosure ditch are: 3927 ± 90 BP (BM-398); 3965 ± 90 BP (BM-399); 4000 ± 90 BP (BM-400). Dates from post-hole 92 are: 3900 ± 90 BP (BM-395); 3950 ± 90 BP (BM-396); 3850 ± 90 BP (BM-397).

3 Cunnington 1929. Re-excavation of the bank and ditch at Woodhenge is reported by Evans and Wainwright 1979.

4 These dates are 3817 ± 74 BP (BM-677) and 3755 ± 54 BP (BM-678).

5 Atkinson's original scheme for the structural sequence at Stonehenge (Atkinson 1979; first edition 1956) was published before the full excavation programme with which he was involved was completed, and these excavations themselves remain unpublished. Although Atkinson has argued that his scheme, which is still generally adopted (cf. RCHME 1979), has required only minor modification (Atkinson 1979: 203ff.), it is likely to be an over-simplification for the structural complexity of the site. For more recent excavations at Stonehenge: J. Evans 1984, with an examination of the structural sequence and a full radiocarbon date list in Pitts 1982. For earlier excavations: Hawley 1924; 1925; 1926; 1928.

Hoare's comment on Stonehenge is worth repeating: 'even the most indifferent passenger over the plain must be attracted by the solitary and magnificent appearance of these ruins; and all with one accord will exclaim, ' "HOW GRAND! HOW WONDER-FUL! HOW INCOMPREHENSIBLE!" ' (Hoare 1810: 152–3).

6 Two radiocarbon dates for antler from the primary silts of the Avenue ditch are 3678 ± 68 BP (BM-1164) and 3720 ± 70 BP (HAR-2013). These are indistinguishable from a date for antler from a pit for one of the inner trilithons (stone 56) of 3670 ± 150 BP (BM-46).

7 The Heel Stone is an unworked sarsen; all the sarsens which make up the stone circle have been extensively worked. The entrance approach through the earthwork has a lengthy and

complex history; the remains include a number of post-holes and additional stone-holes recorded by Hawley. A ditch had been dug around the Heel Stone, and Pitts shows that this ditch cut the stone-hole of the neighbouring stone. Atkinson believed that this ditch had been rapidly infilled.

8   A radiocarbon date for material from one of these pits, Y-hole 30, is 3190 ± 105 BP (I-2445).

9   For a discussion of the Avenue: RCHME 1979: 11–13.

10 The clear chronological distinction between 'communal' and 'single grave' in Britain was originally defined by Thurnam 1869 and 1871.

11 For a simple generative scheme for megalithic and non-megalithic architecture: Kinnes 1975; 1992: 81ff.

12 The way archaeology tends to create a historical coherence to explain historically diverse materials will be discussed in ch. 4.

13 Daniel accepted the diverse conditions under which megalithic tombs would have been constructed whilst still referring to the 'powerful, compelling, Aegean-inspired religion that made them build their tombs' (1963: 136).

14 Goody distinguishes between religions which depend upon different modes of communication. 'Literary religions have some kind of autonomous boundary. Practitioners are committed to one alone and may be defined by their attachment to a Holy Book.' By contrast, he claims, oral traditions espouse a general morality, a way of life which is open-ended; 'in African languages, I can find no equivalent for the western word "religion" ' (1986: 4–5).

15 Colin Richards discusses the experience, in terms of physical conditions and bodily movement, of entering such monuments, and the way an understanding of order may have been drawn from such experiences (1992).

The reworking of experience through interpretation can also be the reworking of a text: 'fortunately, modern theological argument about the actual meaning of the bible is irrelevant to our present purpose. It is not necessary . . . to determine whether or not Christianity is itself intrinsically anthropocentric. The point is that in the early modern periods its leading English exponents . . . undoubtedly were' (K. Thomas 1983: 24).

16 Ancestral rites are generally accepted as lying at the heart of activities associated with neolithic mortuary monuments. For an earlier development of the issues discussed here: Barrett 1988b.

17 The making of an 'intermediary' period between life and death in funerary rites was identified by Hertz (1907) and drawn into a more general class of transition rites by Van Gennep (1960). The importance of the liminal period for the creation of a transformation between fixed states has been developed by Turner (1977) and Bloch (1985). For a general discussion of burial rites: Huntington and Metcalf 1979.

18 'Rather than regarding megaliths as filled with a pre-given meaning which has to be thawed out, we should, as Barthes suggested for the plays of Racine . . ., regard them as an "empty site" eternally open to signification. This openness creates a paradigmatic relationship to society, which allows megaliths to establish ties to any historical moment and culture . . .' (Olsen 1990: 199).

19 For a consideration of how megalithic monuments were drawn into a wider range of activities, in which the architectural features operated as foci for those activities: Lynch 1973; Case 1973: 193ff.; Fleming 1973.

20 For general models of land use in the upper Kennet valley: R. Smith 1984; Whittle 1977:

18–24, and 1990b.

21 For excavation at West Kennet: Piggott 1962. For a survey of the long mounds in the Avebury area: Barker 1985.

22 For an interpretation of the West Kennet chambers representing a single spatial order: Kinnes 1981, fig. 6.10A; Thomas and Whittle 1986.

23 The radiocarbon dates from West Kennet are all for human skeletal material from primary levels in the chambers. They are: 4825 ± 90 BP (OxA-449), 4700 ± 80 BP (OxA-450) and 4780 ± 90 BP (OxA-451): Gillespie et al. 1985.

24 For a general consideration of formation processes involved in burial deposits: O'Shea 1984; Tainter 1978.

25 For the general argument of an emergent 'prestige exchange' network: Thorpe and Richards 1984; Braithwaite 1984; Shennan 1986.

26 For an example of the archaeological analysis of proposed cycles of symbolic investment through grave and votive deposition: Parker Pearson 1984.

27 This point was first noted by Whittle 1981: 329 and further developed by Braithwaite 1984.

28 Cunnington 1929: 13. Cunnington claims that 'the skull appears to have been cleft before burial'.

3

The Archaeology of Ritual

Introduction

Sir Edmund Leach once said that although archaeologists, armed with increasingly refined recovery techniques, were able to describe past physical
environments and the physical consequences of the actions of humans who
had occupied those environments, they were none the less unable to understand the motivations for those actions. These motivations arose from specific
and socially embedded beliefs, they were creative and original, they constituted the flows of 'information' operating within the extinct 'social system'.
It is the inner workings of these systems which Leach believed always lay
beyond archaeological investigation (Leach 1973).

The belief that archaeology is constrained in what it can say by the
fundamental limitations of the material evidence is a view too well rehearsed
to be of any interest to us here. These constraints appear to result from the fact
that the evidence is 'no more' than a residue resulting from human action. The
relationship between the expressed motivations and reasoning of the agents,
and the physical consequences of their actions may often seem arbitrary and
thus beyond archaeological recovery. This is a rather peculiar assumption,
given that knowledge and motivations are created within, and by reference to,
given material conditions. If we recognize that knowledge is implicitly
involved in action, then we may wonder why something of that knowledge
is not also embedded in the material conditions and consequences of
that action.[1]

The problem for archaeology is not so much a constraint arising from the
essential characteristics of our evidence, but rather the limited perceptions
which we are prepared to employ in an archaeological interpretation of the

past. Our knowledge is not grounded upon the material evidence itself, but arises from the interpretive strategies which we are prepared to bring to bear upon that evidence.[2]

One of the currently accepted limitations, constraining all archaeological investigation, is that human knowledge is discursive and as such can be revealed only through language, as either spoken or inscribed. The archaeologist neither hears the spoken word, nor understands how to read the vast majority of the encoded texts. Thus, whilst the anthropologist might ask 'what do you mean by doing that?', no such option is available to the archaeologist. It is this rupture between the agent's expressively motivated actions, with their immediately understood and contextually specific meanings, and the distanciated physical remnants of those actions, which seems to define the challenge of archaeological interpretation. Archaeology currently labours under the misapprehension that an understanding of other people is gained only through a close proximity which allows either for talk or for an available translation of the spoken and written word. However, as *all* knowledges of others involve interpretation, there can be no moment when anyone else is immediately revealed to us. What the archaeologist must discuss is the nature of the interpretive challenge. That interpretive challenge has to recognize that the question of knowledge concerns not a truth of what was once known but how was it possible to claim to know, to interpret and thus make sense of the world ('how do you make sense of this or believe it to be "true"?'). In other words, the object of archaeological enquiry is not to recover some transcendental truth available to the past and to the present, but to reveal the conditions under which certain knowledges become possible.

There is an additional point which must be noted, although I do not wish to develop it here. This is the questionable emphasis which is currently placed upon a linguistic model for knowledge. If knowledge enables action, then all practical actions may be regarded as knowledgeable, in as much as they involve sensory expectations being carried forward into practice. If this is accepted, then we must allow for non-linguistic and pre-linguistic knowledges, as practical ways of knowing the world, but which informants would have considerable difficulty in ever expressing verbally. This may help us to understand, for example, why people who may not 'know' the meaning of certain actions, such as some rituals, will still feel committed to maintaining their practice.[3]

Hopefully these few comments are understandable in the light of our discussion of the henge monuments and the mortuary deposits. We have not uncovered what those monuments meant, and this does not matter for they were never the expression of a single truth. Instead, we have understood how the logic of the known world could have been revealed and sustained, thought and acted through afresh, as various traditions of knowing were reworked upon the available physical resources. It is this form of archaeological interpretation which we must carry forward, by considering how the moments of revelation, achieved in these particular contexts, played back upon other regions of social experience. Such an examination requires that we think about the nature of social existence as built from a network of engagements between people, where the remembered and prejudicial experiences gained in life are carried forward into each new engagement. In this way each interpretive reading, by archaeologists or the agents they study, is either confirmed as empirically valid, or is challenged by the unexpected conditions, or by the unintended consequences, of action.

'Fields of Discourse' – The Regionalized Nature of Social Practices

Social life is lived out as a 'seriality of encounters' between people.[4] Amongst the societal conditions which are the object of this study, such encounters can be characterized as having been highly localized, involving the face-to-face co-presence of the participants.[5] All such encounters occupy regions, or fields, of time-space. Part of the strategies by which such engagements were lived involved using mechanisms to signal the bounding of these regions, bracketing them by various techniques which opened and closed the temporal frame of each engagement. These techniques may include the entry into another's presence, the turning and positioning of the body, vocal cues and the physical demarcation of space.

This basic characterization of social life, which emphasizes how agents regionalize the routine projects of their lives, has, at a purely descriptive level, been explored in the 'time-geography' of Hagerstrand and others.[6] The fundamental principle of this approach is the indivisibility of the human body, and upon that principle time-geography traces the movement of the individual from one locale to another. Each locale is characterized as a setting where a particular group of individuals are brought together for a particular period of time. That allocation of time-space is dedicated to a range of activities which are bracketed off from other activities, not simply in terms of the spatial location where those activities take place, but also in terms of the period of time allocated to them. The individual thus enters and leaves the presence of others in the routine trajectory between, say 'home' and 'workplace'. This involves the practical allocation of time-space to engagements between people and resources, as well as the allocation of time to the movement between each locale.

There are a number of refinements now required to this basic scheme, enabling us to relate it back to the material discussed in the opening chapters, and forward to the question of ritual which will be examined below.

The relationship between the enclosures, as architectural settings, and the regionalized practices which took place within them has already been discussed. Regionalization was not simply defined by physical barriers, but by the strategic deployment of the human body. In the case of Avebury, we have glimpsed the way this architectural resource allowed for a complex interplay of regionalized fields of activity which, when operating alongside each other, erected a contrast between the restricted and hidden regions within the Sanctuary or the Cove and the lengthy display of the processional route. This network of people moving from place to place through time might appear to have expressed a narrative sequence of events.[7]

Time-space allocations constitute the practical reality which people both create and recognize as constituting their own world. They are not a given framework to which the individual agent must necessarily submit, but they are created out of the resources, both material and temporal, which are available to those agents. Time-space allocations are brought into being as agents rework their own understanding of the world and their control over those resources. Thus people carry their memories of how to operate forward into future engagements; they reinvent the time-space matrices which guarantee their own ontological security. This is the point which underlies the analysis already undertaken of Avebury and Durrington. If regionalization is one of the strategies which brings a particular social reality into being, then we, as the external observers who write of the possible ways regionalization was made effective, are always rewriting history. There is no methodology which will discover an absolute network of time-space allocations by which one reality of the past may be described, for no single reality has ever existed. What an interpretive archaeology achieves is an understanding of what *may have been possible* within certain material conditions. This is not 'merely' a speculative programme, as I hope to show throughout this book, but it is certainly an open-ended project in which we must re-evaluate the pasts which we have created.

Let us now extend the insights made available by time-geography away from the simple descriptive framework, towards an understanding of how different social realities were brought into being. Analytically, what time-geography offers is the image of an individual's life made up of a pathway along which a number of places are visited in turn. Many places are simply passed through, others represent 'stations' where time is consumed. These 'stations' or locales are thus distributed serially and are interspersed by periods which are required by the individual both to separate those locales and to move between them. As a process of constituting a social reality, the significance of each locale is determined not only by what takes place there and then, but by what has gone before and what comes after. In other words, it is determined by the memories and the expectations of the participants. Thus an understanding of 'place' depends upon its context within time, a time-context built up from a number of differing trajectories as people meet and then part. What we must do is to attempt to capture something of this duality where what occurs at one moment is given significance by that which is absent, having come before, or that which will take place after.[8]

To emphasize the importance of this issue we can refer back to the material which was discussed earlier. An understanding of the practices which took place in the context of either the enclosure or the mortuary ritual must consider how these practices referred to other, absent places from which the practitioners came and to which they may have returned. I hope to demonstrate here and in chapter 6 that this point is fundamental to our entire study; it is the means by which we can begin to understand the history of the period.

Encounters between people occupy regions, or fields, of time-space, and in their routine, day-to-day activities, people normally move easily between and within such regions. They are practically aware of, and are routinely competent in the use of, the various bracketing mechanisms by which they enter and leave each region, and by which they move from one regionalized setting to another. In some cases the bracketing mechanisms are understated, almost casual, elsewhere they may be more formal and explicit. Between the fifth and the second millennia we might accept that the major allocations of time were those given over to the localized company of others in the routine settings of domestic space and in the labour of production which drew upon nature's own resources. This working upon nature would have determined the *tempo* of life, reproducing a temporal structure which harmonized the routines of life with the 'natural' cycles of the day and night and the passing of the seasons.

Within each field of action a range of specific signalling mechanisms will have been used to bracket that field and to speak and act within it. The competent use of such mechanisms is part of each agent's practical ability in 'knowing how to go on' (Giddens 1979; 1981: 27), in which talk represents the 'casual exchange of conversation in settings of day-to-day life' (Giddens 1987: 99). Talk is executed with reference to a world of experience which is common to the participants (the interlocutors) and where the disposition and movements of their bodies, the use of clothing, architecture and portable artefacts are essential props to speaking effectively. Material culture becomes a system of signification, it is meaningfully constituted by being referred to in talk and in action, by framing the actions and guiding the movements of the interlocutors, and by being exchanged between them.

Communication comprises two elements: the means of transmission and the means of interpretation, and knowing what is said is an issue of interpretation. The first element (transmission) can be regarded as the code which enables and which structures the intention into the doing and the saying. The second element (interpretation) is built from memories and expectations about how the code may be validly used, and this draws upon the range of experiences and expectations which the 'listener' or 'reader' brings with them to any moment of discourse. The ability to speak with the expectation of being understood, and to listen and comprehend, returns us to the interlocutors' practical competence, and their acceptance of the routine *habitus* of cultural existence through which an understanding of the world is structured.[9] The meaning of what is said is therefore found in that space occurring between the act of talking and the range of possible interpretations of what that talk is 'saying'. The power of any discourse involves the strategic deployment of the code in such a way as to limit the options of possible interpretation.[10] Routine actions tend to operate as an empirical confirmation of a range of culturally derived expectations; ontological security is provided because the world is routinely experienced as working in the way it is expected to work. That such ontological security may be challenged by the failure of those expectations seems obvious (cf. Sahlins 1987).

The meaning of any form of communication is always situated within a time-frame extending from the intentions behind the 'saying' or 'doing' through its execution to its interpretation. In talk, the field of discourse is localized, and its temporal duration contains this period of intention–execution–interpretation. Although bracketed from other regions of time-space, each is none the less open because each participant is always pre-informed by a cluster of (perhaps divergent) cultural expectations and by their capabilities in using a range of cultural resources, including language. Each participant may also view one encounter as a necessary part of carrying forward a longer-term project. Thus arises the duality between the moments of communication between agents, and the long-term structures which those moments reproduce. In the small-scale societies under examination here those longer-term structures will have been, primarily, the allocations of resources associated with the reproduction of the natural world. As each agent carried the project of their own lives forward, their own subjectivities were built by submitting to the discipline of a cultural *habitus* which enabled them to act effectively. Their understanding of that *habitus* may have been expressed in terms of a sequence of metaphorical associations where, for example, the seriality of their own lifetime projects was mapped against the cyclical renewal of nature itself (cf. Bourdieu 1977: 143ff.).

As time-geography demonstrates, encounters between people are linked by the paths those same people trace in their movement through time-space. Such paths map personal biographies, they are brought into being as agents employ the cultural resources available to them, and by so doing come to understand something of their own being. Material culture, employed within one field of discourse, can be inscribed with meanings which may be recalled in another, thus guiding the actions in other places and at other times. Giddens has called those objects which 'escape from contexts of presence' and 'incorporate "extended" forms of signification' *cultural objects*.[11] Written texts are the most obvious examples of such objects where traces, encoded upon a durable medium in one context, provide a code from which meanings may be derived in another. Texts therefore gain a degree of autonomy as they break free from the intentions and references of authorship and address the expectations of others situated in quite different horizons of interpretation.

Much of the foregoing has extended, rather more abstractly, the discussion in the first two chapters. The architecture of the henges and the various forms of mortuary deposit were a cultural resource which, when inhabited, enabled certain meanings to be assigned to actions and people by the participants. The cultural resource had no inherent meaning, but contributed towards the structuring of knowledge only when situated in a particular social practice and interpretive framework. The various forms of monument have been described as being developed through time as certain 'structural principles' were reworked upon the increasingly elaborate material residues. The recursive relationship between action and its material context has been stressed. The argument here is that those who understood what took place at these different locales did so by drawing not simply upon the resources present and internal to that regionalized action, but by recalling other understandings and other experiences absent from that moment and that place. Thus the proposed ceremonies and rituals which were performed at these locales have to be situated within a larger context, and this raises a further issue.

If the agent moved from one field of time-space to another by carrying certain memories into their experiences at that place, then we might consider how knowledges derived from these different fields operated one in relation to the other. People build an ability to speak and understand each other based upon different experiences and different expectations. How were different forms of knowledge confirmed or challenged, how did dominant understandings of cultural order arise and how were they maintained? Some hint of how we might approach this issue has already been given. In the first two chapters we have considered how actions, orientated towards death rituals, ancestors and perhaps gods, could have reinscribed particular expectations of cultural order with new meanings. The contrast between what is envisaged as being possible through ritual and ceremonial practices and what has been discussed in this chapter in terms of practical day-to-day activities now demands a clearer definition. Do rituals create particular forms of knowledge, and if so, how might such knowledges operate in relation to other more routine understandings of the world?

Ritual

Archaeologists have tended to see rituals as producing overarching cosmologies, a world-view to which all members of that social group would subscribe. These cosmologies are equated with ideological forms of knowledge, where ideology is taken to represent a 'false' knowledge which 'masks' the images of a 'reality'. Such a notion, as Foucault (1980: 118) objected, sets ideology in opposition to something which is taken to count as 'truth'. Identification of a 'falsehood' presupposes the existence of a 'truth'. The opposition cannot be sustained; to know is to enable, to give the power to act and, as has been argued above, all actions draw upon a knowledge and carry expectations about the culturally mediated truth of the world. Cultural expectations of truth are realized in all actions.

The truth:falsehood dichotomy therefore has political consequences. To identify a claim to knowledge as a falsehood is an attempt to curtail the voices of others and their ability to challenge the authority of certain accepted actions. The struggle for truth is culturally and historically situated, and it permeates all forms of discourse. Ideological knowledges cannot be simply equated with forces which sustain asymmetries of social power by masking the 'truth' of those inequalities.[12] Social authority is routinely exercised where the day-to-day discourse between all social agents reworks the practical, taken-for-granted knowledges which reproduce these asymmetries without any necessary recourse to some dominant ideological scheme.[13]

If ideology is to be rescued as an analytically useful concept which defines a particular mode of knowledge, then the simple truth:falsehood dichotomy must be abandoned, and a more careful evaluation made of the way different forms of knowledge/power are reproduced. By isolating ritual as a distinct region of social practice we must necessarily examine the extent to which such practices constitute a means of knowing which has social consequences distinct from those of other, more routine practices.

Let us begin by taking all discourse as analogous to language use, and follow Ricoeur who sees this use realized in the events of either speaking or writing (Ricoeur 1981: 197). As we have seen, meaning is not inherent to the code but arises between the moment the code is mobilized and the moment of interpretation which seeks meaning from the consequences of that use (from the movement of the body, the sound of talk or from the written text). Interpretation can be characterized as a disciplinary procedure because only a limited range of dispositions capable of reading the code are accepted as valid. Although these dispositions arise in the disciplinary context of the inter-preter, the empirical realization that a meaning (understandable and logical with reference to the generally accepted norms of communication) has been recovered is enough to lead that interpreter to accept the validity of the interpretive procedures which they have employed.

To pursue the analogy further, I wish to maintain the distinction between the discourse of *talk* and the discourse of *text*, because this general distinction will prove useful in our analysis of ritual. Let us remind ourselves that those involved in talking are held in a local, face-to-face region of time-space where the ability to communicate depends upon the pre-expectations which the interlocutors bring with them to this practice, as well as their abilities to monitor the effects of this use of language. Thus, whilst drawing upon experi-ences from beyond the immediate region of language use, talk is none the less executed with reference to a world of experience common to the interlocutors. Consequently, the relationship between intended meaning and interpretation normally seems unproblematically open to negotiation between the par-ticipants of face-to-face communication.

Texts, on the other hand, break free from the immediate intentions and references of the author and become resituated in other frames of reference which belong to the reader. They highlight the ambiguous relationship between the reader and the author.[14] Contemporary critiques emphasize the absence of the author from the text, denying that any reading can ever recover the author's intentions. Consequently, the emphasis shifts away from the author's intentions and is placed upon the structure of the code itself and the way it addresses the reader's own expectations. In effect, the text creates its own readers. This is as may be, but I want to preserve the disciplinary distinction between the expectations of talk and of reading as they appear to operate to the practitioner. In talk, meaning appears as the negotiated out-come of a relationship between practitioners who are present, whilst reading recognizes that the acts and the intentions of authorship are absent from the context of the reader. Texts therefore embody a concept of distanciation, they originate from some other time and from some other place and they hold out the illusion that the author may be recovered through an accurate reading of the text. In other words, to accept the existence of a text is to accept the existence of an absent author.

The expectations of talk and of reading are therefore different. Whilst the former operates as a relatively open negotiation of meaning in a frame of reference held in common between the interlocutors, the latter accepts the permanency of the texts, reading them in the attempt to recover the meanings originally inscribed upon that durable medium by an absent or distanciated author. The 'truth' of the text appears to originate in the moments of authorship and to be revealed within the text itself; it appears to lie beyond the direct control of the reader. Talk and writing/reading define different modes of discourse. They actively construct different concepts of time-space and differences in the ways the material conditions of life may be employed and understood. In talk, material culture seems to offer an immediate frame of reference for the interlocutors whilst, when employed as 'cultural objects', material culture as text appears to have broken free from the context of authorship and to present the reader with an encoded and distanciated message. To engage in talk involves an almost casual discovery of meaning while the text's assertion makes explicit the challenge of interpretation.

What matters here is the way disciplinary expectations enable different relations of presence/absence to be brought into being through discourse. This difference is a powerful element in the structuring principles of ritual. In social life people move, serially, from one region of discourse to another. Ritual discourse is constituted through the expectations of the reader, where a truth may appear to be discursively recovered from the encoded medium of the ritual performance. That medium includes not only symbolic paraphernalia or material culture, but also the bodies and utterances of the participants as they submit to what are regarded as customary practices and, by so doing, bring the ritual process into being. The performance creates the text whose truths, in turn, reveal the existence of other worlds behind it, worlds of ancestors, gods and spirits. The participants of these rituals create, or 'write', the text, but their actions as readers accept an absent author – metaphysical authors in other worlds now open to the gaze of the practitioner.

Maurice Bloch has developed the argument that different forms of knowledge are created through differently constructed experiences of the same world. He distinguishes between knowledges which are learnt out of an everyday experience with an acculturated world, the *habitus* described by

Bourdieu, and those ideological forms of knowledge which are brought into being through ritual.[15] Thus, he argues, we should

> try not to think of knowledge as a whole, either unitary or segmented, but to see it as the momentary crystallisation of different processes which interact on each other, to focus on the processes of formation and their interaction rather than their finished product. (Bloch 1985: 34)

That 'process of formation' recognizes that ritual knowledges are not constituted simply by what happens in the ritual itself (the form of the ritual practice examined by Bloch is an issue upon which we shall comment below) but by the disciplinary expectations which the practitioners bring with them to the regionalized discourse of ritual (Asad 1987; Barrett 1991).

We are now in a position to regard ritual as a process which *creates* a regime of truth and a recognition that the origin of that truth lies beyond the immediate world. This is a different perception from that which expects ritual to *reflect* some pre-existing belief or creed. To return to my opening remarks, the fact that the archaeologist cannot ask the participant 'what do you mean by doing that?' hardly matters in this case, for the question is redundant. More to the point is to seek an understanding of the strategic deployment of resources, made possible by ritual, and the consequences of those practices for other regions of social discourse. It is here that the archaeologist should have something to say.

Rituals carve out regions of time-space; they are bracketed off from other regions of social discourse by a structure which, as Victor Turner demonstrated, is primarily concerned with a social transformation between 'relatively fixed or stable conditions' (Turner 1967: 23). The boundaries of ritual are defined as stable, seemingly autonomous social categories (such as living:dead). The movement between these categories in the period of liminality (dying/death/burial), which is situated at the very heart of the ritual process, only goes to reaffirm their original significance. Bloch has argued that the potency of the ritual message lies precisely in its power to rework and transform social categories through a period of 'anti-structure'. In doing so an alternative image of the world becomes available, and this process, Bloch continues to argue, creates certain dominant values of social order which may be appropriated by those who officiate in the ritual.

Rituals speak of worlds beyond their own boundaries and objectify values which originate beyond the world of lived experience. We can now consider the images which have been evoked with reference to such sites as Avebury and West Kennet. Those who officiated and who occupied the central stage in the ritual displays which were executed at these places did so because their claims to such roles were regarded as legitimate. Rituals may have reinscribed that authority with values which appeared to derive from some external, metaphysical source, and in doing so sacred analogies for that more secular authority may have emerged. None the less, whilst such forms of 'worldly' authority were in this way enhanced, those officiating may also have been placed at some risk because other participants were able to evaluate empirically their ability to speak and act competently and with proper effect within the ritual discourse. It was always open to question whether or not the ritual would work.

Ritual practices enabled those who participated to rework a wide range of their collective experiences against a 'text' whose origin and authority derived from some other, sacred world. The sacred was brought into being by the ritual, and when the sacred was experienced and interpreted then aspects of routine, day-to-day life may have been found to have originated there. Turner identified the role of 'dominant symbols' in ritual as a mechanism to construct a condensed body of symbolic referents, representing axiomatic values which are sustained throughout the ritual cycle and towards which other symbols and experiences may be aligned by metaphoric and metonymic association. Generally agreed, if only vaguely formulated, values may in this way have re-emerged in the interpretations offered for a ritual narrative by the various participants.

There is no single and shared cosmology expressed by ritual. Anthropologists have in the past expected, and have thus tended to invent, too great a level of coherency and order in explaining the rituals they have observed.[16] Rituals may enable a range of readings to be made of general cosmological order, and the extent to which these support and extend political authority derived from other sources of knowledge needs to be examined and demonstrated, and not assumed.

Ritual Discourse in the Late Neolithic

The complex interplay of expectation and experience out of which meaning is constructed requires that we situate any region of social practice, such as ritual, in a network of longer-term projects through which the participants lived their lives. This shift of emphasis seeks an understanding of the way the localized region of social practice (the ritual) contributed to the structuring of longer-term projects and the part it played in the structuring of the social system itself. The opening chapters have been concerned with regions occupied by the practitioners of ritual and ceremony, and we have sought to understand how each region of ritual practice may have been structured. These practices carried forward the longer-term and the larger-scale institutional arrangements of the social system.

One way of expressing this duality of the practice and its location within the social system is to consider how ritual was situated in the time-space networks of other daily and seasonal routines. I do not intend by this to raise a simple dichotomy between 'ritual' and 'secular', but the preceding argument does mean that people were able to make some sense of the ritual 'texts' because they moved between the conditions of routine, day-to-day practice and the discursive moments of ritual and sacrifice. Where and how did people occupy the landscape so that the expectations of routine daily practices could be sustained, carried forward into, and transformed by, the ritualized encounters which we have already described?

Our understanding of those areas with which we are concerned, the chalk uplands at the head of the Kennet valley and to the west of the Wiltshire Avon around Durrington and Stonehenge, is necessarily generalized simply because the available information on settlement and land use remains so elusive. However, this in itself tells us something: that the settlement locations do not appear to have involved any extensive form of ditched enclosure or the construction of deep storage pits, that they may not have been long-lived and densely settled and thus did not result in the substantial accumulation of domestic debris. All these factors, along with the very real possibility that the overall density of settlement on the chalk hills was limited, has resulted in the accumulation of a relatively limited range of archaeological deposits relating to settlement activity.

The chalk uplands in the fifth millennium have been described as marginal to the areas of contemporary settlement, and contrasted with the fourth millennium onwards in which numerous monuments, if not settlements, are encountered. The contrast between the fifth and the fourth millennia seems to reflect the division between the gatherer/hunter economies of the Mesolithic and the 'agricultural' economies of the Neolithic. Our understanding of the former period in this area is scant. Artefacts of this date are defined by the conventions of lithic technology, and such material is sparsely distributed along the margins of the river valleys. Our information on the Neolithic derives from monuments, giving indications of their function, and from the buried soils and ditch deposits which indicate changing regimes of vegetational cover and land use before and after their construction. In the most general of terms, the monuments of the fourth and third millennia were built in an increasingly open environment, although the scale of the clearances of tree cover may have varied. The particular subsistence strategies with which these clearances are associated is unclear. Cultivation is in some cases assumed, but less often demonstrated, and the ultimate development seems to have been towards the creation of areas of grassland.

The contrast between the Mesolithic and the Neolithic is normally presented as essentially a contrast in available subsistence resources, the latter representing the adoption of domesticated animals and cultivation. The resultant models have tended to present images of either the displacement of gatherer/hunters by agriculturalists – who had moved in a fairly steady fashion across Europe – or of a lengthy period of transformation for the gatherer/hunter communities, during which time the agricultural resources which had become available were finally adopted under the pressure of shifting environmental constraints. Contact between the two contrasting subsistence systems seems to lead either to the displacement, or the absorption, of one by the other. In these simple terms the question remains as to how the various forms of monumentality which are associated with the Neolithic were integrated into the agricultural system. Case argued that such monuments as the causewayed enclosures and long mounds must be the product of a late phase of stable adjustment by a colonizing Neolithic, whilst Renfrew has suggested that the megalithic monuments of Atlantic Europe were a territorial adjustment by an agricultural system faced with limited resources of land (Case 1969; Renfrew 1976).

Alternatively, other writers have emphasized the importance of the transformation of social structure over subsistence resources. Bender (1978), for example, argues that social relations and social change should be conceived as operating independently of subsistence specifics, and J. Thomas (1988b) sees the Neolithic as a transformation in relations of production which is bound together at the 'ideological level'. In Thomas's model the ritualized and ceremonial practices implicit in the organization of the monumentality of the fourth and third millennia were integral to neolithic practices; they reworked relations of social obligation through which subsistence resources, whatever they may have been, were deployed.

It would seem that the question of a gatherer/hunter to neolithic transition is open to a more radical revision, one which might usefully begin by abandoning these labels altogether and with them assumptions about the appropriate subsistence strategies by which each should be defined. In place of questions of systemic change at the subsistence level (gatherers to farmers) we may then begin an investigation of the structuring of social practices between the fifth and third millennia, with the aim of elucidating how routine strategies of subsistence reproduction were mediated through increasingly elaborate ritualized encounters at certain places in the reproductive cycle.

These are fundamental issues. Their implications extend well beyond the current area of study and they are issues which we will cover in some detail in chapter 6. That discussion will place the history of land use from the fifth to the third millennia against our understanding of second millennium land use. Before undertaking that discussion, however, we must set in place the groundwork for an understanding of the later period. This will be done by examining firstly one of the classic 'problems' of the early second millennium, the introduction of beaker ceramics, before turning to look at the history of mortuary practices as they can be traced to the middle of the second millennium.

NOTES

1 As Renfrew commented, with reference to Leach's original assertion: 'The dissociation between "material residues" and "sociology" does establish . . . a curious polarisation between mind and matter which the best of present anthropological work . . . has managed to avoid' (1977: 90).

2 This point establishes the basis for an 'interpretive archaeology', a theme to which we will return throughout, and the implications of which will be considered in more detail in ch. 7.

3 For criticisms of the currently dominant 'linguistic' models of culture: Bloch 1991, Hodder 1989.

4 For the seriality of social life: Giddens 1984: 73ff.

5 It is essential to recognize that the memory of other values, peoples and places are carried into such local engagements. In this way such engagements can never be regarded as being closed.

6 Pred (1977) has referred to the 'choreography' of human existence. For work concerned with the temporal and spatial structuring of social relations: Gregory and Urry 1985.

7 The contrast may be described as one between regions of 'low presence availability' and 'high presence availability'.

8 I attempt here to recognize some of the criticisms of Yates (1990) as directed towards my earlier discussion of time-space fields (Barrett 1988a).

9 'The word *disposition* seems particularly suited to express what is covered by the concept of habitus (defined as a system of dispositions). It expresses . . . a *way of being*, a *habitual state* (especially of the body) and, in particular, a *predisposition, tendency, propensity* or *inclination*' (Bourdieu 1977: 214 fn.1).

10 Asad has identified 'authoritative discourse' as that 'which seeks continually to preempt the space of radically opposed utterances' (Asad 1979: 621).

11 Giddens 1987: 100. Moore (1986) also discusses the issue of distanciation, and Ray (1988) stresses the importance of material culture in being able to presence values which originate beyond the discourse which employs those objects.

12   Others have attempted a more exclusive, if not terribly satisfactory, definition of ideology: 'Ideology is therefore not to be equated with all social practice, but only with that which is generated by and tends to reproduce conflicts in interest' (Miller and Tilley 1984: 14).

13   For the critique of the 'dominant ideology thesis': Abercrombie, Hill and Turner 1980.

14   In talk, where face-to-face negotiation of meaning appears to arise between the participants, the complexity of the interpretive process is almost hidden from those participants because they naturally appear to 'see' what each other means. With the written text, the absence of the author makes the interpretive responsibilities of the reader explicit. This is why it is asserted that text precedes speech in our understanding of the processes of discourse.

15   Bloch develops an argument against models for the social determinacy of knowledge, because in such models it is logically impossible to establish the basis for languages which talk about and criticize that social context: Bloch 1977 and 1985.

16   Asad argues against ritual as constituting a single cosmology, recognizing it instead to be one of a number of competing discourses operating through a network of social practices: Asad 1979.

4

The Beaker Complex: An Archaeological Text

It is quite usual to depict the history of archaeology as the simple progression from a pre-nineteenth-century antiquarianism to a 'modern' archaeology which is defined by the adoption of the currently agreed conventions of methodological rigour. Antiquarians appear as mere collectors, whereas modern archaeology appears to have established a more searching investigation of the material through a wide range of explicitly formulated, analytical techniques. Such a history is reassuring for it provides for a feeling of 'development' and 'progress' in the discipline. However, this vague evolutionary scheme can also be used against itself, for what has really changed?

If antiquarians were no more than collectors of antiquities, then such a description would fit a great deal of current archaeological work. True, the modern-day antiquary/archaeologist collects more, exercises greater care and precision in the recovery of material, and operates with more elaborate methods of cataloguing, description and archive management, as well as being more concerned with stratigraphic context; it would be surprising if this were not so. Archaeology has also developed a clearer understanding of the intellectual demands which are made by the challenge of historical interpretation. None the less, throughout the history of antiquarian and archaeological research, the image of discovery – the unearthing of new finds – remains constant.[1] When Wheeler wrote that archaeologists dig up 'people not things'[2] he was perhaps expressing more frustration than sense. The frustration is commonly felt, for *behind* the discoveries unearthed must surely lie the lives of people. The question which both the antiquary and the archaeologist have faced is the same: how are those people to be reached? The answer, when it comes, also seems to be the same: through yet more discoveries which reveal an even more detailed pattern of regularity in the material.

Much that passes for methodological development in archaeology is concerned with pattern recognition. This includes the classification of artefacts and monuments, stratigraphic sequences of association, and the patterns of distribution. Where patterns exist then it is reasonably assumed that they result from some past process. The archaeological purpose has been to describe such patterns and then to identify the generative processes. In this way the dynamic past may be revealed through the study of its surviving traces in the present (cf. Binford 1977). We have already commented upon the way this reasoning implicitly informs the idea of an 'archaeological record'.[3] Obviously not all archaeological patterns are the products of human behaviour because natural agencies have also operated upon these materials, but the more precisely we can explain the patterning in the archaeological record the better will be our understanding of the past. The conclusion which dominates current archaeological thinking is that the recovery of the past is primarily a methodological issue. It requires the recognition of patterns in the material, and the linking of those patterns to some dynamic cause. These are regarded as questions of methodology simply because they require agreed procedures to be applied and to ensure that the results are generally understood. If such requirements are not fulfilled, so the reasoning goes, agreed methodological procedures will have collapsed, and there will be no common grounding for any archaeological interpretation. In its place we will be reduced to trading in speculative commentaries regarding the past.

To suggest that this kind of reasoning severely curtails the potential of archaeology is not to reject the importance of methodology. The point is that an adequate and critical knowledge of the past requires the construction of a competent body of theory, by which I mean the ability to re-evaluate the intellectual basis of our own procedures. Only then will we be able to undertake the fundamental task of re-assessing the currently agreed conceptual categories which give meaning to our observations and thus underpin our methodologies.

A commentary on some aspects of current archaeological practice has already been presented. I have been concerned to question the idea that truths about the human past are mapped directly upon the evidence, as if that evidence created a form of material record which simply awaits our transcription. A pattern of architectural features, for example, does not in itself reveal the practices by which that architecture was occupied and thus interpreted. Nor does an architectural form necessarily reflect the execution of a single planned concept; it may emerge in the cumulative operation of a number of long-term building projects. Mortuary remains are also a direct reflection neither of the organization of a society, nor of a single ideological image of that society, but they were a medium employed to establish a specific set of relations between people via the transformation from life to death.

Both these studies, of architecture and of mortuary remains, have led to a more general axiom, that material resources were implicated in the social practices which we are attempting to investigate: social practices in which the meaning of the material world was itself rediscovered. If we are going to interpret these historical conditions then we cannot approach the evidence as if it were an uncontentious record of some 'process', suggesting that the question of 'how do we give meaning to the archaeological record?' simply posed a methodological dilemma which, once answered, will result in revealing the past to us. The meaning of the material is specific to the contexts of discourse in which it was (and is) employed. Signifiers will shift in meaning according to the way propositions were made and inferences drawn. The creation of a political hegemony across a number of regions of social discourse always involves establishing a specific set of limited expectations in those practices so that only certain readings of an authoritative code prove adequate.

To give things meaning therefore belongs to the strategies of political control and resistance, and this is true of archaeological practice as well as the social practices which the archaeologist is investigating. The archaeological programme can no longer be the value-free exercise of a methodological consensus; rather it is during our struggle to create history that we give some meaning to the material fragments at our disposal. Such meanings will be ambiguous, perhaps fleeting, in an archaeology which is not simply a procedure of discovering the patterns in things, but is primarily a mode of discourse by which our contentious and partial histories will be written.[4] The way we will understand the archaeological evidence is, therefore, not via some once and for all methodological procedure, but by the active and imaginative creation of history.

The Beaker Network

Beakers are a well-known form of pottery vessel which belonged to the very end of the third and the beginning of the second millennium. In their classic form each vessel has a wide belly and flaring neck and is often decorated with zones of impressed decoration across its entire outer surface.[5] Although by no means continuous, the distribution of this type of vessel is extensive throughout Europe, and by the end of the nineteenth century this distribution pattern seemed secure enough to be taken to reflect a pan-European phenomenon, demanding in turn the discovery of the single process which lay behind its

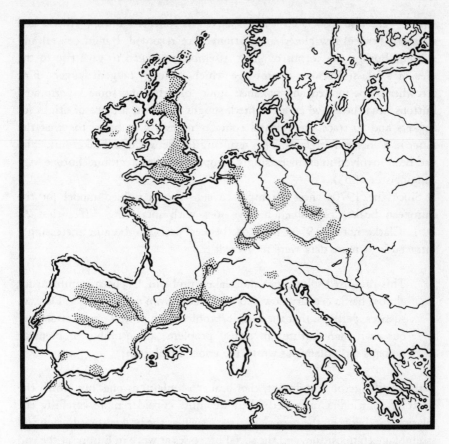

Figure 4.1   The main concentrations of Bell Beaker finds in Europe. (After Harrison 1980)

formation (figure 4.1). Naturally enough that process was originally described in the form of a cultural analysis, and the 'beaker problem' became one of tracing out the distribution pattern as representing a cultural migration from some undetermined place of origin. In Britain, the initial synthesis was established by the work of Thurnam and Abercromby, where the beaker assemblage is most obviously defined in mortuary deposits. Both Thurnam (1871) and Abercromby (1912: 9–92) depended heavily in their own studies upon material collected by earlier barrow excavators. The established view was that the British material represented a distinct cultural horizon which also marked a change to 'single grave' burial and the introduction of metallurgy (cf. Abercromby 1912: 9). However, when a European scale of analysis was adopted it became increasingly necessary to incorporate into any cultural explanation of the ceramic sequences the evidence of those other objects which were also associated with beakers. In southern Europe (Iberia and southern France) few closed associations were recorded, but in central and western Europe the corpus of grave assemblages began to give rise to the idea of a 'classic' beaker assemblage which includes tanged daggers, flint arrowheads, perforated and polished stone 'bracers', and some v-perforated buttons.[6] Syntheses, when attempted, sought to define a place of origin for beakers and to trace the cultural contacts necessary to bring together the range of associated artefacts. This resulting image was of a 'beaker folk' who had been involved in an increasingly complex migration around Europe (e.g. Sangmeister 1963).

Since the 1970s these attempts to construct a unified model for the European beaker phenomenon have met with increasing difficulties. As D. L. Clarke noted (1976: 460), the beaker 'problem' became increasingly intractable as more data were recovered:

> This promised solution to the beaker 'problem' has been imminent for almost half a century now and yet recedes from our grasp. . . . Dare we suspect, perhaps, that the beaker 'problem' is a philosophical artefact of our own manufacture, an unreal problem, an insoluble problem or perhaps a problem not worth the effort of solution?

If the challenge of abandoning the 'beaker problem' as one 'not worth the effort of solution' is accepted, then we must consider more carefully the relationship between the material pattern, such as the beaker distribution and assemblage composition, and the social processes at work in Europe at the end of the third millennium. As Clarke recognized, this is a question of interpretive theory and not a matter of more data. The implication is that the pattern in the archaeological record of a large-scale phenomenon may be no more than the cumulative and distanciated remnants of a variety of processes: the coherence may be illusory.

The problem often appears to be one of scale. The European-wide scale of the beaker distribution is normally regarded as requiring a similarly large-scale explanation.[7] We will approach this question of scale by looking at the way the distribution of material continues to dominate our perceptions, before discussing some of the underlying social complexities.

Questions of Scale: (1) Physical Distribution

We have already noted that the archaeological pattern of beakers and their associations is geographically extensive, and that any explanation has to confront this question of scale. *Culture* has proved a remarkably strong analytical concept for the syntheses of the large quantities of stylistic information which archaeologists have collected over the years. The assumption has been that clusters of similar traits reflect the operation of commonly held beliefs and, coupled with the idea that belief was socially determined, it is possible to understand the attraction of the idea that the distribution of similar stylistic traits must reflect the extent of an underlying social determinate. The historical issues which cultural archaeology attempts to examine include the identification of the region of origin of these beliefs (i.e. cultural origins), and their spread (by the diffusion of influence or by the migration of people). This is precisely the problematic which Clarke (1976: 460) identified as failing in beaker studies: 'the problem becomes one of "origins". Rival hypotheses for beaker origins and dispersion compete one against another in terms of various universal cultural explanations, operating upon general classifications with simple cultural models.'

Criticism of the cultural approach has been accompanied by detailed studies of beaker assemblages which demonstrate the crudity of the cultural classification. This classification has tended to isolate a limited selection of the more distinctive traits (for example the beaker vessel) which were part of far more diverse artefact assemblages, and to map the distribution of these restricted traits simply in terms of presence/absence. Detailed and local studies of the full range of the material corpus now indicate that there are no grounds for assuming the existence of a uniform cultural assemblage. The beaker vessel itself seems to have been adopted within locally specific sequences of ceramic development, where it occurs in very different frequencies. As Clarke (1976: 461) noted: 'Beakers present different phenomena in different areas of their occurrence. In some areas we have thousands of beaker sites (Britain) in other equally well researched areas there are relatively few finds (Denmark).' In his study of the 'cultural' traits represented by four regional grave assemblages between Germany, Bohemia, Moravia and Hungary, Shennan has shown how the frequency of many of these traits varies from one region to another. It is not possible to explain the variation in terms of a uniformly consistent diffusion of cultural influence across central Europe, but rather that the grave rituals in each region seem to have drawn differentially upon a wide range of material resources. None the less, the decorated beaker, copper daggers, stone wrist guards and perhaps v-perforated buttons do represent a small, but more consistent, element within these divergent assemblages. The distribution patterns are of local variation; it is only with the addition of a small number of more widespread elements that we can recognize a 'classic beaker assemblage', encountered in both central and western Europe (Shennan 1978). 'It is now becoming clear . . . that Bell Beakers appeared initially almost universally as a new form of fine pottery in the context of the local pottery assemblages of particular regions' (Shennan 1986: 138).

Although local studies have begun to break down the idea of a European-wide uniformity in the 'beaker culture', the problem remains of how to explain the very much more complex pattern of regional distributions. Clarke discussed this pattern in terms of a 'beaker network', where local variation in the proportion of decorated beakers might have been the consequence of a system of production and exchange dependent upon the restricted distribution of good quality clay sources. The implication is that regional studies will ultimately contribute to understanding the synthesized totality of the 'beaker network'. It is perhaps in these terms that Shennan has commented that

> it seems clear that regions whose forms of organisation were very different were taking part in the Bell Beaker phenomenon: exchanging and imitating Bell Beaker pottery and other items, but also to varying degrees following new modes of burial practice whose appearance was associated with Bell Beaker material. (1986: 141)

There is, therefore, still the feeling of a coherency in at least some elements of the distribution pattern; to what extent must this be interpreted as indicative of a common process?

One of the main concentrations of beaker material in Europe occurs in the British Isles. The distribution of the British material falls into a number of regional clusters, mainly representing the distribution of the grave assemblages (figure 4.2), but with some quite extensive 'domestic' assemblages occurring alongside.[8] One such regional concentration of burial associations occurs on the chalk uplands of Wessex, and extends onto the river terraces of the upper Thames basin. In studying the Wessex material in particular, Shennan has argued that its appearance represents a break with the established forms of political authority which had been associated with the construction and the use of the henges. This returns us to his argument concerning the significance of the 'single grave' mortuary evidence (above, p. 40) where, it will be remembered, he suggests that the new grave rites were associated with 'the rise of an ideology which sought to legitimate social differentiation . . . through the use of . . . prestige items and ritual symbols' (Shennan 1982: 156) and in which beakers were 'exotic or high quality items, to indicate differentiation, including prestige, in a way which had not previously occurred' (1982: 159). The archaeological recognition of prestige material rests upon those exotic, 'prestige goods' being identified by 'their exotic or special nature and, for such items as the copper daggers at least, the

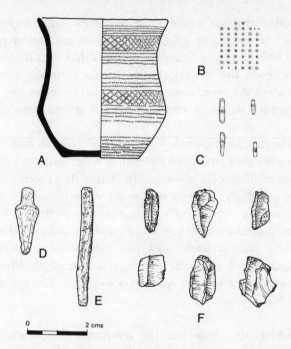

Figure 4.2 A beaker grave assemblage. Artefacts from the primary grave deposit at Chilbolton, Hampshire, which comprise: the beaker (A); *c.* 55 stone beads (B); two pairs of gold hair ornaments – an additional small gold bead not illustrated (C); a tanged copper dagger (D); a red deer antler spatula (E); a group of flint flakes (F). (After Russel 1990)

limited number of occurrences' (1986: 141). The new forms of political authority are thus suggested to have arisen through 'the consumption in burial of prestige items and symbols obtained by means of contacts with high-ranking groups elsewhere' (1986: 143).

The main strands of the argument can now be summarized. It states that the early second millennium saw a break with earlier modes of political authority which was achieved through the use of a new and exotic range of symbolic resources. These resources were employed in such a way as to make explicit the distinction between those who had access to them and those who did not. We have already considered parts of this argument in connection with the changes in mortuary rituals which Shennan has linked to this horizon of exotic material. We must now look in more detail at the nature of these 'exotics'.

In his more recent work Shennan (1986) has drawn upon a very similar model for the period which proposes the existence of two conflicting modes of political authority. One, associated with the henges, is characterized as a 'ritual-authority structure' where positions of rank and seniority were reproduced in such a way as to avoid overt conflict over hierarchy. This was achieved by linking age or lineage seniority directly to relations with the ancestors and gods. In the ways already discussed, lineage elders may have acted on behalf of the entire community in ritual performances. By contrast, a 'prestige-goods economy' is characterized as a system in which

> access to ritual and esoteric knowledge becomes an object of competition, rather than an ordering principle which eliminates competition; creation of alliances is opportunistic, rather than determined by genealogical proximity; defining status and access to status is a function of direct political control; political/economic bases depend on direct controls over resources and the production and circulation of wealth items, including insignia whose allocation defines status position, and the prestige goods on which the reproduction of social life depends. Prestige goods economies are relatively open and fluid. (Thorpe and Richards 1984: 68)

Thorpe and Richards propose that the 'commoner' groups who were held in a relatively low position within the ritual-authority structure eventually broke with that structure by entering the open and competitive networks of a prestige-goods economy. This resulted in the ultimate collapse of the more rigid political structures of the third millennium.

There are two observations which may be made. First, the different political structures are presented as abstract models which are claimed to have a 'good fit' against the patterns in the archaeological record. Second, these models, and the patterns which describe the material and against which the models are matched, erect a contrast between the *internal* or indigenous structure of ritual authority, represented by the communal earthworks of the henges, and *external* networks of exotic material (defined as prestige goods) which were used in a different form of depositional display, most notably in the graves (cf. Braithwaite 1984). The identification of external and exotic contacts obviously fits well with the traditional perception of the beaker phenomenon.

Questions of Scale: (2) Human Agency

Cultural archaeology operated as if society existed prior to individual agency, with people behaving in certain ways because those ways were socially determined. People entered into a society by submitting to its rules and to its conventions. There was no place here for the concept of a human agency which carried forward the project of a social reality. However, the critique of 'culture', established in the 1960s and 1970s, arose not from a reworking of the underlying social theory, but from the need to abandon a concept which was so restrictive, that patterns recognizable in the archaeological evidence could only be explained by reference to a single determinate (Binford 1962).

The argument which has been developed here is that archaeologists should seek to understand how people may once have lived out their lives, and not limit themselves to the more restricted quest of interpreting the archaeological record. These are not one and the same thing. Those lives were lived as routines which were built as people engaged with the empirical realities which they recognized as being available to them. Such engagements could only have arisen from positions of informed pre-understanding. This is an archaeology of memory and of practice, where traditions are the dispositions towards understanding which people routinely displayed by their actions. Practices are therefore lived in the 'gamble' played with nature, where action takes place with reference to both physical conditions and to other people. Traditions are thus enabling and they are carried forward in the action and discourse of human agency. As I have argued in the preceding chapter, such traditions may attempt to gain an overriding legitimacy by the references they make to explicit schemes of cosmological order.

Material culture operates dualistically when drawn into any such discourse. It pre-exists that discourse, for example in the way architecture operates as a frame of reference which people enter and from which they fix their own position in relation to others. Similarly, clothing helps to project and to stage the presence of the agent. The architectural spaces and the form of the clothing may, however, be invested with new meanings according to context and when employed within that discourse. Material resources become the objects upon which action works as well as its medium.

Whilst routine practices seemingly recreate certain material resources (fields are ploughed and sown in a fashion which seems endlessly repeated from season to season), cumulative material effects also arise from unchanging practices. Field lynchets form and soil nutrients leach away, unacknowledged material changes which operate against the very practices which have created them. In the same way the steady architectural embellishment of certain buildings, whilst following the routine logic of spatial arrangements, may create increasingly 'baroque' forms, transforming the actions they were intended to contain.[9]

All practices embody a duality; the time-space frame of the practice itself, and the pre-existing stocks of knowledge and physical resources upon which the agents draw in the reproduction of long-term traditions. This duality thus situates practice within traditional knowledges and the distanciated clutter of cultural artefacts which lie around and to hand to be worked, rethought or abandoned. The day-to-day routines with their cyclical repetition of traditional practices give rise to the institutional qualities of these practices as they outlive the moments of their execution. Traditional practices therefore extend deeply in time-space, thus taking on the characteristics of institutions. Institutions describe common orientations of action and common sets of material resources, and the existence of common linguistic conventions in the reproduction of such conditions will be important. The reach of such institutions in the fourth to second millennia may have been slight in comparison with the embedded institutional arrangements of the modern world. None the less, we have noted the way in which common resources of knowledge may have been employed over very long periods of time to create the conditions of a political hegemony, and the way common orientations of action could unite the practices of a widely dispersed population.

Material culture has its own history. The material resources upon which actions draw outlive and extend beyond the scale of the various interventions of agency upon which they depend for their reproduction. The material consequences of action can obviously outlive their active deployment in a given historical tradition. The distanciated cultural objects become abandoned, forgotten, partly destroyed, reinvented or incorporated almost unnoticed into another world.

One form of rediscovery and reworking occurs in the modern tradition of archaeology, where archaeologists, who are situated outside the localized and day-to-day practices of the past, work that material residue into the tradition of a contemporary knowledge called history. History's only claim to an authenticity with the past is that it employs the same antique fragments in its modern discourse.

Culture was an archaeological invention. The fragmentary material remains which have accumulated over the centuries, when viewed in their surviving totality, take on a structured and ordered appearance of their own. Similar forms of artefact may have arisen widely in time and space. These systemic patterns are the consequences of localized and variant practices, and it is at this local, contextualized level that they must be understood. Cultures are our invented classes of empirical order which create their own problematic. By inventing 'Culture' archaeology had invented the issues which then dominated its research.

The artefacts which now make up the contemporary 'archaeological record' appear, to the archaeological reader, as a text which holds out the promise of revealing its author as the past. Archaeological practice is situated quite differently in relation to these 'authentic' texts when compared with those distant practices which previously occupied and sought to read this material. Archaeology must examine its own practices in relation to the other it seeks to understand. For example, beakers as exotica is surely no more than a reading of the archaeological record situated in the contexts of museums, archives, academic publications and travel grants. Who would have seen or have known of the geographical extent of these artefacts in the second millennium BC?

Too much of current archaeological research is dedicated to writing the history of *things*. This antiquarianism assumes that if the patterns of material debris are adequately recorded then, by using the correct methodological devices, the people will somehow emerge from behind the material. Time and space are simply used as descriptive parameters, to define chronological sequences and spatial distributions. However, the chronology and the spatial distribution of things must be situated in the time-space contexts of those practices which generated them. We might define the genesis of a contemporary archaeology as the moment when the full recognition of the implications of this shift in perception becomes generally accepted.

It has not been my intention to deny that unusual and exotic objects have the power to evoke the esoteric sources of knowledge to which an elite may lay claim (Helms 1988). But archaeologists are in danger of creating political structures of long-distance exchange from their own reading of material distributions which, in the case of the third and early second millennium, took centuries to accumulate. There are two quite different interpretive strategies at work here, each focusing upon the same artefacts but each separated by some four thousand years and each situating those artefacts in quite different perspectives of time-space.

The Beaker Problem

The distribution of beakers and their associations represents the concretion of material laid down over the centuries. That concretion was precipitated from local practices and there seems little point in attempting a synthesis of all these processes. Our understanding of the period will emerge from attempts to situate each strategy in a context of local practice and tradition, and it should not be surprising to find that these local studies provide increasingly divergent views on the 'beaker problem' rather than a common thread of coherency. This issue is important because, despite statements to the contrary, the beaker problem is still discussed as if it were the issue for study. That issue is defined empirically by the widespread distribution of beaker-type vessels and associated artefacts. The definition of such a distribution pattern raises issues of 'exchange' (even 'long-distance' exchange implying a distinct set of exchange mechanisms) and the language of description slips into the language of a proposed explanation with the introduction of such terms as 'exotica'. Internal mechanisms now appear to operate with reference to external exchange. Consequently, the prestige-goods model is employed, not from a clear analysis of any local political situation, but from an adherence to the beaker problem.

In the Wessex case the contrast between internal mechanisms and external exchange is translated into a contrast between two political structures, one of ritual authority associated with the henges, the other arising from the control of prestige goods and associated with a separate set of beaker depositional contexts. The latter, so it is argued, led to the eclipse of the former. One way forward would be to trace the evidence we have for the period between about 2000 and 1600 BC and search for a dislocation in the kinds of political authority we have already discussed. Whatever uncertainties remain about the southern British beaker chronology, we do remain justified in seeing this as representing the major period of beaker use.[10] Part of the detail of the argument pursued here, that concerning single grave burial, has already been rehearsed in chapter 2 and it will be picked up again in the next chapter.

Of the five large Wessex henge complexes originally discussed by Renfrew, Durrington and Mount Pleasant have been the most extensively excavated.[11] In addition, Mount Pleasant, situated to the east of the modern Dorset town of Dorchester, is in an area of more recent and intensive archaeological survey.[12] Given this later work, it may now be worthwhile to examine in some detail the Mount Pleasant and Dorchester area (figure 4.3).

The topography of the area is important. To the south it is bounded by the chalk uplands of the Dorset ridgeway, and to the north by the river Frome, upon which the modern town of Dorchester lies. Between the two is an outlying spur of the ridgeway, extending from Maiden Castle and dropping eastward to the Alington ridge. This spur is bounded north and south by the rivers Frome and South Winterborne. Until the early 1970s our understanding of the distribution of prehistoric monuments was determined by the history of relatively recent agricultural activity, where earthworks survived on the traditional pastures of the chalk uplands and were destroyed on the more

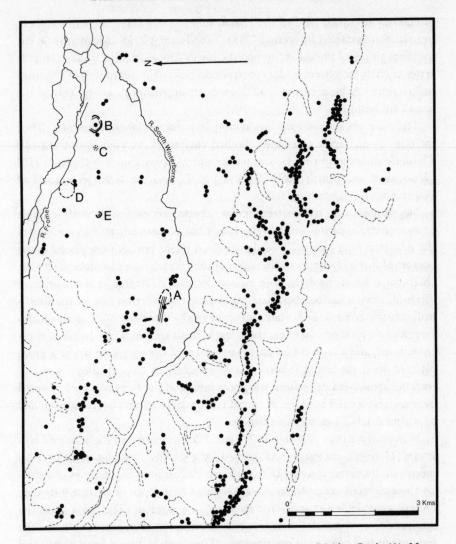

Figure 4.3 Map of the area around Mount Pleasant showing: Maiden Castle (A); Mount Pleasant (B); Flagstones (C); Dorchester Palisaded Enclosure (D); and Maumbury Rings (E).

intensively used land of the valleys. Recent work has begun to alter that perception.

By the mid fourth millennium woodland clearance is attested on the upper chalk spur, associated with the construction of the causewayed enclosure at Maiden Castle.[13] In the second half of that millennium a bank barrow was built across the enclosure and there is also evidence for some woodland regeneration. It seems possible that the spur lies above an area of more intensively occupied land in the Frome valley where more extensive areas of grassland are attested by around 2000 (Woodward 1991). It is mainly on the southern slopes of the valley, and on the lower Alington ridge, that a complex series of enclosures were under construction before the beginning of the third millennium. A long barrow had been built at Alington at the end of the fourth millennium.[14]

The later enclosures vary in size and in constructional techniques. They include pit-dug and causewayed ditched enclosures, varying from the small 15-metre diameter pit enclosures on the north-facing slopes of Conygar Hill (Woodward and Smith 1987: 84 and fig. 4), and the larger enclosures of Flagstones and Maumbury Rings.

Flagstones[15] is a 100-metre circular, causwayed enclosure, with a single known entrance facing north-west. It is situated immediately to the east of the Alington long barrow. Two slab-covered infant burials were placed in the bottom of ditch segments to the south of the entrance, and in some places the chalk-cut sides of the ditch bore incised decoration. Antler from the primary ditch-fill gave a radiocarbon date indicating construction late in the fourth millennium. Some later burials also occur in the ditch-fill. Within the enclosure, and on its southern edge, there was a small and undated cluster of three cremations, and a later burial lay at the centre of the enclosure where a grave pit contained the flexed inhumation of an adult. A 'copper alloy rivet' and tranchet arrowhead came from the grave infill and the body was itself covered by a massive sarsen boulder. A round barrow overlay this burial surrounded by a ring ditch 25 metres in diameter.

Maumbury Rings (Bradley 1976) lies 1.5 kilometres to the west of Flagstones. Here the enclosure was marked by a shallow, circular ditch over 50 metres in diameter, into the bottom of which had been dug a series of shafts. Of the excavated examples, one was recorded to a depth of at least 9 metres. Others were shallower and some seem to have intercut. The chalk from the ditch and from the shafts went into the construction of an outer bank, and the monument had been built on grassland. The single entrance faced north, and outside it there may have been at least one standing stone. The shafts were infilled by processes which included some deliberate deposition, of carved chalk, flint and animal bone. The latter included antler and deer skulls, but very little other deer bone was recovered. Antler from the bottom of the deepest shaft gave a radiocarbon determination in the middle of the third millennium BC.[16]

The entrance of the Flagstones enclosure, orientated westwards along the Alington ridge, and that of Maumbury Rings facing north, both face towards modern Dorchester. Here, in the town centre, excavations in Greyhound Yard have revealed a curving arc of 21 post-pits.[17] Cut into the chalk to a maximum depth of 2.5 metres, these pits were ramped for raising posts of between 0.9 and 1.2 metres diameter. Standing to at least 4 metres above the ground surface, the posts would have been fairly evenly spaced, with about a metre between them. The arc was traced in excavations 100 metres to the north, and it is suggested that it belonged to a circular enclosure of 380 metres diameter. Antler fragments from the base of post-pits gave radiocarbon determinations in the second quarter of the third millennium.[18]

The Mount Pleasant henge is within 200 metres of Flagstones, but to the east and away from Dorchester itself (Wainwright 1979). Like the Dorchester site, it is also on the very edge of the chalk, above the Frome flood plain. The henge is an oval enclosure, 370 metres west to east and 340 metres north to south, with four entrances; north, west, south-east and east. Excavations have revealed the complexity of the enclosure sequence, and have investigated a single area within the interior. The henge enclosure has a very unevenly cut ditch with an external bank which lay, like Maumbury, on open grassland. Charcoal from the primary silts at the northern entrance gave radiocarbon dates in the second quarter of the third millennium,[19] and charcoal from the overlying deposits gave a date towards the middle of the third millennium.[20] The single structure uncovered in the interior was a multiple post-setting (figure 4.4). A central area of 12.5 metres diameter was surrounded by five post-rings with an outer diameter of 38 metres. The rings were broken into four regular quadrants, none of which were struck from a common centre. These quadrants defined four corridors running between the outside and the centre. A penannular ditch with external bank was built around this timber structure. The excavator regarded the ditch and the timbers as being contemporary but, whilst the timber building was presumably standing when the ditch was open, a more complex structural sequence may have been at work. The southern corridor was blocked by a single post, and the ditch, with its single causeway, restricted access to the building via the northern corridor. The digging of the ditch could therefore have resulted in a shift in the orientation and given a more limited access to the building. The ditch causeway was itself orientated directly at the northern entrance of the enclosure. Organic material in the primary fill of the ditch gave radiocarbon dates towards the middle of the third millennium.[21]

The initial phases of building activity at Mount Pleasant are therefore broadly contemporary with the construction of Maumbury Rings, and the Greyhound Yard palisade, and slightly later than Flagstones. However, Mount Pleasant also displays a longer *constructional* history than is recognizable at these other sites. The ditch terminals of the western entrance

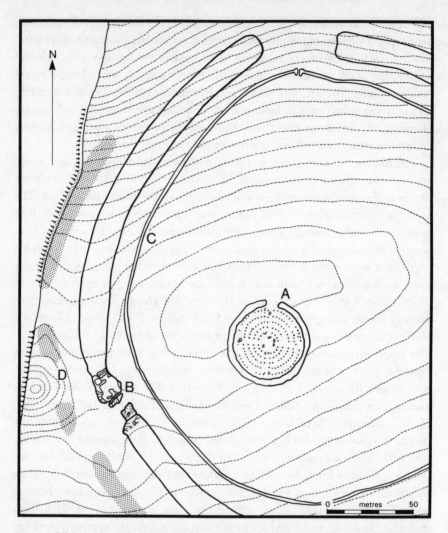

Figure 4.4   Mount Pleasant, showing: the ditched post-ring and stone structures (A); the western entrance narrowed by additional pits (B); the palisade trench (C); the Conquer Barrow (D); (After Wainwright 1979)

were extended by cutting additional pits which reduced the causeway width to 5 metres. Antler from the primary silts of these pits gave dates in the last quarter of the third millennium.[22] A flanged bronze axe was placed in the deposits which formed above these primary silts. But the western and the south-eastern entrances were also effectively closed by the construction of a palisade around the inner edge of the ditch. The timbers for this were close-set in a continuous foundation trench, unlike the earlier structure at Greyhound Yard, Dorchester. The palisade trench at Mount Pleasant, between 1 and 2 metres wide and between 2.5 and 3.0 metres deep, held posts between 0.3 and 0.5 metres thick which, it is estimated, rose to a height of 6 metres. Two of the original entrances were maintained through this stockade, those in the north and east, but they were drastically reduced in width. The posts at the entrances were larger than those on the remainder of the perimeter, and the gap between them at the eastern entrance could have been no more than 0.7 metres. The northern entrance was not fully excavated but was of a similar dimension (figure 4.4). An antler pick from the foundation trench and a sample of the timber gave dates at around 2000 BC.[23] The northern terminal of the bank at the western entrance had a round mound built upon it (the 'Conquer Barrow'). This is undated. However, if it were contemporary with the palisade, then anyone standing on the top of that mound/platform would have seen into the enclosure.

Activity inside the enclosure, broadly contemporary with the construction of the palisade, occurs in the area of the earlier timber structure. By now the timbers must either have decayed or have been removed, but the main organization of the building, with its central area and axial corridors, was maintained by a series of sarsen monoliths and pits. In the centre, four sarsen uprights form the west, north and eastern sides of a 6-metre square, and sarsens also mark the ends of the north and western corridors. The end of the eastern corridor may have been marked by a pit or possibly by a sarsen. Flakes from the dressing of sarsen and the stone mauls used in that operation were deposited in the partly silted ditch; charcoal associated with one such deposit gave a date around 2000 BC.[24]

The Dorchester area, south of the Frome, now provides evidence for the building and development of monuments which took place over the last three quarters of the third millennium, up to the very period in which beakers came into use. What can be made of this evidence? There are two possible readings of the material. First, that the changes after c.2400 BC, as at Durrington Walls, represent a marked dislocation in the way these monuments were used. That dislocation conforms to the beginning of the period in which beakers were used in grave assemblages in Wessex and would, on the face of it, support the idea of some kind of political disruption at this time (cf. Braithwaite 1984: 98). Alternatively, and this is the interpretation which is followed here, whilst there were obvious changes in the organization of the monuments, these are best understood as part of a long-term continuity and evolution in political strategies.

The problems of the possible chronological resolution in our understanding of the history of the monuments has already been discussed. We know little of either the organization or the later use of the Dorchester (Greyhound Yard) site; the timbers decayed *in situ* and they may have stood for well over a century after construction. At Maumbury Rings the pits, with their deliberate deposits, seem to have been infilled rapidly, but it is unlikely that the original excavator would have recognized any re-excavation of those pits, if it had occurred. Certainly the Maumbury enclosure had a long life as a standing earthwork. At Flagstones the central burial represents a later use of the enclosure. However, the issue in all these cases is not one of the structural sequence so much as of understanding how the building projects intervened in the political realities of the period.

From the middle of the third millennium, monument building began on the southern slopes of the upper reaches of the Frome. This was some centuries after the building of the causewayed enclosure and bank barrow on the Maiden Castle spur, and the indications are of woodland regeneration occurring on these uplands at this time. The working of ecologically varied resources along the valley and on the hills necessitated the movement, dispersal and congregation of people, a pattern of movement mapped in terms of place and of season. The placing and the orientation of the monuments would have both harmonized with, and intervened in, this topographical structure. Entrances faced towards the Frome because the siting of the enclosures conformed with the grain of the occupied topography. The topography was reworked by these monuments when people moved into the more specific and increasingly restricted spaces which they defined. No evidence for processional ways currently exists, although the orientation of both Flagstones and Maumbury towards the Dorchester (Greyhound Yard) enclosure might indicate that a unity could have been achieved through processions between these different places. Indeed, it has been suggested that the entrance of the Dorchester (Greyhound Yard) enclosure might lie to the south, and thus face towards Maumbury Rings (Lawson 1990: 277). The increasingly restricted operation of such places is best exemplified by Mount Pleasant. Each structural addition to this site had the effect of closing down the options of movement and of restricting the observation of activities both within and beyond the monument. The ditch around the timber setting directed its axis towards the north entrance of the henge. The west entrance was reduced in width, and then blocked with the construction of the palisade. Only the north and east entrances remained open, and these were eventually restricted by very narrow gates. Here are the elements of a technology of the 'individual': entrances which permit only one person to cross the threshold at a time, the possible construction of an elevated platform (the Conquer Barrow), and the restricted area of the stone setting which may have actually faced away from the open, north entrance. The increasing regionalization of this locale seems to have worked progressively down to a level which focused upon the individual agent who, approaching these places, was unable to see what lay beyond the immediate barrier, or who was hidden from the wider view, or the agent who was foregrounded by either their entry or their exit from the palisade, or by their positioning on the platform.

Beaker sherds from Mount Pleasant occur in the palisade trench. They were also recovered from the southern terminal of the ditch which had been dug around the timber setting, but in the secondary silts and associated with the debris of stone-working. Instead of seeing the adoption of beakers as part of an alternative political strategy it is quite possible to regard their use in Wessex as, at least partly, contingent upon the political changes brought about by these ceremonial enclosures. These, I have argued, contributed towards the construction of a ritual elite who, at certain moments, may have spoken and acted on behalf of the wider community. Whatever their original, and continuing, claim to assert this authority – be it age, gender, lineage – that authority was transformed by their involvement in these increasingly elaborate ceremonial practices. A new form of person was created in this way, one who perhaps belonged to an increasingly remote and sacred community and who, through forms of dress and through the food and drink consumed at moments of ritual display, may have emphasized their proximity to the gods or the ancestors or to other forms of esoteric knowledge.

The artefacts signifying such an elite could be referred to as 'prestige goods', but their operation is quite different from that proposed by Thorpe and Richards. The distinction concerns the context in which such material was circulating. Friedman and Rowlands proposed a general model to describe a range of specific evolutionary developments which could arise from a 'tribal' system of social reproduction. The potential trajectories in this model originate from a system where

> local production predominates in the development of differential prestige and ranking and where an independent exchange sphere of valuables or prestige goods does not exist. Such goods do, of course, circulate, and the more hierarchical the societies become the more distantly produced valuables enter into exchange cycles. We have assumed, however, that such articles have merely sumptuary value and are not in themselves subject to independent accumulation nor a source of direct economic control. (Friedman and Rowlands 1977: 214)

This contrasts with political structures where local productive strategies may be transformed by elite control over prestige goods. Here, the way such materials

> circulate over wide areas is the basis of political-economic power because such goods are necessary for the marriage and other obligatory payments of all groups. In this way the prestige goods accumulated through long distance contacts are converted directly into control over labour. (1977: 214)

This second case approximates to the role Thorpe and Richards envisage for beaker-associated material. Friedman and Rowlands suggest that the potential development of such systems is 'unclear', although they allow that access to exotic goods may be the 'basis for a development of increasing hierarchisation', a development most likely to occur on the periphery of state systems (1977: 214).

Our understanding of a particular form of political reproduction depends upon our ability to situate it within its own specific historical and material context. This is more than the application of a general model to a pattern described in the material record, simply hoping that the goodness of fit between the two is adequate. The local historical development which has been traced here is of an emergent elite who, whilst increasingly concerned to signify their identity by mode of dress and the deployment of specific ritual items, did not achieve their position through the control of such paraphernalia. Beaker vessels may have been drawn into these strategies, and in some areas the vessel and specific dress items were further employed within quite specific funerary rituals. However, this does not appear to be a feature of the burial rituals known in the immediate vicinity of the Mount Pleasant complex. None the less, it may be that a further extension of a local elite's attempts to establish their own immediate history, through rites of inheritance, took the form of burial rituals which situated the grave in this already ritually ordered landscape. Funerary rituals which now employed earth-dug graves become increasingly recognizable in the Dorchester area from the opening decades of the second millennium, even if beakers were rarely incorporated in the burial assemblage (Bellamy 1991). These graves presumably include the early burials beneath mounds in the well-known barrow cemeteries on the uplands of the Dorset Ridgeway, and in the more recently recognized barrow cemetery on the Alington ridge. It is in the latter area that we find the inhumation grave placed centrally within the Flagstones enclosure.

The third millennium as a whole is a period in which a complex body of artefacts may, at particular moments, have been used to define people and actions, leaving the archaeological traces of such strategies in distinct and often localized patterns of assemblage variation. These categories share widespread geographical similarities, a feature of late neolithic ceramics which is shared by beakers, and which is the physical residue of centuries of use. These patterns are not indicators of 'external' exchange: to what are they external? The very term is a misnomer, for the strategies may have been almost obsessively *internal* in the way they defined categories of people. Things moved because people moved, and the movement and distribution of people involved their ability to relocate themselves, or to be relocated, within the matrix of obligations which sustained those networks of power. It was not an adherence to ethnic identity which defined the subject but their submission to forms of authority, such as the lineage, and these forms of authority created their own histories which could be reinvented to incorporate the fluctuating demands of political affiliation. These were the oral histories recounted in the rituals and legends of a region and which employed the monuments themselves as their immediate points of reference.

NOTES

1 'A problem in archaeology has always been that its method has provided the dominant metaphor for its interpretation. Before all else, archaeology has been about discovery' (Miller and Tilley 1984: 1).

2 M. Wheeler 1956: 17. Wheeler went on to appeal for an interpretation of the evidence 'with a controlled imagination that inevitably partakes of the qualities of art and even of philosophy' (1956: 229).

3 Above, p. 12. For comments on the idea of an 'archaeological record' see Patrik 1985.

4 I accept the point which Mark Edmonds has made to me, that however ambiguous and contingent the meanings are which adhere to the material, they are created in intellectual labour, through the logical and critical process of drawing inferences. They therefore require our intellectual commitment and they are open to evaluation.

5 For general surveys of this material: Harrison 1980; Mercer 1977; Waldren and Kennard 1987. Problems in the definition of beaker ceramics do occur; see for example the comments by Barfield, Waldren and Topp in Waldren and Kennard 1987: 5–22.

6 See Shennan 1986 for a discussion of the 'classic bell beaker grave inventory'.

7 'These very large-scale phenomena demand equally large-scale explanations' (Sherratt 1987: 88).

8 The basic description of British grave assemblages remains Clarke 1970, but with the critical reviews of Lanting and van der Waals 1972, Burgess 1979 and Case 1977. For a review of 'domestic' assemblages: Gibson 1982.

9   I owe the idea of a 'baroque' development of an architectural form, resulting from its otherwise routine development and embellishment, to Roland Fletcher. See also Fletcher 1984.

10 For the most recent programme concerned with the radiocarbon dating of British beaker-associated material: Kinnes et al. 1991.

11 A third of the large Wessex henges, that at Marden, has also been investigated by excavation: Wainwright 1971.

12 For the Mount Pleasant excavations: Wainwright 1979. More recent excavation in the Dorchester area has been summarized by Woodward and Smith 1987. For a general statement of landscape development in the area: Woodward 1991: 127ff. and Woodward et al. in Sharples 1991: 9–36. For an interim report on this work: Lawson 1990.

13 For the Maiden Castle causewayed enclosure: R. Wheeler 1943: 18–24 and 80–6; Sharples 1991: 49–54.

14 For the Alington long barrow: Davies, Stacey and Woodward 1985: 103. Radiocarbon date of antler(?) in the northern ditch: 4450 ± 80 BP (HAR-8579).

15 Flagstones: Woodward and Smith 1987: 81–4. Radiocarbon date of an antler pick from the primary ditch-fill: 4030 ± 100 BP (HAR-8578).

16 Maumbury Rings radiocarbon date of antler: 3970 ± 70 BP (BM-2282N).

17 For Greyhound Yard: Woodward, Davies and Graham 1984.

18 Greyhound Yard radiocarbon date of antler: 4020 ± 80 BP (HAR-6663). A second date of charcoal gives: 4140 ± 90 BP (HAR-6689).

19 Mount Pleasant radiocarbon dates of charcoal: 4058 ± 71 BP and 4048 ± 54 BP (BM-792, 793).

20 Mount Pleasant radiocarbon date of charcoal: 3891 ± 66 BP (BM-791).

21 Mount Pleasant radiocarbon dates of charcoal: 3911 ± 89 BP (BM-663); antler 3941 ± 72 BP (BM-666); animal bone 3989 ± 84 BP (BM-667).

22 Mount Pleasant radiocarbon dates of antler: 3734 ± 41 BP and 3728 ± 59 BP (BM-645, 646)

23 Mount Pleasant radiocarbon date of antler pick: 3637 ±63 BP (BM-662); charcoal 3645 ± 43 BP (BM-665).

24 Mount Pleasant radiocarbon date of charcoal: 3630 ± 60 BP (BM-668).

5

An End to Remembrance

The Construction of Memory

John Aubrey has been accredited with the rediscovery of Avebury: 'he came across Avebury when he was hunting in 1649, and "was wonderfully surprised at the sight of these vast stones of which I had never heard before" ' (Malone 1989: 22). His rediscovery was achieved through a programme of survey and description which brought the monument to the notice of antiquarian scholarship. Such a rediscovery marks the first reference to the monument in the narrative traditions of antiquarian archaeology to which we still adhere. From that moment Avebury became a recognizable part of our own intellectual history, and as such this rediscovery is akin to the European 'discovery' of the new world, a world which had long been known and inhabited by others. Avebury was also inhabited before Aubrey first saw it and wrote of its existence. The Saxon church was built just outside the earthwork and the Saxon village also seems to have lain beyond the enclosure. The site of the church remains to this day although the modern village now sprawls through the centre of the henge. Avebury may have been rediscovered and described afresh within an academic tradition of knowledge by Aubrey, but it will always have had its place within other knowledges.

Aubrey was born in Wiltshire at Malmesbury and he grew up in the county, but despite this local upbringing and his wide interests, his own testimony implies that word of the monument had never reached him. Stukeley, a century later, recorded the destruction of stones by the local populace, and stone felling had certainly taken place in the medieval period.[1] Avebury was known locally but it is as if the significance of the monument was being worked against, the stone felling having the effect of slowly eradicating its physical trace. Rediscovery has meant preservation and reconstruction. Different ways of talking about the past must operate through a different rhetoric; as a local working against the material remains (a 'forgetting' or 'casting-out'), and as the preservation of that material by an interested and diverse community of visitors ('rediscovery').[2]

Our understanding of Avebury, as with the other Wessex henges and the mortuary monuments of the fourth and third millennia, depends upon our ability to create an image of the social practices in which to situate these monuments. These practices are written into existence by the historian who must assume that the monuments facilitated a certain order in the distribution of human relations. Thus, the building and the use of these monuments have always involved acts of rediscovery and remembrance by which traditions of knowledge and of a more general moral order were recalled and sustained. The avenues and the stone and timber settings once acted as the mnemonic devices enabling the effective reworking of oral testimonies and ritualistic display. Given the large numbers of people likely to have been involved in some of these undertakings, something clearly happened in the four thousand years between the earlier use of Avebury and the necessity for Aubrey to 'rediscover' it in the early seventeenth century AD. A widely shared language of description and interpretation no longer existed. At some point particular traditions of remembrance must have begun to fall away; the processions may have become less frequent, the cycles of renewal were broken and the numbers attending dwindled. Archaeologically we can isolate some of the physical indications of these changing practices although, as we have seen, our understanding of the chronology of this process is at best uncertain. The evidence is perhaps the clearest at Mount Pleasant; the timber palisade was partly burnt and dismantled, and sometime late in the first century BC the sarsen stone setting was broken up and replaced by a timber round house and grain storage pits.

Traditional archaeology tends to treat changes in the use of a particular category of monument as indicating a transformation in the 'underlying' social organization which had used such monuments. The case which has been made here is that the rituals executed at the henges were created out of expectations derived from elsewhere, and that these rituals, by confirming those expectations, returned to address future experiences. The rituals were situated in a time-space network of social practice – they were executed at certain moments and places within the flow of human experience. A single monument-type cannot be used to characterize the operation of such networks. Changes in the use of monuments may imply changes in certain of these practices, but there were also strands of continuity, and it is the operation of this more complex lattice of social trajectories which we need to evaluate. What was transformed and what was held in place in the social practices of the mid to late second millennium?

The practical contingencies of everyday life were regularly reworked by their metaphorical association with particular values of political, religious and moral order. But options existed, and similar routine experiences could have been associated with different metaphysical values. This construction of different chains of metaphorical association would have established expectations which were then carried forward into experience. This would introduce what Sahlins has so clearly described as the moment of empirical risk. People bring explicitly formulated cultural categories into play against differently grounded conditions of reality:

> The gamble is that referential action, by placing *a priori* concepts in correspondence with external objects, will imply some *unforeseen* effects which cannot be ignored. Besides, as action involves a thinking subject (or subjects), related to the sign in the capacity of the agent, the cultural scheme is put in double jeopardy, subjectively as well as objectively: subjectively, by the people's interested use of signs in their own projects; objectively, as meaning is risked in a cosmos fully capable of contradicting the symbolic systems that are preserved to describe it. (Sahlins 1987: 149)

The risk is always present that a discourse which was once politically dominant may become distant or irrelevant to the experiences it continually seeks to address. From the changing perspectives of the routines of everyday life, the ritualized practices executed at the henges could have become unintelligible, irrelevant or have been more directly challenged by knowledges and truths built out of an engagement with different symbolic resources. The irrelevancy of these once dominant associations would have ensured an end to the acts of remembrance. It seems feasible to identify two possible conditions under which this transformation in practice may have occurred. Both concern the structuring of time and space, one through the conditions connected with the change in burial rituals already considered in the second chapter, the other with the way the resources of nature were appropriated. We will consider the latter condition in the next chapter and I hope to demonstrate that the two were necessarily linked. This linkage is not one of an emergent, functional incompatibility between two autonomous elements of a social and ecological 'system'.[3] Rather, our priority continues to be to understand the transformation as the product of lives which were able to create new forms of human existence. This is a transformation in the possibilities of interpretation. It arises as memories of prior experiences (themselves interpretations) were used to make sense of the present.

Burial and the Mapping of Genealogy

Three observations were made in the second chapter about the nature of the mortuary rituals of the fourth and the third millennia: first, that most of the earlier monumentality associated with these rituals seems to have been directed towards establishing a fixed place as the architectural context for the execution of ancestor rites. The resources required for those rites were certainly built in part from the products of funerary rituals (obviously including the deposits of human remains), and funerary rituals will have continued to operate with reference to ancestral monuments (independent of whether or not all the dead were included in those monuments). None the less, if the dominant metaphor in death rituals was the ancestral presence, then the organization of funerary rites will have been routinely subsumed within an overarching order structured by reference to this generalized ancestral group.

Second, funerary rituals are generally as much concerned with a transformation in the conditions and status of the mourners as they are with a transformation in the status of the deceased. It is through funerary rituals that rights and obligations are relocated amongst the living as a consequence of the deaths which they celebrate.

Third, it was the increasing use of dug graves which heralded the most notable change in funerary rituals at the end of the third millennium and which rendered the physical consequences of those rituals, the grave assemblage, such an obvious feature for archaeological analysis. The inhumation tradition, for example, represents a marked development in mortuary rituals, not because the corpse was occasionally accompanied by grave-goods, but because the grave, acting as a container, now fixed the point in the landscape where the dead were individually deposited. This fixed deposit of the individual now contrasted with the place of ancestral presence where the individual corpse, if deposited at all, may eventually have been broken up or represented by fragmentary skeletal material.

Social practice establishes the relationship between people, material and symbolic resources. Funerary rituals can be understood as the deployment of a particular range of symbolic resources, which include the corpse, to redefine some of the principles out of which relationships between the living are defined. Those relationships are partly recognized by reference to the transformation of death where the burial ritual creates an image which can only be understood, or 'read', through the memories each participant brings with them to that ritual. The grave rituals which were established by the end of the third millennium involved a re-inscription of the immediate landscape by marking the moment at which the burial rite ended with the fixed place of the grave. We are now in a position to consider how this particular strategy operated to build, over the centuries of the second millennium, new perceptions of each community's own identity.

Categories of Death

The 1980s witnessed the publication of many excavations undertaken on Wessex round barrows in the late 1950s and early 1960s.[4] These earthwork mounds are classically identified as the funerary monuments of the early Bronze Age, although the architectural tradition of the round barrow, which either covered or contained funerary deposits, is one whose origins lies in the Neolithic of the fourth millennium.[5] The patterns which are now recoverable as archaeological deposits (including the position of the grave, the mound architecture and the grave assemblage) arose from the strategic deployment of an available architectural order. Inhumation and cremation rituals, and the various options concerning the placing of the final deposit, the grave design and the grave assemblage, all these operated in a frame of reference defined by a cemetery whose architectural form was continually being transformed by the practices which that cemetery served to accommodate. As we shall see, the interplay between the inhumation and cremation rituals and the architecture of the cemetery contributed towards the creation of new forms of historical reality.[6]

In the second chapter we examined the link between the particular development of inhumation rituals and the use of the grave. Each burial rite changed, however subtly, the form of the landscape; the passage to death occurred at that one place and future deaths would have been defined with reference to those which had gone before. This re-inscription of the burial ground, where each succeeding deposit structured the options available to future action, as well as creating its own identity by reference to the past, is what distinguishes these traditions from burials which reworked the same generalized location, be it an ancestral tomb or some other mode of disposal. Obviously the grave itself is not strictly necessary for such a strategy to have operated effectively and late Neolithic burials are known where the corpse appears to have been placed upon the ground surface and then covered with a mound.[7] None the less, the effect – the creation of place – is ultimately the same.

In the Stonehenge environs, oval or sub-rectangular grave pits cut up to a metre into the chalk are the more common receptacle for the earliest inhumations which form the primary deposits below many of the round barrows. There are other similarities between the burials in this area. The corpse was normally flexed or bound in a foetal position and lay facing east,[8] and when included in the grave, the pottery beaker was often placed behind the feet and buttocks. The grave was then infilled by chalk rubble, surmounted by a low mound and surrounded by a shallow circular ditch.[9] These observations do no more than reflect normative patterns of deposition, arising out of the regular deployment of certain principles of *difference*: between an east or west orientation, in the topography of the human body and the form it takes in birth and at death, in the materials of chalk and turf, and in closing off the area of burial from the outside. It was these principles which enabled the creation not only of the patterns of similarity which we recount today, but also the abnormalities; they allowed for the creation of ideas of what was possible and what was not possible, the creation of different categories of death. The principles are therefore present not only where we meet the pattern of recurrent associations, but also where those associations are absent or are refused. Convention and routine, and the unconventional, thus define each other.

The construction of differences in the nature of death can be illustrated by the evidence recovered from two of the barrows in Shrewton parish.[10] Beneath Shrewton barrow 24 the initial burial was of an adult male; the body had been contracted and lay facing east with a beaker placed at its heels. The grave pit was infilled with chalk rubble mixed with loam and was covered by a small mound of chalk and earth derived from a surrounding circle of quarry pits. The barrow was part of a cemetery of similar mounds which eventually developed along the axis of a broad spur of the chalk hill. Shrewton barrow 23, on the other hand, was built away from this main nucleus of the barrow cemetery. The grave pit contained the body of a middle-aged female who had suffered from severe osteoarthritis. The body was slightly flexed and faced west, towards the line of a bank and a north–south row of posts against which the grave pit had been dug. A rubbing stone was placed immediately behind the head. The chalk upcast from the grave-pit was piled to the east of the grave and was not used as backfilling; instead the grave was infilled with turf, and during this process a small bronze awl was added to the grave-fill. The posts were withdrawn from their pits at about this time and the cremated remains of a young adult were tipped into one of them. A turf mound was raised over the entire area without the use of chalk and without a surrounding ditch.

The location of the grave, the nature and arrangement of the grave assemblage, and the closing of the grave, all these made an image of death. The artefacts and raw materials were the referents, the means by which the dead were known and through which they could be recognized. We must consider this 'making of the dead' in a little more detail because it was partly through this process that the living communities reworked aspects of their own identities.

The process of 'making' is one which moves towards a reflexivity. This movement is from the creative, practical use of resources to an understanding of the objective reality which that practice has brought into being. The analogy is the movement from the writing of a text to its contemplation by either the author or some other reader. Such a contemplation may also recognize, in the material consequences of those earlier actions, 'new' resources which had now become available as a potential medium of future practice. The making of each death will have structured the material conditions against which each future burial ritual will have been worked. I want to follow through the implications of this argument and develop the themes examined in chapter 2 (the way funeral rituals are partly structured by the mortuary architecture they inhabit) and chapter 3 (the kinds of truth which were embodied in the practice of the ritual). The argument will involve our recognizing the possible 'moments' of reflection where an order, having been built within a ritualized practice, was recognized by the objectified truths which appeared then to be realized by that practice. The way those truths were understood would be a guide for future actions. Such 'moments', it will be argued, isolated categories of death by reference to the treatment of the corpse and the means of its final disposal.

Categories among the dead were created through funeral rituals which culminated in rites of re-incorporation. The argument has already been outlined in chapter 2, that one moment of reflexive understanding in the inhumation rite was reached with the creation of the grave assemblage. Such assemblages played the mediating role through which the category of death was secured. Cremation rituals were differently structured. Rites of re-incorporation were likely to have been initiated by the lighting of the pyre, while the last obligations demanded of the mourners would have focused upon the final deposition or dispersal of the ashes. Placing the dead recognized the wider contexts of reference within which an individual death was situated because the reference to *place* allowed for the reference to ancestors or to genealogical succession.[11] It was by creating these conditions that the participants were able to speak of their own renewed or transformed identities among the communities to which they would return. The path taken out of the state of mourning was accompanied by a recognition of renewed obligations between the living which involved some explicit reference to the death so recently defined.

Situated at these moments the agent would have achieved a means of expressing an understanding both of what had been created, and of what was then necessary in terms of further action. They would have understood themselves in moments which were suspended between references back to the deceased – and its place amongst the dead – and forward in the effective creation of new realities.

The dead are created out of the treatment of the corpse, which in the case of inhumation involves its preparation, transportation to the grave, and deposition and the subsequent infilling of the grave pit. Artefacts which accompanied the corpse into the grave derived from three different types of context: decorative material attached to the corpse, material placed in the grave around the corpse, and material discarded by the mourners.[12] Obviously the distinction between these categories may blur; for example, the body may have been decorated once it had been placed in the grave or the final acts of mourning may have included a requirement to make an offering to the dead. At other times the distinction may be clearer, as in the case of Hemp Knoll already described (above, p. 62), where some artefacts were thrown into the grave as it was being infilled, as distinct from the beaker which was placed in the coffin.

Although similar items may have been used both to dress the living and to adorn the corpse, we must distinguish between the two. The way the different assemblages were formed, and the way the various items were treated, may have evoked a contrast between death and life, and the adornment of the corpse was obviously not as part of its own self-conscious display as in the dress of the living.[13] Certain items of adornment appear to have been intimately associated with the corpse throughout the funeral ritual. The primary inhumation grave from Chilbolton, Hampshire, for example, produced four gold hair ornaments or 'earrings' and a tubular gold bead from the area around the skull.[14] Such material may well have been attached to the corpse, perhaps in the hair, throughout the funeral (figure 4.2). Elsewhere there are hints that other items of dress were placed next to the body only after it had been put in the grave. Necklaces are one example of how decorative items may have been used in these different moments of depositional context. In Shrewton barrow 5J a grave, seemingly dug down through a pre-existing mound, contained the contracted corpse of an elderly female. She lay facing south, and around her neck, presumably where it was fixed before the corpse had been deposited, was a necklace. In contrast, Shrewton barrow 5L produced a necklace of seven beads which seems to have been used to secure the neck of a bag containing the cremated remains of a young female. This was buried next to a pit, also containing a cremation, which was situated centrally beneath the mound. Quite clearly this necklace could not have passed through the pyre and thus did not accompany the corpse throughout the funeral rites.[15]

Once the corpse was placed in the grave, and if not sealed in a coffin, then other items could be arranged immediately around it. The corpse acted as the dominant referent for the construction of this grave assemblage by determining its arrangement in the grave. Beakers were put in the grave at this point (we have already noted the inauspicious location of many of these vessels in relation to the corpse) and they represent the most commonly recognizable medium of exchange given by the mourners at the close of the earlier inhumation rituals. Some daggers were also added to the grave assemblages at this point, and this particular use of the dagger will be of significance when we come to consider cremation deposits. In the case of the disturbed primary inhumation grave at Chilbolton, a copper dagger, possibly in a sheath, stood point upwards against a beaker and behind the lower part of the body. In the primary grave beneath barrow 5K at Shrewton (figure 5.1), a beaker had been placed 'clasped between the man's hands' and a small copper dagger, enclosed in a wrapping of fabric and moss, was set on two chalk pebbles between the chest and left arm of the contracted corpse.[16] Clearly neither dagger was attached to the attire of the corpse and both had been placed in the grave after the body was deposited.[17]

The inhumation ritual involved the preparation of the grave, the preparation and transportation of the corpse, and its deposition.[18] That final act marked the place, and affirmed the category, of death. It also formed the reflexive moment when the category was finally realized by a series of exchanges between the mourners and the grave. These exchanges drew upon a restricted range of artefacts which were then placed in subsidiary positions around the corpse itself. The funeral was then brought to a close with the infilling of the grave and the withdrawal of the mourners.

By putting certain artefacts in the grave, the mourners not only created an image of death but also said something of themselves by the types of exchanges they were either able, prepared or thought it necessary to make. This moment of exchange could obviously have been used strategically by employing items which had a restricted circulation, and much could be made of the way complex grave assemblages indicate not so much the status of the

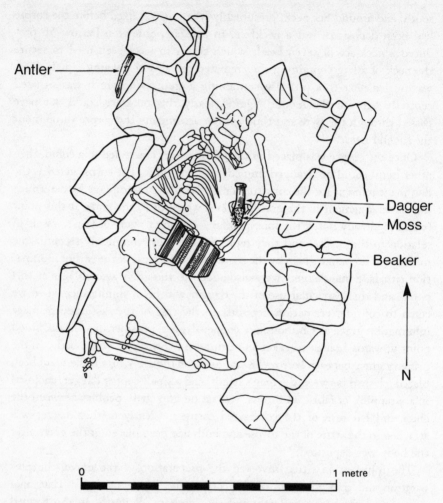

Antler

Dagger
Moss

Beaker

N

0   1 metre

Figure 5.1 The primary burial at Shrewton 5K surrounded by chalk blocks and a series of
objects placed in the grave around the body. (After Green and Rollo-Smith 1984)

deceased as the ability of the mourners to reiterate their own power to
sacrifice.[19] The memories of earlier exchanges by which these same items were
procured would have been evoked by these deposits. Certainly it is possible to
identify periods when some funerals terminated in moments of quite considerable display, as in the primary inhumation grave below the Bush Barrow
which remains the classic example.[20] This corpse was put not in a grave but
on the old land surface, not flexed but prone on its back. Here is the image of
a text written out around and on the corpse, using an elaborate and extended

range of artefacts which few would have been able to emulate. These items were placed above the head and down the right hand (easterly) side of the body, with one sheet-gold plate placed on its chest. All the items were arranged once the body was in place and must all have been almost immediately buried within the initial deposits of the covering mound.[21]

If the inhumation rituals fixed the place and moment at which both the dead and the mourners moved from the liminality of the funeral rite – the deceased passing over into death and the mourners beginning their own return to the living – then cremation rituals established a more complex analogy between place and the transitional moments of the rite. The funeral pyre itself became the place where the deceased was finally released from mortal existence, whilst the disposal of the ashes became far more of a focus for the enactment of the final obligations demanded of the mourners.

Cremations were being deposited in the burial grounds by the early second millennium. They may have been an early feature in the development of the funerary architecture and they certainly represent primary deposits around which enclosures were built and over which mounds were raised.[22] As with the inhumations, considerable variation exists in the nature of these primary deposits, although some of the basic principles employed in the ritual can still be recognized.

In the case of Shrewton barrow 5D an oval pit, less than half a metre deep, received the cremated remains of at least one adult male. These may have been contained in an organic bag and had been placed on the floor of the pit, which then seems to have been backfilled with turf.[23] The cremation pit lay centrally within at least two rings of stakes, possibly fence lines, and there is the suggestion of an entrance passage through these from the south-west. Such stake circles occur elsewhere, and in the case of the poorly recorded excavations of Winterbourne Stoke barrows G47, 49 and 50, it has also been argued that some kind of entrance arrangement can be recognized approaching from the east or south-east in each of these cases (Gingell 1988: 59–60, 64, 66). Such an arrangement reminds us that the place of deposition was understood as a place of approach and of departure for those engaged in the ritual. It was these participants who had collected the cremated bone from the pyre, perhaps cleaned it, and then brought it to the burial pit, and it was they who also deposited any additional material with the cremation. Edmondsham barrow G2 is in north Dorset and away from the main group of burials we have been discussing (Proudfoot 1963: 395ff.). Here the pyre had originally covered an area at least 1 metre in diameter and was built to cremate the corpse of a young adult male (figure 5.2). The bones were then collected, although some fragments remained amongst the ashes of the pyre, and they were placed in an

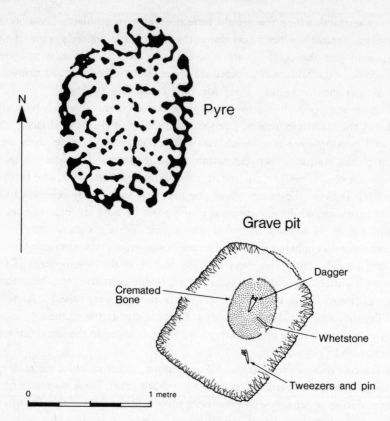

Figure 5.2   Edmondsham Barrow G2, showing the relationship between the pyre and the grave pit. (After Proudfoot 1963)

ash-free pile on the floor of a rectangular grave pit dug immediately to the south-east of the pyre. The pit was less than a half-metre deep and, from the nature of the fill, seems to have been excavated after the firing of the pyre. A whetstone was deposited amongst the bone whilst a sheathed dagger was placed on top of the cremation. A little to the south and separate from this deposit lay a pair of bone tweezers and a bone pin. None of the artefacts appear to have passed through the pyre. The grave was then infilled with turf and covered by a cairn of clean chalk, the top of which was disturbed before it, and the area of the pyre, became covered by a turf mound, itself then capped by chalk derived from a surrounding ditch.

Another example involving the deposition of a cremation immediately alongside the pyre comes from Amesbury barrow 39, which was built just to the south of the line of the Stonehenge avenue. Excavated originally by Cunnington early in the nineteenth century it was re-excavated in 1960. The cremation of a young adult male had been collected from the pyre and then deposited again to the east of the pyre, but this time on the old land surface. The bone was accompanied by a conical jet button, two fusiform jet beads, eighteen amber beads and one possible amber button. The covering mound of turf must have been built almost immediately thus protecting these deposits. The mound was later capped by chalk dug from a surrounding ditch (Ashbee 1981).

Other cremations have been found in primary positions beneath the barrows which were scattered across the hillsides to the east of the Wiltshire Avon. Amesbury barrow G61a is one. It contained two adjacent grave deposits within the area enclosed by a single oval ditch. One of these graves was a rectangular pit, and contained a pile of cremated bone probably belonging to a single adult. In the same pit, but immediately to the north of the cremation, lay a string of beads which included faience, amber, steatite and cowrie shells. A bronze awl and a small upright vessel were placed over the necklace, and against the vessel lay a beaver incisor. Another fragment of bronze lay close by. The vessel contained another amber bead, a fossil crinoid stem and two small flint flakes. The pit was then infilled with a chalky loam. Amesbury barrow G58 covered a central rectangular grave pit, across the floor of which was scattered a layer of wood ash on which was deposited, in a clearly delimited almost rectangular pile, the cremated remains of an adult, possibly female. To one side of this deposit lay a dagger and half an iron pyrites nodule. The dagger blade with its horn hilt was in a hide sheath and the entire object had been wrapped in moss and then cloth. The grave pit was infilled with chalk rubble before being covered by a turf mound, again capped by chalk.[24]

We have remarked upon the use of daggers and necklaces in inhumation rituals and we have noted that these may be among the items deposited once the human remains were in place. The choice of such objects is significant. They are artefacts which would have been worn by the living, but they are not entering the grave simply as items of dress even if, as in the case of the necklace from Shrewton 5J (above, p. 116), some were attached to the corpse itself. These items helped to objectify the image of a death and each object spoke of its own history and its association with specific practices (figure 5.3). Some of the necklaces were probably of considerable antiquity, the remnants of earlier strings and pendants and comprising a number of different types of bead.[25] Does this hint at the extent to which these necklaces had circulated

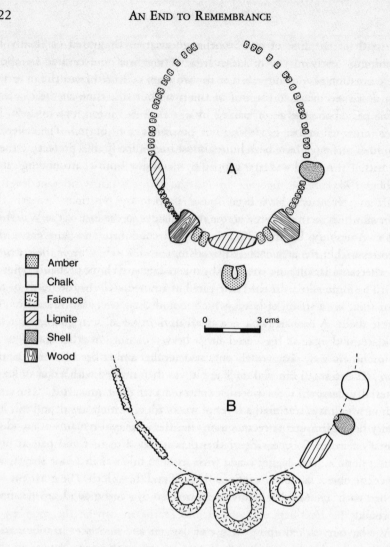

Figure 5.3 Necklaces from Shrewton Barrow 5J (A) and Shrewton Barrow 5L (B). Each represents the accumulation of different materials, and thus perhaps different exchange histories. (After Green and Rollo-Smith 1984)

among the living – given and then worn, split and subdivided, indicators of a status bestowed or won from others, the kinds of exchange which created categories of kin, marriage partners, the signs of personal veneration? If so, that same language of interpersonal exchange was being used to talk metaphorically of the relationships by which the dead and their line could be described. It is hardly surprising that the grave associations should be so restricted in the range of items or that those items should occur with such remarkable uniformity over large areas of northern and central Europe.[26] These assemblages do not represent the arbitrary sacrifice of wealth but rather the use of a specific assemblage of signifiers which marked out the relationship of one person to another. That assemblage excluded items representative of other forms of exchange, although at moments of high drama and display even these items, normally excluded, were used in the funeral display; witness the baton, the mace and the axe from the Bush Barrow. By putting that particular assemblage together around the corpse a quite different level of moral and political order was being addressed.

In addition to these decorative items other objects, such as 'awls', razors and tweezers, are occasionally recovered. In the Edmondsham grave the tweezers and the pin had been placed to one side of the cremation whilst the whetstone and dagger were amongst and on top of the bone deposit (figure 5.2). The former items should be treated separately, and they are much more a feature of cremation deposits in general than they are of inhumations. The simplest way to consider this non-decorative material is to identify it with those items which had been used either in the preparation of the corpse or by the mourners and, polluted by this association, were then deposited in the grave. Tweezers, razors and awls are all tools for the modification of some material, at least the former being connected with the human body. The state of mourning may have required some minor form of mutilation, and this has in fact been glimpsed once and with dramatic clarity. At Winterslow G3 a cremation, covered by an inverted urn, was found to be accompanied by a small pile of human eyebrow hair from more than one individual along with a bronze razor.[27] Such a deposit as this reinforces our view that it was the deposition of cremated remains, separate from the firing of the corpse, that expressed the final acts and obligations of the mourners; the moment of transition out of mourning was now separated from the transformation into death.

Placing the Dead

If the grave was the medium in which an objective category of death was confirmed and the obligations of the mourners also realized, then the position of the grave in relation to other burials enabled those categories to be situated historically. All the evidence indicates that a complex intercutting and spatial referencing occurred in the digging of the individual graves, with the consequent definition of historical precedence. A direct construction of sequential deposition is encountered in a number of beaker graves, for example, although two cases are enough to make the point.

A grave pit, a little over one metre deep, lay beneath Shrewton barrow 24. Into this was placed the contracted body of an adult male, lying on its left side and facing east. Between the buttocks and the feet lay the beaker. The grave had then been infilled with chalk rubble and loam and was then covered by a small mound of chalk and earth derived from the encircling ring of quarry pits. After a period of time, long enough for the quarry pits to silt and for turf to have grown over the site, a second grave pit was cut through the centre of the mound and down through the fill of the first. This second grave received the contracted body of a young male which lay facing west, although the skull was found detached and lying on the chest of the skeleton. Sherds of three beakers lay in front of the corpse, and it has been suggested that these were residual material caught up by the infilling of the grave. Once it had been infilled with 'fine chalk dust and loam' the grave was covered by a mound reconstituted and enlarged by the addition of turves and a chalk capping derived from a second and larger ditch (Green and Rollo Smith 1984: 285). A number of points could be made concerning the treatment of the second corpse, its orientation and the fragmentary nature of the possible grave deposits, but all we will do here is emphasize that by inserting that burial into the earlier grave a sequential relationship was established and the significance of that one place was reaffirmed. The first burial determined precisely the placing of the second; it created the image of a primacy and of an origin, that this was an order which could be described historically. Death now allowed for the specific reaffirmation of relationships back through the preceding generations.

When a grave was selected and reopened one legitimate route to the past was established and others were refused. To found a grave or a burial ground could be to lay claim to future obligations of veneration. Although most graves would have had to be re-excavated for the addition of any further deposits, a more complex technology is sometimes encountered which seems to have been designed to leave the grave visible or even to have prepared it for future access. Amesbury barrow G51, lying just to the south of the Stone-henge cursus, was excavated at the beginning of the nineteenth century and again in 1960 (Ashbee 1978). The later excavation revealed a central grave pit containing a rectangular timber structure around the lower footings of which was packed a solid chalk rubble. The recent excavator suggests the rubble was cemented by water which had washed down from the sloping roof of the timber 'mortuary house'. The implication is that 'a house-like rectangular structure was half buried, but exposed and visible in the grave pit for a measurable period before the barrow was built'.[28] On the floor of this 'house' lay an inhumation accompanied by a beaker, both of which had been recovered by the earlier excavators. The grave pit was eventually infilled with a loose chalk mix, probably upcast derived from digging the grave pit, and the covering mound was further enlarged by additions of loam and then chalk derived from an encircling, causewayed ditch. At some later stage the buried timber building collapsed. The earlier excavators had also recovered two central inhumations, one placed above the other, and both above the primary burial. The relationship of these burials to the timber mortuary house, the grave-fill and the mound is unknown. Two further burials, one from the upper portion of the mound and one from the ditch, were also recovered in 1960.

By reusing any cemetery, choices were demanded between re-opening a particular grave, placing the burial next to another, or establishing a new and isolated siting for the grave. The requirement was always present, demanding each succeeding funeral to make some reference to those burials which had gone before. A new kind of history was being written in these rites.

The complex developments in the cemetery architecture and the funerary practices of the early second millennium were the medium for a historical narrative whose metaphors were the spatial relationships which evoked the image of time. The generalized past which had once belonged to the ancestors was now fragmented and the living forged new relationships between themselves and the dead; in this way they had found other ways of distinguishing between themselves. In his study of early Bronze Age round barrows Garwood (1991) has emphasized the considerable diversity in practices represented, reflecting the diverse strategies through which alliances among the living were given historical precedence. None the less Garwood also accepts that a very generalized sequence is perceptible in the architectural development of the burial mounds during the first half of the second millennium. This development, which he describes as running from mounds with free-standing pre-mound timber structures or revetted mounds to single phase unrevetted turf mounds which did not cover earlier timber structures, is one which should also be set against the long-recognized shift towards an increasingly widespread adoption of cremation. By the end of the millennium cremation deposits become the norm in cemetery archaeology, and it is important to understand the extent to which the two processes, the evolving mound structure and the more general adoption of cremation, were related.[29]

Despite the uncertainties of the chronology, it is still reasonable to accept that the beaker graves are amongst the earliest examples of the inhumation tradition in southern Britain. The quite regular reopening of these graves has

Figure 5.4   Bronze Age round barrow on Normanton Down, representing in its final phases
of development a substantial earthwork monument.

been noted, and from late in the third millennium cemeteries were established where both inhumations and cremations were most often covered by
low mounds and sometimes encircled by shallow ditches. Other means of
enclosing the grave existed, such as the flint and sarsen bank around the
grave at West Overton G6b.[30] One grave therefore established the spatial
parameters in which future deposits had to operate. The later deposits had
either to be dug into the primary grave, placed next to it within the enclosed
space, inserted in the ditch (or, as in the West Overton G6b example, beneath
the bank), or immediately outside the enclosure. In this initial phase of
development the emphasis was to gain access to the earlier grave, to locate
burials next to that grave, or to establish a new primary grave.

Grave assemblages and the dead meant nothing in themselves. Their
significance was expressed only by the remembered or claimed demands of
relationship, and these could be situated historically by reference to the other
graves within the cemetery. The importance of the spatial interplay between
the grave deposits, evoking the imagery of a genealogy, has already been
stressed. The addition of turf and chalk to the primary mounds changed the
material conditions under which future histories were written. The early
emphasis upon the place of the grave, where the grave was accessible and
could be reopened or have further deposits placed around it, was displaced
during the second millennium. Whereas the earlier covering mounds, with
their slight encircling ditches and fence lines, did little more than mark the
place of deposition, the more substantial earthwork, perhaps of recognizable
antiquity, became itself the focus for deposits which were either placed high

in the mound or on its margins (figure 5.4). It is this shift in the reference made by the deposition of human remains, away from the grave to the monument itself, which is also accompanied by the general move towards cremation. The culmination of the funeral rite was now at the pyre and the mourners brought the ashes back to an ancestral burial mound.

The contrast in these different forms of cemetery mound can be represented as stages in the development of some single monuments. This is well illustrated by two barrows from Launceston Down, Dorset, where the primary graves beneath each were originally covered by small chalk and turf mounds and were reopened on several occasions. The mounds were then more substantially enlarged by turf and chalk and further burials were placed high in these mounds and at their margins (Green, Lynch and White 1982). Similar developments can be traced among many of the cemeteries so far discussed, even though recent excavations have done little to elucidate our understanding of the later stages of mound development. The enlargement of many of the mounds by the addition first of turf and then of a chalk capping is a relatively common feature among the barrow cemeteries of the Avon valley. Amesbury barrow G71 exemplifies the sequence. The initial monument comprised a grave pit within a stake circle and ring ditch. The grave was reopened and was ultimately covered by a spread of chalk and surrounded by further rings of fence-line. The later monument then took on quite a different character; the turf mound was capped by a layer of chalk derived from a larger surrounding ditch and the capped mound was used as a platform upon which a pyre was established. Cremations were buried high in the mound before the surface of the platform was itself covered by another turf stack and surrounding chalk revetment. A small group of cremations and inhumations were then inserted into the heavily silted ditch on the south-east side of the mound.[31]

The burial rituals of the early second millennium reaffirmed the category and status of the dead and, in turn, that of the mourners. These categories were situated historically by funerary rituals which used the place of the grave as their text. To break open the grave or to excavate next to it was to give tangible expression to the sequence of individual lives. However, the development of the cemetery mounds in their monumental form eventually replaced the immediate availability of that original deposit with the images of more distant origins. The generalized ancestral origins perceptible to the communities of the fourth and third millennia were thus displaced during the second millennium. Lines of specific genealogical identity were constructed whose own origins then came to be fixed by mythological images of increasingly more distant times. It was in those distant and mythological ages that the inaccessible and heroic figures had lived and died who now lay buried beneath the massive turf and chalk-capped tumuli. The homage was paid by the mourners who carried the ashes of their own kin to the earlier burial mounds for interment. The ritual of cremation heightened the drama and the distance separating the particular death and the origins of the lineage to which it belonged, a distance surely acknowledged by depositing the ashes on the very margins of the mound.

Each of the major henge complexes in southern Britain is the focus for a significantly higher concentration of round barrows than are found elsewhere on the uplands, a pattern which can be extended to the river gravels of the upper Thames basin.[32] The burials were situated on the margins of the enclosures and not within them. In the case of the late Neolithic ceremonial enclosures around Mount Pleasant, for example, the main development of the barrow cemeteries lies to the south on the upland margins of the valley along the Dorset Ridgeway (Woodward 1991). Similarly, despite the proximity of many of the burial grounds to Stonehenge, that monument was not itself the focus for these cemeteries. The earliest phase of Stonehenge, an embanked enclosure, certainly predates the establishment of the formal burial grounds. The stone circles, built inside the earlier earthwork, came after a period of abandonment, and they are contemporary with the development of the cemeteries. These developments, at Stonehenge and of the barrows, represent two different ritual practices on this particular area of upland. The barrows were built with direct reference to a number of local features, including earlier monuments and the local topography. Durrington Walls lies away from the main cemetery clusters towards the Avon valley, and the chronological problems of relating late activity there with the development of Stonehenge has already been discussed (above, p. 41ff.). What is indicated is that the upland margins around Durrington had, by the second millennium, come to be described by reference to a different ritual and funerary programme. The evidence for the contemporary vegetational cover suggests that this process was accompanied by some clearance of scrub, and the creation of large tracts of grassland.[33]

The uplands around Stonehenge and the Dorset Ridgeway were gradually transformed from the end of the third to the end of the second millennium. The burial mounds now emerged as the most significant, permanent points of reference to anyone wishing either to locate themselves in that landscape or to describe the setting of the plain and the ridgeway; they still work that way today. The barrows embodied their own transformation, from grave-markers to silent and distant monuments, a transformation effected by the passage of time and by a usage which shifted its emphasis from the specific location of the grave to the veneration of the monument itself. Over the course of the second millennium new histories were being created; they may have been told as stories and celebrated in ritual but their reality was understood from the more mundane perspectives of day-to-day existence. If these different forms of remembrance also accompanied an increasing feeling of irrelevance for the great enclosed arena and processional avenues of traditional ceremonial display then it is to those routines of everyday life that we must now turn, for it was in these lives that the meaning of the rituals was to be read.

NOTES

1. I. F. Smith 1965: p1.25 records Keiller's discovery of the body of a fourteenth-century 'barber surgeon' crushed beneath one of the felled stones.
2. Burl quotes Charleton who, in 1633, published the following comment: 'Monuments themselves are subject to Forgetfulness, even while they remain. . . . They usually stand rather as dead objects of popular wonder, and occasions of Fables, than as certain records of Antiquity' (Burl 1992: 171).
3. Such an approach would return us to 'systems thinking' in which semi-autonomous processes seem to operate independently of human agency. It is this type of approach which Renfrew (1984), among others, has taken to characterize 'processual archaeology' (see ch. 7 below). A consideration of agency must recognize that memory, expectation and desire enable the agent to move between experiences, places and times.
4. This was a programme of rescue excavation initiated by the then Ministry of Works. For an early attempt to synthesize some of the first results of this programme, and to consider those results against the background of the barrow excavations of the late eighteenth and nineteenth centuries: Ashbee 1960.
5. For the evidence of Neolithic round mounds: Kinnes 1979.
6. For a discussion of the contrast between inhumation and cremation rituals: Barrett and Needham 1988: 130ff. and Barrett 1990a. For the construction of genealogy through burial rites: Garwood 1991.
7. For example, Handley Barrow PR27: Pitt Rivers 1898: 136ff.
8. Many accounts stress the importance of the orientation of the corpse in the grave as indicated by the position of the head. However, as a flexed body lies on its side it may be more important to consider the direction the body faces, rather than which end of the grave pit contains the head.
9. These general patterns can be recognized in the Shrewton barrow cemetery: Green and Rollo-Smith 1984.
10. Green and Rollo-Smith 1984. See here figure 2.1 above.
11. Garwood distinguished between the relatively passive recognition of a generalized body of ancestors and the more actively constructed concept of ancestry: Garwood 1991.
12. Other sources for artefacts recovered from grave-fills obviously exist. They include the residual material caught up in the backfilling of the grave or even objects inside the body, such as arrowheads (cf. H. S. Green in Evans 1984: 19).
13. Pader (1982) discusses dress in relation to Anglo-Saxon burial without making a clear

enough distinction between dressing the living and adorning the dead. Items may be transformed when moved between these two contexts, such as the breaking of the stone 'wrist-guard' in the Barnack grave (Donaldson 1977: 209). Needham has also identified early Bronze Age ornaments which are excluded from use in burial (Needham 1988: 233).

14   For Chilbolton: Russel 1990. Although gold ornaments, similar to those from Chilbolton, have in the past been interpreted as earrings, Sherratt's interpretation of them as hair ornaments seems the more likely (Sherratt 1986).

15   For Shrewton 5J: Green and Rollo-Smith 1984: 273–5.

16   For Shrewton 5K: Green and Rollo-Smith 1984: 275–9.

17   For an earlier discussion of the role of the dagger: Barrett 1985 and Needham 1988.

18   Evidence concerning the preparation of the grave pit includes the engraving on the wall of the grave of Shrewton 5K (Green and Rollo-Smith 1984: 275) and the indications that the grave of West Overton G6b had remained open for some time before the burial (Smith and Simpson 1966: 127). Evidence for a possible bier has been claimed at Sutton Veny (Johnson 1980: 36).

19   The importance of the grave as the place for the display of sacrifice and consumption has been widely discussed, e.g.: Bradley 1984: 84ff. and Kristiansen 1978.

20   Our understanding of the Bush Barrow assemblage depends upon the early nineteenth-century description (Hoare 1810: 202–4). Ashbee's reconstruction of the burial deposit (1960: fig. 24) is questionable in some details when read against this ambiguous earlier account. The position of the axe, for example, which may or may not have been hafted, is simply recorded as near the shoulders with no particular side of the body given.

21   This form of burial display, where a number of individual artefact deposits, or groups of artefacts, are laid out around the body is a feature of a number of other 'rich' grave assemblages from Bronze Age Europe. This includes the Leubingen and Helmsdorf graves (Piggott 1965: 129 and fig. 67) and the 'first' Breton grave series which includes graves into which groups of artefacts have been deposited, some in organic containers (Briard 1984: 54ff.).

22   Currently available radiocarbon dates indicate that cremation is certainly a contemporary rite alongside the earliest inhumations associated with beakers in southern Britain.

23   For Shrewton 5D: Green and Rollo-Smith 1984: 265–7. There are some indications in the Shrewton cemetery that turf was fairly regularly used, as opposed to chalk, for infilling cremation graves.

24   For Amesbury G61a and G58: Ashbee 1985. For a comparable assemblage of dagger, amber and jet beads, and an awl accompanying a cremation, see Winterbourne Stoke G47: Gingell 1988: 60–1.

25   Another example of a composite necklace of shale, amber and faience beads was found associated with a cremation beneath the bell barrow Upton Lovell G1 (Annable and Simpson 1964: 54, nos 340–342).

26   This point returns us to the discussion of the 'classic' bell beaker assemblages of Europe. For work on amber ornaments in Britain: Beck and Shennan 1991.

27   I am grateful to Leslie Grinsell for details of this grave assemblage: Grinsell 1950.

28   Ashbee 1978: 8. Another possible timber structure set within a grave pit has been identified in the excavation of the Fordington Farm round barrow (Bellamy 1991).

29   'In this period [c.1650–1400 BC] . . . cremation, especially in-urned cremation, was the dominant form of burial throughout these islands, and inhumations practically disappeared' (Burgess 1980: 115).

30 For West Overton G6b: Smith and Simpson 1966.

31 For Amesbury G71: Christie 1967.

32 Fleming (1971) discusses the nature of the barrow distributions in Wessex in detail. For the correlation of the barrow cemetery distributions with the distribution of the henges: Renfrew 1973.

33 Fleming (1971) links the distribution of the round barrow cemeteries with areas of upland pasture.

6

Time and Place: The Formation of the Agricultural Landscape

Introduction

Building the various enclosures, mortuary structures and tombs represented a considerable investment of time and labour. So, indeed, did the effort expended in their ritual and ceremonial use. However, that effort was invested in long-term projects which extended over some two to three millennia and the investment must have been only a fraction of the total energy reserves demanded by more mundane, everyday activities. If the lengthy rituals at Avebury or at Durrington, or the ancestral rites at West Kennet, were regularly executed they will still only have occupied the smaller part either of the year or of an individual's lifetime. And even at their most elaborate, the architecture of each place and the ceremonial activities which were employed there extended over only a limited portion of the occupied land surface.

When they are expressed as a fraction of the lived allocation of time and space, and when they are set against the more densely occupied background of cultivation plots, pasturage and woodland, then ritual and ceremonial activities begin to appear almost marginal. That marginality can also be expressed in other ways. The restricted spaces of the henges operated as mechanisms of exclusion, areas reserved only for initiates. The chambers of many ancestral tombs must have functioned in a similar way. Burial rituals obviously occurred frequently, driven by the relatively haphazard intervention of death. Funerary processions and the cremation pyres will have been regularly observed, and the funeral celebrations were shared by many members of the community. But the uniqueness of a grave assemblage such as that from Bush Barrow is all too easily overlooked. Here, briefly and at the end of the funeral rites, were gathered together a quite unusual collection of elaborate but small artefacts. They were immediately buried beneath a covering mound. Few people will have witnessed this although others will have heard tell of it, and the detail of each telling may, for a while at least, have grown more elaborate with the passing of time. Archaeologists have begun to tell those stories again as they regularly reproduce the images of the artefacts in their publications and their lectures, and continue to discuss the significance of the burial as if it typified the period. Has our emphasis upon all this material been misguided, a concentration upon 'the abstractions of ideology and ritual' (Whittle 1991: 261), in place of a more worthwhile concern with the 'economic basis' of these times?

I think the question is misleading when expressed simply in this way, as a contrast between the elaborate but marginal ritual experiences and the more routine experiences of economic life. Throughout this book we have attempted to distance ourselves from the tradition of sociological analysis which takes the social totality as its object of study, and which proceeds to define that totality in terms of certain 'basic' or 'essential' attributes. By abandoning these abstractions we have been able to consider how different areas of social practice may have been maintained by agents who, by moving between them, drew the understandings gained in one area into the practical interpretations of another. Thus were symbolic resources carried forward, not as abstract schemes but in the practical dispositions of agents who were themselves constituted in this nexus of social practice. It was by sustaining and reproducing *life* itself that these social conditions were maintained. The 'economic' and the 'ideological' domains offer neither a 'true' nor a 'false' image of some social reality, nor is one in some way marginal to the other. Both were reproduced as the necessary conditions of social life, a body of empirical experience which was drawn into the practical interpretation of the world.

In ritual, meanings are read by practitioners who find some familiarity in the logic of the traditionally constituted text and who bring their own interpretive abilities to bear upon it. These abilities need not be directly acknowledged, and the truths revealed may seem to depend upon the spiritual receptivity of the observer directed towards the 'still, small voice' immanent to the text. Created as a language and a symbolism of metaphor, displaced from the more routine areas of experience, the truth of the ritual will appear to derive from elsewhere. These truths appear timeless, metaphysical, and they address and make real the wider realms of experience. Certainly, as one of the few discursive languages available to express generally held concepts of moral order by reference to the notions of 'truthfulness', 'origins' and 'causes', ritual codes may always be read as representing an ideal and coherent statement of the communities' 'world-view'. Although such statements may rarely express conflicts of interest, appearing to speak instead on behalf of dominant forms of political authority, it does not follow that the ideological domain represents a 'false consciousness' or one which 'masks truth'. Such judgements simply repeat the notion that a true or an absolute description of any social reality is actually possible. The task of archaeology is to understand how the languages and the understandings necessary for living were constructed, defended and held in place by those who occupied and reworked the material conditions which they had available to them. The fragments of those conditions are recoverable today and their redescription in archaeological writing represents a further reworking, this time from perspectives which are situated in the material and social contexts of our modern world.

If the rituals and the ceremonials which we have discussed only occupied the smaller portion of the lives of those who undertook them, we may none the less discount the view that our emphasis has so far missed something more fundamental, namely the conditions of 'economic' life. It was these more 'mundane' experiences which the ritual and ceremonial practices addressed. It was from such mundane practices that some ability to understand, if only partially, the significance, truth or adequacy of each ritual arose. In other words, the culturally interpreted conditions of economic life were read into the interpretation of the ritual, and the truth of the ritual returned to inhabit economic practice. Thus the interpretations which have been offered in the chapters above have in fact been about the structuring of economic practice. Let me stress that this argument does not presume a final determinacy residing in the economic sphere; it simply recognizes how the agent will have operated, situated between these discourses of economic and ritual practices.

This argument makes it analytically necessary to maintain the distinction between the different spheres of discourse/practice across which agency operated. We may distinguish between traditions of knowledge which were reproduced in ritual and which had the potential for being expressed discursively as the principles which underpinned the order of things, and those knowledges which were reproduced in day-to-day activities. Many of the principles contained in the latter would never have found voice, other than in the practical understandings of 'knowing how to go on'. The distinction between the two has been described in terms of a contrast, in which the recognition of the distanciation between the context of the reader and the text of the ritual is compared with the contexts of co-presence in 'talk' and routine practice. But it was by moving between these different regions of social practice that an individual's biography was created and a language found through which the agent could begin to comprehend the world and their place within it. To what extent is it possible for the archaeologist to touch upon and thus to understand those biographies? This understanding must do more than simply expose the logic of the ritual text, or the symbolic logic of material production; in short, it must abandon the structuralist programme. In its place we seek to touch upon lives which found it possible to move, to act and to speak between each text, and so to create for themselves an understanding of the agent's own situated sense of being. The attempt which will be made here begins with those rituals which we have already explored in terms of their internal organization, that is of their code – the material conditions and consequences of those practices and the distribution and actions of people within them. We must now move beyond the code to the situated conditions of its reading. What understandings of the self were to be found within these various forms of ritual through the recognition of their wider relevance in day-to-day experience?

Three ritual codes, those concerned with ancestral rites, ceremonial procession and burial rituals, have been discussed. Each developed with a certain degree of spatial autonomy; ancestral monuments were not incorporated within the major ceremonial enclosures, and when the early burial monuments appeared at the beginning of the second millennium they were sometimes adjacent to, but not generally placed within, the earlier enclosures. None the less, by their execution, explicit references were undoubtedly made to those principles which appeared to be held in common between these different ritual practices. For example, the idea of an ancestral presence could have been evoked with reference to a number of different locations by the deposition of human bone and not restricted simply by reference to the megalithic and non-megalithic mounds. Each form of ritual also displayed a relative autonomy in its own historical development, although the situation here is obviously complex. As suggested in chapter 5, the conditions under which the highly evolved ceremonial practices of the late Neolithic began to decline during the second millennium were contingent upon other forms of ritual practice; the developing burial rituals of the period are obviously likely to have played a part in this process. This brings us to the heart of the analysis which will be pursued here; if different fields of ritual practice appear to have operated in conflict at some point in their history, then this conflict arose not because each offered an alternative and competing medium for display but because each may have addressed, and thus have made comprehensible, differences in the contextual conditions from which they were read. What we need to disentangle is the extent to which this sequence of ritual practices addressed different 'economic' strategies.

The path which our analysis must trace is as follows. In each of the three fields of ritual we must isolate the principles which structured the biographical relationship between the participant and the metaphysical values of the ritual itself. Each biography could be lived because it carried the agent forward in such a way that the various structuring principles were recognizably reproduced in other, diverse areas of social practice. These principles were also the ones an agent might have drawn upon in the unlikely event of being asked to describe their own existence, or the place of the humanity to which they belonged in a wider order of things. Over the entire period with which we are concerned I will argue that the structuring principles involve a transformation between two different concepts of temporality.

The first of these temporalities belonged to the third millennium, but had a history which stretched back through the fourth and probably the fifth millennia. It evoked the idea of human existence as a process of *becoming*, a movement towards a future state which was described by reference to ancestors or to gods and where life itself might be spoken of as ephemeral, as a series of movements through states or as a journey through the world. Perhaps that future was a return to the origin of time, a beginning and an end revealed in the timeless values of the rituals themselves.

The second concept of temporality was constructed out of the practices of the second millennium, and it was where the weight of the past began to bear down upon the agent to fix an existence of *being*, a place and a moment where obligations and authority were situated in the directional flow of time. This may have involved a more complex definition of the person in terms of their status, obligations and their genealogical position.

What we must grasp are the metaphors which made it possible to talk about human existence and thus to act meaningfully. It would be wrong to assume that such contrasting metaphorical chains of reasoning gave rise directly to conflicting images of temporality – in fact different images of temporality may have co-existed. But they do embody quite specific structural implications, and I would argue that by the end of the second millennium the dominant metaphors of life had become those of *being*.

On Becoming

The mortuary monuments of the fourth millennium arose from ritual strategies which fixed places of ancestral veneration upon the landscape. The mechanisms of this process have already been discussed, and the fact that the places selected had always been appreciated as auspicious for the revelation of an ancestral presence seems more than likely. Although some burial rituals may have terminated at these monuments, the overall evidence indicates that contemporary burial rites normally required no specific monumental setting. If individuals, in the company of others, did recognize their identity with, and their obligations towards, these ancestral sites then this effectively established a form of tenurial claim upon that place.

It is important for the development of this argument that we should now follow Ingold's (1986: 130ff.) discussion of *tenure*, and we will do this in two respects. Firstly I take tenure to be concerned with the way resources are contained within a network of social obligation and authority which is reproduced over time. Tenure is the ability to exercise power over 'allocative resources' and it 'is about the ways in which a resource locale is worked or bound into the biography of the subject'.[1] Secondly, in describing the environment across which humans move we must distinguish between the surfaces of the land, places, and the paths facilitating movement from one place to another. Tenure is not simply about claims over areas of land surface, and Ingold extends, somewhat abstractly, our understanding of the way tenure addresses three very different spatial dimensions: it may operate 'zero-dimensionally' on *places*, 'one-dimensionally' on *paths* or tracks and 'two-dimensionally' over the *ground surface*.

Identification with the place of ancestral presence was therefore a form of 'zero-dimensional' tenure in Ingold's terms: it involves no necessary tenurial claim upon areas of land.[2] Such tenure would have been routinely expressed by acknowledging the significance of the place as the landscape was traversed, and also in the moments of ritual veneration which took place at those locations. In both cases the monument was one place on a network of paths along which those who either approached or who passed by the monument moved.

Paths could have been identified by a routine usage expressive of inherited rights of access or of passage across the land. The architecture of the monuments themselves, for example the way the long barrows are sometimes situated along the line of a ridge and with a broad facade across one end, invited a certain regular disposition in the orientation of those who would look towards them or who would approach the mound. However, there are also indications of more formally demarcated paths. The cursus are long parallel-sided enclosures, normally comprising a double line of bank and ditch. The Dorset Cursus is the longest example of such a monument in Britain. In its final form it runs for over ten kilometres, with an internal width between the banks of slightly less than 60 metres. If these were paths or avenues, then they were not open-ended, and the south-western terminal of the Dorset Cursus is enclosed by a substantial earthwork. Bradley's analysis of the monument has enabled him to demonstrate the relatively piecemeal programme of its construction where the line was sighted from one hill-top and ridge to the next. Built towards the end of the fourth millennium, that line ran along Cranborne Chase and close to the line of the watershed from which the rivers drain south-east into the coastal basin. Both the Dorset Cursus and the Stonehenge Cursus are closely associated with earthen long barrows. Long mounds were aligned on the terminals of the Dorset Cursus while another mound lay within and across its path and another was included in the line of the western bank. Other long barrows cluster in the immediate vicinity of the monument. The eastern terminal of the Stonehenge Cursus lies alongside a long barrow (figure 2.1) the profile of which could have been clearly observed by looking down the line of the cursus from the opposite, western terminal.[3]

Movement along these paths will therefore have been made with some reference to the long barrows. A number of long barrows were constructed as part of building the Dorset Cursus. One of the longest uninterrupted views along the line of the cursus is gained between Bottlebush Down and Gussage Cow Down. From Bottlebush Down a long mound dominates the Gussage skyline, and from this position the midwinter sun would also have been observed to set behind that mound. It was only by occupying and by moving along the path of the Cursus, from one skyline to the next, that the overall order of the monument would have become apparent. However, if the cursus defined one path it also cut others.

The topographical setting of the Stonehenge Cursus is such that it divides two blocks of downland, each containing a cluster of long barrows, while the Dorset Cursus lies between the chalk upland of Cranborne Chase and the river valleys. In both cases any movement between these areas would have involved crossing the line of each earthwork. In the case of Cranborne Chase such movement would have conformed with a seasonal migration between the coastal basin, the valleys and the uplands. People might have moved with particular groups of animals or have shifted between differently located seasonal resources (Ingold 1980; 1986: 165ff.). However, any attempt to refine our understanding of this use of the upland faces some quite funda-mental difficulties.

The earthworks of the fourth millennium, the long barrows, causewayed enclosures and cursus, are well known by their siting on the uplands. How-ever, evidence for human activity immediately preceding their construction is more difficult to locate. Flint artefacts which can be typologically assigned to the fifth millennium are largely unattested, seemingly indicative of a lack of settlement. A similar picture occurs in all the upland areas so far discussed.[4] The building of the earliest earthworks might seem to indicate a period of colonization. So lacking are the uplands in earlier material that Bradley (in Barrett, Bradley and Green 1991: 53) has considered the possibility that the 'building of some of the monuments on the Wessex chalk might precede the general establishment of settlement in the area'. In his discussion of the upper reaches of the Kennet valley Whittle has also argued for a significant change in the settlement of the uplands between the end of the fifth and the early fourth millennium. In the earlier period he proposes that gatherer-hunters operated from the middle reaches of the valley, with only occasional incursions onto the hills. In the fourth millennium he claims that the picture changed dramatically, with the location of such earthworks as long barrows and the causewayed enclosure at Windmill Hill on these hills. This, Whittle argues (1990b: 107–8), amounts to 'a process of infill, for more regular economic exploitation and for settlement, even though that need not have been permanent or continuous from the outset'.

The image of a rapid colonization into an upland landscape is at odds with some of the environmental evidence, mainly the snail fauna and soils which derive from the buried surfaces and the deposits which accumulated in humanly dug features. Some of the evidence for pre-building activity beneath the long barrows around Avebury has already been considered. Overall the picture is one where the hills carried an uneven patchwork of pasture, forest and scrub, with some limited traces of cultivation. The Dorset Cursus, for example, passed between open ground and more closed, forested conditions. The history of this vegetational regime is difficult to assess; it may have been the product of a quite lengthy process of clearance associated with both animal management and cultivation.[5]

The historical context of the earliest monument building should now be reconsidered by looking again at the assumptions which currently inform our interpretation of the settlement and environment evidence. The primacy given to flint debitage as the indicator of fifth and early fourth millennium settlement is open to challenge. Such material, including artefacts and working waste, is of central importance in identifying activities including the procurement of the raw material and the maintenance of hunting equipment; in other words, we should interpret the debris as the product of specific activities and not simply as 'calling cards' indicative of any human presence.[6] If the uplands were occupied over much of the fifth millennium for activities which involved little by way of either flint procurement associated with core reduction, or the maintenance of tool kits, or hunting (or the building of earthworks for that matter), then it will be very difficult to identify that occupation archaeologically. Perhaps the importance of the uplands for hunting has been overstated; after all, in the fourth millennium on Cranborne

Chase most of the projectile points come from the coastal areas and not from the chalk (Gardiner in Barrett et al. 1991: 54).

Sites are places of human activity and their locations are normally examined by plotting these locations against their contemporary environmental conditions. The relationship between the two, the site and the environment, is analysed as if the site were the centre from which the resources which lay in its immediate vicinity were exploited. Classically this relationship is portrayed in the abstract modelling of site catchment analysis which situates the site at the centre of an encircling zone of potentially exploitable resources. Such analyses maintain the terminological confusion, which Ingold has criticized, between *territorial behaviour* and *tenure*.[7] Territorial behaviour describes the routine movement of a human population over a particular portion of the land surface. Such a population may advertise its presence at the time, but different groups may be able to negotiate a fairly open access to the same resources, and the territories of a number of such populations may therefore overlap. The means by which access to resources is negotiated, or those resources are controlled, is a question of tenure. Within any territorial pattern of behaviour the three different forms of tenure which Ingold has identified may be in operation, and as Ingold demonstrates it is essential to distinguish between tenure operating over a bounded area of land surface and a pattern of territorial behaviour. To recognize territorial behaviour amongst a human population becomes relatively trivial; it is the mechanisms by which access to resources is negotiated through time which is of greater importance.

The various attempts to present the monuments of the fourth and third millennia as nodes or as centres of clearly defined 'territories' fail to contribute to our understanding of the issue of tenure. Instead we are left with a number of conflicting images. Renfrew's model (1973) of the period presented the long barrows and causewayed enclosures as places situated centrally in their differently scaled political territories. According to this model these territories were gradually combined until, by the third millennium, there emerged a group of larger 'polities'. Bradley, on the other hand, has depicted both the cursus and the long barrows of Cranborne Chase as lying on the 'upper boundary of an enormous triangular territory' the centre of which lay in the coastal basin (Bradley in Barrett et al. 1991: 54). Obviously it will always be possible to locate the geometric centre for a distribution map of points where each point represents a monument or, by using the same data, to generate a network of polygonal territories around each point, but these abstractions need have little significance in terms of the human practices they seek to analyse.

Do those monuments which were built on the chalk in the fourth millennium (the long barrows, causewayed enclosures and the cursus) represent the result of a relatively rapid colonization onto a previously marginal and intermittently occupied upland, the kind of 'infill' envisaged by Whittle for the Avebury area? Perhaps the alternative would be to view the monuments as the products of much longer-term strategies whose origins lay firmly in the fifth millennium. For this argument to carry any weight it will have to accommodate the limited artefactual evidence remaining from the uplands. This may not pose too great a problem if we can assume that the continuity proposed was structured by a tenure restricted to places and to paths. The human presence would have been transient from one place to another as the paths were reworked by movement between local and seasonally variable resources, and by tenurial claims upon migrant animal populations. The paths followed by some portion of the human population may therefore also have been shared by animals, a symbiosis defined more in terms of the pastoralist than of the hunter. The importance of cattle in the use of the upland is illustrated by the butchery and food residues recovered as primary deposits in the Windmill Hill ditches or from the Coneybury Pit on Salisbury Plain. We might also recall the ox skulls beneath the mound of South Street and, at a later date, the ox skin in the grave-fill of the Hemp Knoll barrow.[8]

The cross-cutting of each individual trajectory by an arrival at one place, and by the dissolution of that meeting through departure and by moving on, would have structured people's access to, and their appropriation of, the available resources. The temporal and the spatial referents of these lives would have been known in terms of the seasons and of the distances between places. These were the referents around which the local and the supralocal communities were constructed. The obligations of the latter could, as has long been suggested, have been relived at such places as the causewayed enclosures, where interpersonal obligations were recognized through the exchange of people, food and materials. These sites did not occupy the centres of territories so much as lie at the end of one path and at the beginning of the next. Certain places were the markers of a permanent order; they had always existed and they always would. Perhaps it was the ancestral presence which was the metaphor for that timeless quality, written into the landscape by the routine acts of veneration which led eventually to the construction of the megalithic and non-megalithic long mounds. But that same metaphor was reworked elsewhere with the deposition of human remains in the ditches of many causewayed enclosures.

The adoption of domesticates and, above all, the beginning of cultivation is normally taken to mark the seemingly fundamental transition from gatherer-hunter to farmer. This transition is traditionally described as an evolution out of a state of nature. Gatherer-hunters appear to take the form of communities who

> have yet to bend nature to a social purpose; wholly enmeshed within a web of material relations they are deemed to remain subservient to her demands – hence the persistent inclination to view hunting and gathering societies in terms that are exclusively ecological rather than social. (Ingold 1986: 135)

Meillassoux (1972) maintains an evolutionary division between gatherer-hunters and farmers by repeating Marx's distinction between the ways land functions in different economic formations, either as a 'subject of labour' or as an 'instrument of labour'. The former involves little labour investment as resources are extracted from a land out of which those resources are reproduced through the forces of nature alone. According to this view, neither the land nor its products are bound into the reproduction of social relations. The products of the hunt or of gathering are shared amongst the community without long-term obligations arising from that distribution because no participant can establish a tenurial claim upon the reproduction of the forces of nature. When land becomes an instrument of labour,

> the agricultural team is linked together, at least until the time of cropping, in order for every member to benefit from their joint labour. Furthermore, the vital problem of feeding the cultivator during the non-productive period of labour – between clearing the ground and harvest-time – cannot be solved unless enough of the previous crop is available for this purpose. The members of one agricultural party are consequently linked not only to one another during the non-productive period of work, but also to the working party that produced the food during the previous cycle. Time and continuity become essential features of the economic and social organisation. (Meillassoux 1972: 99)

The uses which have been made of Meillassoux's work in archaeology are not without their problems, arising largely from the assumption that a transformation in the tenurial link between labour and the products of the land is the one determinate distinguishing farming/neolithic societies from those of gatherer-hunters.[9] All social formations are reproduced across time as agents operate within the exchange networks which both transform the material forces of nature into a social product and maintain other authoritative resources such as age, gender and proximity to spiritual or godly powers.

The transformation of social conditions arises from a reworking of these resources and the relative position each takes within the hegemony claimed by dominant forms of discourse.[10] The metaphors of ancestral presence and of ceremonial veneration have been identified as those which dominated the languages of production in the fourth and third millennia. These were the languages which defined as legitimate those tenurial bonds which situated people in place and in time. The argument is close to the suggestion made by Bender when she writes of the way ritual permanence may establish 'a ceremonial and social locus that invokes a delay on *socially* invested time, energy and thought – a place pivotal within the cognitive scheme of things' (1985: 26).

There exists an unwarranted assumption that, because cultivation requires the maintenance of field plots, then the appearance of cultivars at the end of the fifth millennium must also herald the emergence of a predominant concern with the social control of portions of land surface. The social organization of labour, with its access to the resources necessary for cultivation, could have been structured via the seasonal movement of people between relatively widely dispersed places. In her study *The Conditions of Agricultural Growth* Boserup distinguished between different intensities of land use which she defined by the length of the fallow period. These differences are also related to the state of preparation of the land, the technology employed and the form of land tenure (Boserup 1965). The important correlations which she noted between the level of technology, the form of tenure and the length of the fallow period can be accepted without also having to accept her central thesis that population pressure plays the determinate role in the intensification of land use.

We will develop our argument by following Boserup's analysis in distinguishing between *long fallow* systems, classified as forest-fallow and bush-fallow, and the *short fallow* systems which include short periods of grass-fallow, annual cropping and multi-cropping. Obviously the differences between the two systems partly reflect land-use history; in temperate Europe, forest-, bush- and grass-fallow are strategies which would only have been available at different stages in a longer cycle of forest clearing. However, what distinguishes between long and short fallow is more than an adaptive response to different levels of forest clearance; it also involves different technologies of cultivation (between digging sticks and hoes on the one hand and traction ploughing on the other), differences in the organization of labour and, crucially, differences in the form of tenure.

Agricultural systems whose cultivation plots were given over to long periods of fallow, and where some regeneration of vegetation might be expected, would have been cultivated by people whose access to that land was claimed as generalized rights arising from alliances between the members of a wider community. To belong to that community was also to recognize that the land was held in trust by the community itself, the members of which would neither have expected nor have required to make a continuous claim to control a place of cultivation; what mattered was to belong to and reproduce the identity of the community. Long fallow cultivation demanded little investment of agricultural technology, and the expectation was that access to cultivable land was secured as one of the mosaic of resources over which the community exercised its rights. The place of cultivation would therefore have become available for a short period of time, to be relinquished in the knowledge that other places could be claimed in turn.

Archaeological traces of these long fallow systems, other than the negative trace of no surviving early field boundaries and no enclosed settlements, cannot be identified on the Wessex chalk. Outside this area it is possible to identify cultivation of this type among the cairnfields of northern Britain, where short-lived cultivation plots seem to have characterized periods of land colonization during the second millennium BC (Barrett 1989a).

Short fallow systems are where the land was used more intensively, crops being removed with a greater frequency even to the extent of multi-cropping.[11] Such systems demand a different organization of labour, a greater investment in agricultural technology along with the interventions necessary to maintain the land and its fertility. These investments were long-term in the way a particular area of land was maintained from one year to the next by the labour of a particular portion of the community.

All agricultural systems involve a delay between the labour investment of planting and the return derived from the harvest, and all agricultural practices establish a link between the different tasks of planting and harvesting and the allocation of the products of that labour between the various participants. For Meillassoux it is the delay which exists between the labour and resources necessary for planting, and the return of the harvest, which is decisive in distinguishing the social labour of the agriculturalist from the immediate returns available to the gatherer-hunter. Bender (1978) has shown this contrast to be overdrawn, simply because all forms of gift exchange, not only agricultural practices, involve a delayed return. However, in agricultural production itself the further distinction can be made between long and short fallow systems because they operate on the basis of different tenurial expectations, and it is these which structure the way cultivation is reproduced from one generation to the next. Long fallow systems will have enhanced the expectation of the availability of resources (land and co-operative labour) arising from the maintenance of open alliances throughout the wider community. By contrast, short fallow systems will have been reproduced by closing down access to both land and co-operative labour to within a more tightly drawn community whose members were able to sustain their tenurial claims over a specific area of land from one generation to the next and to mobilize a greater level of investment in that land. It was in the latter system that the biographies of the individual came to be tied more closely to a certain portion of land and to a more tightly defined and closed community. The fundamental difference between these two systems lies, as Goody (1976) demonstrated so clearly, in the way inheritance will have operated.

Not every member of the wider community would, or indeed could, have moved on the same paths, or have shared the same seasonal cycle of movement or have been situated in the same networks of exchange. The community was built from a cluster of different biographies strung across different regions of time-space. The differences between people's perceptions of the landscape were the practical realizations of labour which defined what it was to be young or to be old, to be male or to be female.

In the last half of the third millennium ritual texts had emerged, which developed the most elaborate metaphorical representations of place and path and of the sacred identity of the community itself. These representations were enacted at the great ceremonial complexes such as Avebury, Durrington and Mount Pleasant. These monuments lay between the uplands, and the river and lowland basins. The form of the land was itself changing. Substantial forest clearing at this time is indicated by the timber buildings and the palisades, and the particular importance of the forests is also indicated by the predominance of pig over cattle amongst the food refuse on these sites (Grigson 1982).

However intricate these great architectural settings appear to us today, or may become as the result of further fieldwork, we can recognize in them the steady material elaboration of a relatively simple arrangement, the movement along a path, approaching and then departing from some precisely defined place. The enclosure of these places, the formalized processional approaches, and the facades across the entrance ways have already been described. Although the rituals which vitalized these monuments were practised within the increasingly elaborate and enclosed spaces by a sanctified elite, and may have addressed that elite most directly, they will also have been read by a wider audience. All the participants may have recognized in some way (and without necessarily accepting it) the basis of the authority claimed by those who were acting on their behalf. Indeed they may have found it increasingly difficult not to describe that authority in the language of its ritualized imagery. All participants will also have understood something of the fundamental structure of the ritual code as being a recognizable transformation of their own diverse and routine experiences. That broad understanding of what the execution of ritual required is implicit in the successful mobilization of the enormous, co-operative effort demanded by the construction of these monuments. People knew what was needed and they could objectify that knowledge, even if their experiences of the rituals were always going to be partial and subjective. These monuments were the theatres of transitory experience, where the passage of an individual's life could touch upon the presence of ancestors and gods.

Situated between the ritual and the routine, and recognizing the homologies which interwove all into the 'seamless cloth' of cultural life, agents achieved a means of self-reflection, an understanding of their own existence expressed in terms of the obligations they owed, and the demands they could make of others. These extended from immediate kin, through strangers to spirits and ancestors. Individual biographies bound people and cultural resources together, and between the fifth and the third millennia life may have worked itself out as transient, as the labour on a world which was constantly reforming, only for life to return to an origin, the source of the community's own identity, the ancestral home.

If such a commentary as that above appears speculative, then as such it is necessary for through it we can touch upon the possibilities of what may have been, and begin to understand more fully the profound nature of the changes which were brought about during the second millennium.

On Being

The continuity which we have traced between the fifth and the third millennia concerned the structuring of routine practice and the readings of the metaphorical imagery of ritual, an order which was realized in the movement along paths and between places. We have arrived at an understanding of the period which is different from that normally presented. This is because we have rejected the traditional view which takes the adoption of agriculture as representing a major transformation which distinguishes the fourth millennium from the closing centuries of the fifth. The traditional model sees the fourth millennium marking the beginning of a steady process of forest clearance demanded by cultivation, a shift from a human subsistence strategy which was migratory to one which was sedentary, and with a relocation of the main weight of human settlement activity towards the cultivable lands while the uncleared (if managed) forests now defined the margin.

The alternative outlined here displaces the moment of an agricultural transformation of the landscape away from the fourth millennium and into the short fallow systems which, it will be argued, emerged in the second millennium. The difference between the two agricultural systems is between a landscape which was held together by movement across its surface between a constellation of places each of which was loaded with social and religious significances, and a landscape which was viewed from the centre of a domain, with distinct boundaries between an internal world belonging to the household and the self, and the outside world of others. In the latter, it was the centre (the household) and the margins which now become places of particular religious concern. Our terminology is affected by the revision. Words and phrases such as 'centre', 'woodland', 'pasture', 'arable', 'marginal', 'colonization', 'abandonment and regeneration', have very different meanings in the context of land-use systems where tenure is not concerned with the control of bounded areas of land surface in contrast to those in which it is. Time is also differently constituted in the two systems. The movement of the days and seasons remains constant, and with them the recurrent availability of natural resources, but to move from place to place is to move along the cycles of time in contrast to observers who watch the cyclical renewal of the seasons working themselves out upon that portion of the land to which they belong. It is this place-bound sense of *being* which characterizes not the fourth and third millennia but which was constructed during the second millennium and from which it dominated all succeeding periods in our prehistory.

If the adoption of cultivation by the end of the fifth millennium in southern Britain can be understood as occurring in a 'mesolithic' context, in other words as one product of the social alliances of a generalized community, membership of which created paths of access to the ancestors and gods whilst confirming a person's rights of access to places and the physical and spiritual resources which those places contained, then a far more fundamental transformation can be proposed for the second millennium. It was in this period that a place-bound sense of 'being' emerged through the fragmentation of that generalized community into the more closed communities and households. These households or household clusters were the products of a lineal history in which their individual identities were fixed historically and also in relation to the land.

Obviously the case for this transformation in the control of land does not depend upon the presence of cultivation, for this was common to both the long and the short fallow systems. More to the point are the indications of technological change, a more intensive use of the land with short fallow, a concern for the division and demarcation of the land and possible changes in the definition of settlement locations.

Technological change in the methods of cultivation, in particular the adoption of traction ploughing, are difficult to trace given how little information is available concerning the earlier systems of cultivation. The evidence of the South Street long barrow certainly demonstrates the use of traction ploughing at the end of the fourth millennium, but how generally this practice extended is quite unclear.[12] Perhaps the more important indications are those of the intensive regimes of cultivation which resulted in soil erosion. A number of recent surveys have examined the history of chalkland soils and the history of dry valley colluvial deposits. It is generally accepted that these soils underwent considerable change during the periods with which we are concerned, particularly with the truncation of the original and extensive loessic component of the post-glacial soil. However, if this truncation had occurred by the end of the third millennium it is difficult to identify the resulting colluvial deposits.

Colluviation is the result of mechanical erosion or slopewash, and soil erosion rates under the same mechanical conditions of disturbance will depend upon variations in soil type and landform. Forest clearance will almost inevitably result in soil erosion, as will cultivation. Work on chalkland colluvial deposits was initiated in Sussex and Hampshire by Bell (1983) and has now been undertaken elsewhere in Wessex, including work by Entwistle (1989) around Stonehenge and the Wiltshire Avon, and by Evans and Rouse (in Sharples 1991: 15ff.) around Maiden Castle, Dorset. These and other studies make it clear that colluvial deposits are not a general feature of the chalkland – none were found in the environs of Stonehenge, for example. However, where they are found, and where dating evidence exists, substantial deposits do not appear to predate the second millennium, although they do occur after that period and continued to form throughout the first millennium and into the medieval period. Taken at face value this general profile of soil erosion certainly indicates substantial changes in land use during the second millennium, perhaps with some areas of chalk upland witnessing the break-up of quite ancient grassland by the plough.

The sequence of soil erosion correlates with the date of the first recognizable appearance of field lynchets (the so-called 'celtic fields'). The dating of these cultivation plots is in many cases ambiguous; some examples may have been quite short-lived, and as a particular phenomenon they continued to form throughout the first millennium BC and into the first half of the first

Figure 6.1   Late second millennium field-systems on Preshute Down. One of the settlement enclosures is indicated; the circular features are later dew-ponds. (Copyright: Ashmolean Museum, Oxford)

millennium AD (figure 6.1). None the less, it remains difficult to date any of these cultivation systems to before the second millennium BC. Bell has suggested that they represent an attempt to manage soil erosion, with the field edges demarcated by stone clearance forming traps for hillwash, and there is evidence that some of these field systems were changed on their alignments, thus bringing the soils accumulating in lynchets back into cultivation.[13] The relationship is surely more complex, however, with both cultivation plots and soil erosion being indicative of the more regular and intensive cultivation which is the characteristic of short fallow systems. The form and the size of the plots would also indicate the use of the traction plough rather than spade or hoe cultivation.

All these features, the regular availability of the same plots of land and a relatively high level of technological investment enabling intensive cultivation, would have been the product of the regular and frequent involvement of co-operative labour by communities which reproduced a tenurial control over particular areas of land. Such communities must have been able to recognize their own distinctive histories, and thus their own tenurial claims. The earlier pattern of an open and general community was now fragmented, as was the

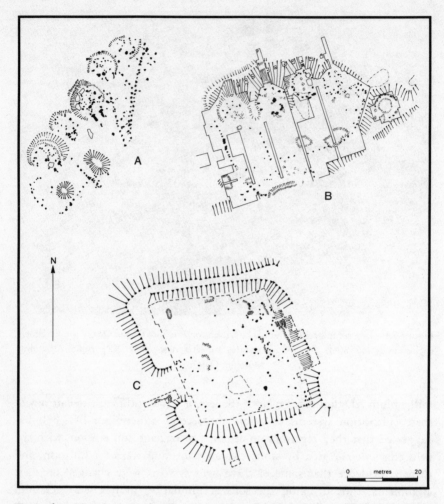

Figure 6.2   Three late second millennium southern British settlements: Black Patch, Sussex (A); Itford Hill enclosure IV, Sussex (B); South Lodge enclosure, Wiltshire (C). (After Drewett 1982; Burstow and Holleymen 1957; Barrett, Bradley and Green 1991)

landscape itself, no longer a constellation of sacred sites linked by paths of access, but a landscape which began to be divided by large tracts of cultivated and enclosed land. Common land and resources undoubtedly remained, but movement across the land might have been curtailed by the physical barriers which appear as an increasingly obvious feature on the upland landscapes from the end of the second millennium.[14]

Fragmentation of both landscape and community is also reflected in the form of the domestic architecture. It was from the end of the second millennium that the first enclosed settlements appear – the only enclosures before this were the communal sites of the causewayed enclosures and the henges. In a number of cases the enclosed settlements are the final phase of a long sequence of activity which begins with open settlement. Enclosures were eventually created out of embankments, fences and occasionally ditches (figure 6.2). In some cases the houses and enclosures became the focus chosen for votive deposits.[15]

How was this transformation achieved? One necessary condition has been traced through the burial rites of the second millennium. The construction of a lineal history now situated the agent within a given past and at the head of a comprehensible future. The earlier community, simply with its horizontal divisions of age and religious authority linking the material and ancestral worlds, was now shot through by the vertical cleavages of lineage and inheritance, of different histories and therefore of different rights. This outcome was not the strategic intention of burial rites which may have begun by simply distinguishing between those differences of rank and of person which were publicly defined by the place each took in ritual and ceremonial practices. But the early barrow cemeteries were instrumental in allowing a different history to be read, a reading which helped to make possible the gradual changes in control over the natural resources to be both understood and given voice. The significance of these material conditions therefore lay in their interpretation. Agents could no longer recognize their identity in the more general community. The chains of metaphorical association by which the agent moved between routine and ritual practices and back, now fixed them in time and spoke to them as members of a differently constituted and more restricted community. The burial mounds, for example, were no longer constructed as a consequence of a burial ritual but had now become a focus of veneration to which the ashes of the dead were carried (figure 6.3).

Other changes, in the organization of the domestic mode of production, the available technology, and the history of the land itself, cleared of trees and scrub, had also to be in place to contribute to the contingency of this moment. In considering the form taken by recent studies which are directed towards an 'engendered archaeology', Conkey and Gero maintain the kind of distinction between the 'ceremonial' and the 'mundane' with which we began this chapter. They note that these writings tend to eschew 'the usual archaeological narratives that showcase the finest material expressions (intertwined with lessons of control over resources or labor), the dazzling displays of "man's" ability as mounted in enormous piles of mammoth bones or towering adobe walls . . .' and in their place focus upon 'interpersonal relations . . . , [an] enquiry . . . into the social dynamics of the everyday activities of prehistoric

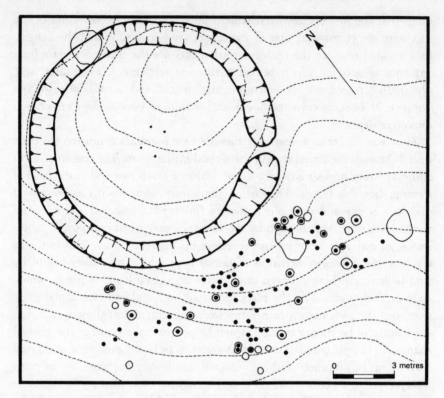

Figure 6.3   Late second millennium cremation cemetery at Simons Ground Barrow B, Dorset. Cremations with urns, some in pits, cluster outside a small round barrow. (After White 1982)

life, activities which comprise most of the hours of prehistoric time for most of the people' (Conkey and Gero 1991: 15). Surely the point is that those 'dazzling displays' were made, interpreted and eventually forgotten by those who walked to the fields in the morning, who tilled the ground, who brought in the harvest. By tracing the paths between these different realms of experience, with their differential routes and moments of access and exclusion, we might begin to understand how women and men were made and the material and symbolic means of their existences transformed.

By the end of the second millennium the landscape was one of extensive field plots with the widespread enclosure of settlement sites. The round barrow cemeteries now lay on the margins of this arable land. These earlier cemeteries were now formed of monumental turf and chalk-clad mounds, and it was to these that the ashes of the dead were often borne.[16] Such acts were expressive of the now distant and perhaps heroic origins which were claimed by those whose political authority was that of the earthly representatives of the lineages and whose own biographies were linked to that of the land and the settlement. Each of these transformations has its own history, each operating through an agency which understood its own actions if not the full resonance of their consequences.

NOTES

1   Ingold 1986: 137. For allocative resources: Giddens 1984: 258. See also Kopytoff 1986 for a discussion of the biographical treatment of material resources.

2   This argument represents a rejection of models which treat megalithic monuments either as territorial markers (Renfrew 1976) or as the markers of some other 'critical resource' (Chapman 1981). For an alternative view of megalithic monuments: Hughes 1988.

3   For the Dorset Cursus: Bradley in Barrett, Bradley and Green 1991: 36ff. For the Stonehenge Cursus: J. Richards 1990: 93ff.

4   For the Stonehenge area, noting the 'little mesolithic background': J. Richards 1990: 263. In the Avebury region Whittle dismisses R. W. Smith's (1984) case for a continuity between the mesolithic and neolithic settlement on the chalk (Whittle 1990b). For Cranborne Chase: Barrett, Bradley and Green 1991: 29ff. For South Dorset: Woodward 1991: 127.

5   A patchwork of vegetational cover is implied by the molluscan evidence from the Dorset Cursus (Bradley et al. in Barrett, Bradley and Green 1991: 18). A comparable picture has been drawn elsewhere, for example the Avebury region (R. Smith 1984) and South Dorset (Woodward 1991).

6   Mellars (1976) analysed the relationship between mesolithic settlement organization and the occurrence of stone tool and waste products, and these issues were then considered in relation to geological sources (Mellars and Reinhart 1978). The need is to take such data forward into a regional 'off-site' perspective (Foley 1981).

7   For the classic statement of site catchment analysis: Vita-Finzi and Higgs 1970. For the rigid, and perhaps misapplied, use of the approach in the analysis of neolithic land use on the chalk uplands: Barker and Webley 1978. For the distinction between territorial behaviour and tenure: Ingold 1986: 130ff.

8   For the Coneybury Pit (or 'anomaly'): J. Richards 1990: 40. For a discussion of the overall importance of animal husbandry in the Neolithic and a consideration of the evidence for grain production at the same time: Entwistle and Grant 1989.

9   This has been the main focus of the critique by Bender (1978 and 1985) who has stressed that other modes of exchange exist which structure gatherer-hunter societies and which embody a delayed return (i.e. the fundamental principle of gift exchange). Bender notes that these mechanisms will continue with the adoption of agriculture. The importance of delayed return mechanisms among gatherer-hunters has also been discussed by Woodburn (1980); see also Layton (1986). Bradley (forthcoming) has considered the implication of these ideas for our understanding of early monument building.

10 Giddens discusses the resources which 'constitute structures of domination' under the two headings of *allocative* and *authoritative* resources (Giddens 1984: 258). For a somewhat

similar discussion of the 'sources of social power': Mann 1986.

11 Boserup 1965: 88ff. Harding (1989) has argued that an important series of changes in agricultural practices can now be recognized as occurring in northern and central Europe during the late Bronze Age, including the beginning of multi-cropping.

12 The adoption of traction ploughing in the European Neolithic is part of Sherratt's 'secondary products revolution' (Sherratt 1981). This model is important because it emphasizes the internal dynamics of evolving agricultural practices. However, as we argue here, these also have to be situated within their social context and it is questionable how far such models can be applied uniformly across the European Neolithic.

13 A clear example of a shift in the alignment of a field system can be seen on an aerial photograph of the Bronze Age field systems on the Marlborough Downs, North Wiltshire, given here as figure 6.1. See also C. M. Piggott 1942 for the associated settlement evidence.

14 Movement within the landscape will have been trasnformed by land enclosure and the formation of regular field plots. This may be seen most clearly on the uplands of Dartmoor in south-west Britain where Bronze Age land divisions, known as *reaves*, cut across earlier lines of land use and access including the alignment of stone rows (Fleming 1988).

15 This occurrence of votive deposits on settlements may be recognized at the South Lodge enclosure (Barrett, Bradley and Green 1991: 225) and at Black Patch, Sussex (Drewett 1982; cf. Barrett 1989b).

16 By the end of the second millennium BC there is evidence for small round barrows being constructed, some near contemporary settlements, and which were used as the focus for the deposition of cremations (e.g. White 1982). Some of these barrow cemeteries almost appear to represent small-scale copies of the older barrow cemeteries (Barrett, Bradley and Green 1991: 25).

7

Making History

Although this book covers a long period of time, the account has described only a small portion of the available evidence, and that from one restricted region in southern Britain. This selection of material and the localized scale of the study reflects our priorities. It was never my intention to catalogue the archaeological monuments and artefacts of the period over some vast geographical canvas. Instead the aim has been to contribute to the history of human agency over the period 2900–1200 BC, and as a consequence we have not been so much concerned with the creation of artefacts as with the creation of the human subject. Obviously artefacts are the medium which allow archaeologists to approach the past, but understanding how people were created as knowing and capable agents extends well beyond an enquiry into how artefacts were created. People therefore make themselves – a creative process which is situated in conditions which are not freely chosen, and which may have consequences which are unintended. Our exploration of some aspects of this process has, I hope, gone some way to answering the questions, posed by Shanks and Tilley (1987a: 27), concerning the structuring of social realities with which we concluded the first chapter (p. 35). I now wish to discuss in more detail the final question which Shanks and Tilley also raise, namely what do we mean when we claim to have gained some knowledge of a past social reality? To pose this question is to enquire further into a theme which has recurred throughout this book, the nature of archaeological practice itself.

Archaeologists in general seem to believe that writing history is equivalent to explaining the material record. We may characterize this consensus model of archaeology as being *representational*, where the evidence is assumed to represent some past event or process. Consequently, the task of archaeology is to identify the event or process to which the record stands as witness. It is as if some aspect of the past was addressing us directly through that record and the fuller and the more complete we can make our analyses of the record, then the fuller and the more complete will be our resulting images of the past. This reasoning assumes not only that the patterns which we observe in the record are the product of historical processes but that these same processes are of relevance to our historical enquiry. Relevance is thus determined by some essence of the material rather than being a matter determined by our own choices. Obviously we can not observe the processes which created the record, but archaeologists do believe that they can understand them through the material, and they also believe that this understanding leads directly to an understanding of history. Inevitably we reach the two conclusions which structure the contemporary archaeological programme: first, that the past has inscribed a truth about itself upon the archaeological record and that by 'explaining' the data we automatically 'explain' the past; second, that the form of the past which we write as history is predetermined by the 'nature' of our data, for no other past can exist outside those data. By way of such reasoning it simply remains the task of archaeology to identify those authentic voices which are present in the data.

The failure of many aspects of this empiricism have been often enough stated to require no more than a brief restatement here. If archaeologists are involved in 'reading' or interpreting the archaeological record, then the regularities which they recognize as structuring the form of that record, and which therefore seem to need explaining, are both identified by and interpreted through the expectations of the archaeologist. The recognition of patterning therefore involves the active participation of the observer, and archaeological data are made up of our responses to the material. This point simply restates the general principle that data are theory-laden and that the search for a neutral language of description is untenable.[1] We must recognize that this is not a 'problem' where the subjective expectations of the observer appear to override and distort an objective truth, and I will argue here that the making of history will always demand the commitment of our own interpretive involvement. If archaeologists do hope to 'explain' their data by reference to some past reality (and this is certainly not the position which I am attempting to develop) then that explanation must involve a self-critical understanding of how those data are made recognizable to the archaeologist via the archaeologist's own pre-expectations. We could go further and say that interpretation precedes data collection for the simple reason that the expectations which structure our observations of data are expectations about the operation of history. In practice most archaeologists manage to avoid coming to terms with this issue because they regard data identification as the product of a value-free methodology rather than a consequence of their own choices.

We could now describe archaeologists as necessarily prejudiced readers of their evidence,[2] and I wish to develop this idea by using, as an example, some recent work on the European Neolithic. Although I will focus upon the work of two authors, Colin Renfrew and Ian Hodder, their writings can be taken to characterize the more general and contrasting approaches in contemporary archaeology which have been labelled as 'processual' and 'post-processual'. These approaches are defined by differences in the significance each gives to archaeological data and the bases upon which interpretations of the past may be validated.

Processual Archaeology

Processual archaeology describes the more recent developments in the approaches originally established as the 'new archaeology' of the 1960s. The prefix *new* (as with the more recent use of the prefix *post* in post-processual archaeology) was intended to imply a fundamental break with those archaeological traditions which had gone before. New or processual archaeology was therefore developed in opposition to the cultural archaeology which had been practised in the first half of the twentieth century. It was claimed that traditional archaeology assumed that patterns in the archaeological record were largely the product of the normative behaviour of particular social or ethnic populations.[3] In contrast, processual archaeology asserted that the patterns result not from a single, undifferentiated process (socially or culturally determined behaviour) but from a series of diverse and identifiable processes which operated in a single 'socio-cultural' system.[4] The operation of the systemically internal and dynamic relationships between these processes, and the articulation of the resulting system with processes which were external to it, were taken to be the forces of historical transformation.

The contrast which new archaeology sought to establish between cultural and processual archaeology is between the idea of society operating as a homogeneous totality, held together by shared and socially determined beliefs, and society as a heterogeneous organizational system. Both approaches would seem to think of societies as bounded entities where, in the ideas of processual archaeology, the degree of internal heterogeneity marks the level of the social system's organizational complexity. Changes in the status or in the organization of society generally arise either from external contact in the case of cultural archaeology, or from internal dynamics in the case of new/processual archaeology. There is one further contrast between the two approaches which we should note. Explanations of social change which are written in terms of cultural archaeology and diffusion deal with specific historical circumstances and specific cultural traits. Processual archaeology's concern with organizational principles, on the other hand, has allowed it to offer explanations which are claimed to have a more general applicability. A processual analysis of one organizational system should therefore aim to clarify our understanding of the historical development of all those systems which share similiar organizational properties. In this way processual archaeology has operated on the assumption that an explanation established for one case study could then be deployed and evaluated cross-culturally.

In Renfrew's work the terms 'society', 'social system' and 'social organization' appear synonymous, and one of the main themes in his research has been to address the methodological question of 'how can the archaeologist reconstruct the social organization of prehistoric communities?'[5] Renfrew suggests that the spatial distribution of contemporary phenomena, a material pattern of artefacts and sites, directly reflects the spatial organization of the activities which gave rise to those phenomena. In other words, spatial patterns of heterogeneity in the record reflect the organizational heterogeneity of the historical system. Because the specialist activities which constitute the organizational structure of the social system are likely to be located at different places in the landscape of that system, then 'the evolution of human society can profitably be considered in terms of spatial patterning' (Renfrew 1977: 89).

Renfrew's study (1973) of the Neolithic of southern Britain was originally offered as an example of such an analysis. The study described the regional development of a sequence of monuments and carefully avoided any explanatory reference to diffusionist influences originating from outside the system. Renfrew used three pieces of information which enabled him to construct a model for the internal evolution of the neolithic social system. These were: the spatial distribution of the monuments, the labour estimates calculated for their construction, and the chronology of the monuments. In his model the sequence of monuments represented an evolving hierarchy in the quantities of labour actually mobilized for their construction, a hierarchy which ran from the non-megalithic long mounds at the lower end of the scale (with slightly more labour demanded by the construction of the megalithic mounds), through the early neolithic causewayed enclosures to the major henges, the Dorset Cursus and Silbury Hill, and culminating in the sarsen construction of Stonehenge III. All these monuments lie on the chalk uplands of central Wessex, but additional features in their distribution were also discernible.

The long mounds are among the earliest monuments and they occur in five main clusters. Within each cluster some additional grouping of mounds may also be recognized and Renfrew claimed that the fairly regular spacing between the mounds in each of these clusters indicated that each mound lay within the territory of an individual community. Each cluster of long mounds also tends to conform with the distribution of individual causewayed enclosures which represented the next level in labour energy demanded by their construction. Because a number of long mounds are seen to cluster around the location of individual enclosures, the 'hierarchy of effort for the causewayed enclosures and long barrows is matched by one of distribution' (1973: 548). The pattern can now be described as one of individual territories (figure 7.1), each of which contained a group of long mounds and a causewayed enclosure.

Although the actual distributions are not quite as clear-cut as the model implies, his proposed territorial divisions are matched in the late Neolithic by the distribution of the five large henge complexes. In this later period Renfrew suggested that 'we are perhaps entitled to think in terms of an increased population and a more developed social hierarchy' (1973: 551). And with the case of Silbury Hill and Stonehenge III, 'we might well think in terms of a further co-operation between different regions, a "confederation" like that of the Creek Indians in the eighteenth century. Or better, we might envisage the five Wessex chiefdoms coalescing into one greater chiefdom with five constituent tribes' (1973: 552).

The model therefore describes a group of evolving chiefdoms attested by their ability to co-ordinate the labour required to build the causewayed enclosures and whose dependent populations and organizational capacities continued to grow in the late Neolithic, enabling the construction of the henges and, ultimately, the building of Stonehenge III as the apparently dominant centre. As this study was a preliminary investigation by Renfrew which aimed at explaining some of the classic monuments of British prehistory in terms of social evolution, it is hardly surprising that there are now problems with accepting the patterns as they were originally outlined. Renfrew himself recognized that his proposed territorial patterns were a simplification, and he also accepted that uncertainties existed when a monument such as the Dorset Cursus was incorporated into the overall scheme. Since the late 1970s our understanding of all these monuments has increased and we need no longer accept either the proposed sequence of monument building or the labour estimates.[6] However, there are other, more general issues concerning such models of social evolution which demand comment. The main principles employed in Renfrew's model may be summarized as follows:

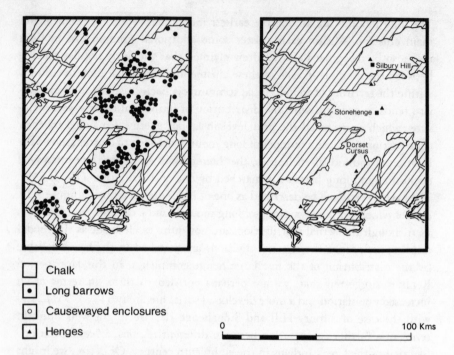

☐ Chalk

● Long barrows

◎ Causewayed enclosures

▲ Henges

0   100 Kms

Figure 7.1 Renfrew's model for the social evolution of the Neolithic in southern Britain, indicated by the increasing scale of labour demands for monument construction and the 'centralized' distribution of those monuments. (After Renfrew 1973)

1   Societies may be considered as systems which have a real existence, and may be characterized in terms of their organizational principles. Ancient societies made themselves archaeologically visible because they organized material resources and thus left material correlates as a record of their existence.

2   These organizational systems which 'administer' people and resources imply 'government (with the exercise of power) and resource allocation. Both imply some partition of the world into persons and resources governed or allocated, and those which fall out of the control of the administration, and hence by their very nature some kind of a delineation of an entity, the polity' (Renfrew 1977: 98). Societies are thus bounded, they have a territorial integrity; polities have a continuous territorial jurisdication over their domain (Renfrew 1984: 55).

3   Because societies appear as bounded systems, it is possible to undertake comparative studies and to construct generalizations concerning the regularities shared by societies of the same type. Thus 'the explanatory

principles adduced for one society will be applicable to certain other societies in appropriate circumstances' (Renfrew 1982: 13).

Explanation, Renfrew suggests (1982: 8–9), makes phenomena comprehensible to an observer: a process akin to the translation of the unfamiliar into the language and frame of reference which is shared by the observer. Renfrew's 'social archaeology' makes the archaeological record comprehensible by treating it as if it were the product of particular social processes which were situated in larger and more complex systems. These social systems are understandable because we can describe them in more abstract terms which subsume these particular processes to a set of general, and familiar, organizational principles. To explain is therefore to isolate those general principles and not to focus upon the uniqueness of the past event; it is to move from the particular to the more general (or abstract). 'To know *what* happened in the past is not sufficient: The aim is to understand *why* it happened. . . . In order to explain it, it is necessary first to compare and then to go further and to generalise' (Renfrew 1979: 3).

What we in fact discover is not a particular past but our ability to make a history which we recognize and which we are prepared to accept as the author of the material record. We find Renfrew's account of the Neolithic monuments understandable because it describes them, not as an encounter with the historically specific and the unfamiliar, but as the representational products of social processes which are comprehensible to us because those processes occur more generally and are part of our own experiences. Surely we must pay closer attention to the way this comprehension requires the translation of the distant and the unfamiliar into that which is familiar. It is a past which is grasped, ordered and described in the only terms available, the product of a conceptual framework which we may routinely employ in understanding our contemporary world. Renfrew's analysis has effectively read many of our own assumptions about the general operation of human society into the material. The past which he presents to us, and which we seem to recognize as the author of the record, is therefore of our making. To understand that past requires therefore that we critically evaluate our own making of it as history.

The identification of a social totality such as the 'chiefdom' is problematic, and generalizations about such totalities tend to attribute to them the structural properties of the modern state. To a certain extent this is exemplified in the assumption, implicit in Renfrew's use of the descriptive term *polity*, that social totalities display a territorial integrity. Whilst such a term may be applicable to the study of the early state, or to other types of centralized regional administration (and it was first employed in an examination of the 'rise of civilization' in the Aegean), it cannot be adopted unproblematically in the general theorization of all social totalities.[7]

States occupy regions within wider social formations; they arise out of a claimed jurisdiction over a specific territory which is sustained by the ability to mobilize the resources to monitor and administer the reproduction of certain key social relations within that territory. 'States involve the reflexive monitoring of aspects of the reproduction of the social system subject to their rule' (Giddens 1985: 17). The resources of control, the state apparatus, include the control of violence through the establishment of legitimate armed force and bureaucratic controls dependent upon the technologies of writing (Giddens 1985: 41). Understanding the operation of the state therefore involves analysing the processes involved in reproducing and extending forms of authoritative surveillance and administration.

In early states the range and degree to which the technologies of surveillance were able to penetrate more extensive social practices was restricted, and the city state represents the geographically limited domain over which most of these intensive forms of control operated. It is this image of a centrally located body of political authority which was capable of appropriating and defining a totality (the 'polity') which we have already challenged as a source for our own understanding of the late Neolithic.

Institutional forms of surveillance such as the census, taxation, legality or military terror, operating over a claimed territory of jurisdiction from one or more centres within that territory, both characterize early states and distinguish them from non-state systems. The difference is in the operation of alternative forms of 'social power'. Mann distinguishes between *authoritative power* which is reproduced by the duality of definite commands and conscious obedience, and *diffused power* which 'spreads in a more spontaneous, unconscious, decentred way through a population'. The latter resides in routine, day-to-day practices, being expressed through 'an understanding that these practices are natural or moral or result from self-evident common interest' (Mann 1986: 8). Both forms of power may be reproduced extensively, over far-flung territories, or within more limited and perhaps highly structured locales. The state emerges through the instrumental mobilization of forms of authoritative power which may enter the lives of its subjects over a wide territorial jurisdication. Such forms of power occupy the various forms of disciplinary institutions which secure the compliance of its subjects. The city plays a fundamental role in storing the authoritative and technological means of control, such as bureaucratic archives.

Early cities take a number of forms, although a commonly shared feature is the ceremonial and religious centre (e.g. Wheatley 1971). We should distinguish between the ceremonial centres of state and non-state systems, not simply in terms of form but in the way each lies at a nodal point in differently operating regions of authoritative discourse. The long-term organization of building practices and the relatively simple architectural competences which we have suggested were mobilized for the building of the henge complexes contrast sharply with the way resources were controlled in some early states. Wheatley, in his survey of the ceremonial centres of early states, emphasizes not only the massive labour requirements, but the relatively short period over which they were recruited, and goes on to consider the methods by which such mobilization may occur. In the case of the palace at Nagaoka in ancient Japan, and in the construction of the surrounding city, for example: 'all the provinces were ordered to render at once their taxes for the whole year, together with a levy of materials' (Wheatley 1971: 258). It is the absence of such a centralized and coercive means of procurement, along with the absence of a permanent bureaucracy, which we have taken to characterize the Neolithic case.

In contrast with Renfrew's model, our history of the Neolithic has been constructed with the use of an interpretive programme which is partly dedicated to preserving the radical differences which exist between state and non-state systems.[8] Our characterization of the period has depended upon maintaining the absence of a resource of extensive and authoritative power which was also the site of personal power: 'The chief is not a commander; the people of the tribe are under no obligation to obey. *The space of the chieftainship is not the locus of power*, and the "profile" of the primitive chief in no way foreshadows that of the future despot' (Clastres 1977: 174). In our late Neolithic we have not discovered (because we have not looked for) autocratic chiefs who expressed their will, and thus made themselves known to us, by mobilizing the resources required for the construction of the great ceremonial centres of the period; the hand of Atkinson's autocratic chief no longer lies behind the construction of Stonehenge. On the contrary, we have examined the ways it might have proved possible, from the fourth millennium onwards, to focus a diverse and extensive range of experiences upon a series of common interpretive schemes which recognized the existence of a sacred or metaphysical community, and the technical ways in which that interpretive programme was constructed. Those who mediated these interpretive practices did so more out of their obligation to the community itself than as an exercise of individual power, and although that obligation could be seen to have a sacred derivation, with the consequence that what had once been a pragmatic identification of responsibilities may have increasingly appeared to have had a supernatural derivation, none the less:

The chief is there to serve society; it is society as such – the real locus of power – that exercises its authority over the chief. That is why it is impossible for the chief to reverse that relationship for his own ends, to put society in his service, to exercise what is termed power over the tribe: primitive society would never tolerate having a chief transform himself into a despot. (Clastres 1977: 175)

Post-Processual Archaeology

While processual archaeology seeks to make the past comprehensible by identifying it as the product of a number of general processes, which include human behavioural traits along with natural and social processes, so post-processual archaeology has sought to recognize the past as the product of multiple and specific moments of cultural creation. The latter has been strategically concerned to rescue the position of human agency from being consigned to the fully determined product of its own social context.

In identifying a 'post-processual' tradition in archaeology, Hodder has emphasized the contrast between portraying people as responding to external stimuli, or as creating their own realities by negotiating 'social rules, creating and transforming the social structure' (1985: 2). To adopt the second perspective involves abandoning the search for uniform responses directly determined by external stimuli. Human responses to given material conditions must now be regarded as culturally mediated – people 'learn how to cope in the world and . . . find certain strategies [which] work for them and make sense to them' (1985: 4). Two important points about the contrast between processual and post-processual archaeology must be identified.

First, both approaches claim to have discovered something which is generally true about what it is to be human. They claim that regularities displayed in the behaviour of human populations derive either from the behavioural responses to material stimuli (and which include social structural stimuli), or from the strategic deployment of historically specific knowledges and assumptions about how the world might be expected to work. In the latter case these knowledges also operate to sustain different forms of social authority. It would seem reasonable to view human populations as being reproduced by biological beings *who are always capable of rethinking the realities which they inhabit*. The question sometimes seems to turn upon the emphasis which we, in our various analyses, are prepared to place upon either the behavioural determinates or the cognitive procedures operating within these populations.

The point made in this book is that agency involves the transformation of the biological being into a social being through knowledgeable action, where 'being social involves *consciousness*' (Ingold 1986: 136).

Second, if the different emphases which we employ to understand others are taken to have a general application in understanding all humanity (which, for them to operate, they must) then they will also be principles which we will employ in understanding ourselves, and they will also inform our own attitudes towards the validation of archaeological knowledge. If we were to follow the processual line of reasoning which emphasizes the underlying regularities determining human behaviour, then we would also expect to establish, by cross-cultural analysis, what those regularities are and we would accept, as relatively uncontentious, the claimed discovery of 'high-order' generalizations or even 'laws' about human behaviour. We would also seek the methodological procedures which would validate those discoveries. On the other hand if, as post-processualists, we emphasize the historically specific ways knowledge-claims operate as strategies of social reproduction, then we will not only proceed by citing specific instances of such practices to demonstrate our point, but further, we will accept that our own writings are also components of contemporary social strategies. Different traditions of historical writing will be regarded as the products of potentially competing social strategies, and any claim to a general truth in such constructions will be regarded with the deepest of suspicion. Both processual and post-processual approaches draw upon specific studies to sustain their more generalized principles, with processual archaeology emphasizing the truth of the underlying determinates behind human actions and post-processual archaeology emphasizing that all truths are relative to their historical circumstances. If post-processual archaeology has demonstrated that processual archaeology is also strategically embedded within a particular historical programme, perhaps seeking to sustain the hegemony of the western scientific tradition, then it must similarly expose its own strategic intent to scrutiny.[9] Paradoxically, if post-processual archaeology is accepted as an attempt to open up all programmes of historical enquiry to a level of evaluation which radically questions, rather than confirms, their truth-claims, then I would suggest that this programme is closer to the original objectives of the new archaeology than the current programme of processual archaeology with its emphasis upon the unambiguous evaluation of data and its repeatedly stated desire to limit the scope of archaeological enquiry.

Social actions are mediated through traditions of knowledge and, as a consequence, social systems must be thought of as being brought into existence as the recursive products of human agency. The principles out of which agency is structured are the object of our enquiry, and for that enquiry to operate archaeologically it must consider the place of material culture within social practice. If these principles are accepted, and if our own historical enquiry is similarly regarded as a contemporary and historically specific strategy, then we must rethink the relationship between: our own actions in creating archaeological knowledge; the historical conditions which we seek to study; and the material evidence which we employ in that study. It would seem that our own understanding of past human agency, as well as the traditions of knowledge employed by agents who once acted out those understandings of the world in which they lived, have both required working upon a commonly shared set of materials, although from very different historical circumstances of expectation and experience. These materials which survive today as the fragments from antiquity are the materials which we choose to regard as the evidence for the past.

Let us start with the proposition that material culture is 'meaningfully constituted' through social practice. One reading of this proposition would be to assume that culturally specific meanings were once inscribed upon the durable medium of material culture which has by chance survived to form a record of those meanings. Patrik has characterized this position as one which treats archaeological evidence as a textual record.[10] However, the problem with this approach is that it leads archaeologists to ask such questions as 'what was meant by this particular depositional pattern or this particular style of artefact decoration?' The active involvement of agency in making history appears to be that of the author who once inscribed those messages upon the medium and whose meaningful intentions must be revealed through archaeological anlaysis. But, given that these encoded messages are deciphered *by us* from the context of our own experiences (i.e. situated within specific and quite different social contexts) what is the status of our contemporary readings of these codes (cf. Barrett 1987)? The naive position which treats the record as a transmitter of meaning and which assumes that some authentic, original meaning can be recovered by discovering what single meaning is represented by the record, simply cannot be sustained. It wrongly assumes that there was once a single recognizable meaning assigned to these things and it also gives no active involvement to our own agency in bringing that history into being.

Hodder has written of a contextual archaeology which makes artefacts meaningful by situating them in contexts which are the products of a universal structure. This structure, he suggests, generates the practice of material language use and it therefore appears to represent a kind of uniformitarian principle linking us with the past:

Clearly, if the past material culture language had no common features, words, grammar or structure with contemporary verbal language, then . . . reading [it] would be difficult if not impossible, especially since the surviving text is partial and fragmentary in addition to being simply different. However I wish to argue that there are some very simple rules underlying all languages – or at least underlying the ways in which *homo sapiens sapiens* at all times and all places give meaning to things. (1991: 126)

The archaeological programme he develops seeks to 'identify the meaning content behind [the objects archaeologists excavate], . . . examining how the ideas denoted by material symbols . . . play a part in structuring society' (1991: 125). The meaning content is one which Hodder identifies with the 'public and social concepts which are reproduced in the practices of daily life' (1991: 128), and because these concepts structure institutionalized practices they will also be embedded in the material record of those practices. The archaeologist may recover these patterns, and recognize them as the representational, material encoding of structural principles, although: 'success in such endeavours depends upon including as much information as is available on the historical contexts and association of traits, styles and organizational design properties, as well as a reconstruction of the active use of such traits in social strategies' (1991: 127).

This recognition of the material code extends the traditional, empirical programme of archaeology away from the study of individual categories of evidence towards an understanding of a total material universe within which patterns of association and exclusion between material categories may be recognized. These patterns are no longer taken to be the result of the adaptive properties of the social system; rather they are assumed to have resulted from practices that employed conceptual categories which structured these ancient societies. If the structure of the code appears immediately present in the record, as Hodder appears to imply, then 'the problem comes in the interpretation' (1991: 126) for we have still not established our own place in the creation of such interpretations.

Interpretation gives meaning to the code by employing what Hodder has referred to as a 'deep abstraction'. For example, the

abstract opposition between culture and nature may link together the degree to which settlements are 'defended' or bounded, and the relative proportions of wild and domesticated animals found in these settlements. . . . [W]here the dichotomy is . . . marked the boundaries around settlements may be more substantial, houses . . . more elaborate, and even pottery more decorated (as marking the 'domestication' of food products . . .). . . . It is not immediately apparent that boundaries around settlements, pottery decoration and the proportions of wild and domesticated animal bones have anything to do with each other. The provision of a 'deep' abstraction suddenly makes sense of the varied pieces of information as they change through time. (1991: 138)

The epistemological status of these abstractions is obviously vital but remains unclear in Hodder's account. We are forced to ask whose 'knowledge' this is, and to wonder if this is no more than the usual structuralist claim to have discovered some fundamental truth about others through the application of the current western linguistic obsession. Are we able to make any assessment regarding the extent to which such choices of historical narrative have broken free from any engagement with other human realities which once existed and are now merely creating a 'past as an arena for the playing out of different social values and interests' (Hodder 1984: 31)?

In his later study of the European Neolithic Hodder argues that the abstractions which we employ are not in fact of our making; rather it is we who are made by our desire to engage with certain pre-existing intellectual traditions. The abstractions which he employs to give meaning to a diverse and complex set of material codes, allowing for the 'discovery' of the principles which may have structured the European Neolithic, are *domus*, *foris* and *agrios*, terms with Indo-European roots. He writes:

I have not wanted to write a prehistory of words or concepts . . . [but] to show that the concepts through which we think the origins of agriculture are constructed in the past, perhaps even in the very distant past. I wanted to play on . . . words . . . to show how our acceptance of certain ideas is partly dependent on the words and associated assumptions through which we think. . . . [T]he persuasiveness of an argument about the pre-historic past depends at least partly on structures of language which may have very early origins. But there is also some room for individual agency. I have had to choose which words to use and I have had to interpret the data in terms of those words. (1990: 276)

Hodder, in effect, claims to have discovered his Neolithic by discovering himself, by choosing a way of thinking.

Artefacts mean nothing. It is only when they are interpreted through practice that they become invested with meanings and may then act as props for the strategies of social life. Any empirical enquiry is an active, selective and prejudiced experience whose descriptions of a reality are driven by a desire to know that reality in a certain way. Such an enquiry involves carrying an interpretive programme into experience, and it is structured according to expectations about the way such realities should or might operate.

Artefacts are meaningfully constituted by being incorporated in such interpretive strategies, and this is true whether we are considering the path of contemporary archaeological enquiry (as Hodder recognizes) or the historical paths of other agencies which, I argue, are the object of archaeological enquiry. The human subject in all periods is the product of the active, biographical engagement which agency establishes with an external reality. Biographies are not determined by the external conditions which they inhabit but are created out of the possible ways the actor can move into that world and operate effectively through an ability to read the world for meaning.

History is made by the engagement of knowledgeable beings with the material conditions of their existence; it requires human action in the world, the reworking and transformation of a material reality. That reworking is interpretive, in as much as it demands an ability to monitor, both practically and discursively, conditions, desires, actions and consequences. Interpretation therefore requires an encounter which is informed by certain expectations about the world and about the agent's place within it. People draw upon experiences to interpret the conditions which confront them and to formulate expectations about what is possible in action, given those conditions. By taking expectations forward in this way agency not only transforms and reproduces its material conditions but it also recreates itself.

There is no single history. There are programmes of interpretation which have appeared effective or to have been thwarted in the actions which flow from them. Those interpretive programmes obviously have certain historically specific material and social consequences because they orientate human action towards its material conditions in some way. The historian or the archaeologist may work upon the fragmented residues of past material conditions, not to find what lay behind them – the 'reality' to which they correspond, not to discover 'the history' or 'the meanings' which they record, but to construct a past through their own interpretive endeavours. There is no actual past state of history 'out there' which is represented by our data and which is waiting for us to discover it. And there is no absolute against which to measure the accuracy of our own narratives about the past. All we have are the contexts of our desires to know a past, positions from which we may then examine the material conditions which others, at other times and from other perspectives, also sought to understand. We should treat this material as a medium from which it is always possible to create meaning, rather than a record which is involved in the transmission of meaning. By so doing we seek to understand something of how those other interpretations may have been formed, how prejudices which are other than our own may have operated upon that same material.

The particular writing of a past attempted in this book becomes possible when we accept that we can understand something of these other interpretive regimes. These understandings, which we express here as a narrative of history, represent one kind of narrative tradition, but all traditions of historical writing are representative of the relationship which is forged by us with those others whose lives have preceded our own.[11] Hodder is correct to state that we know the past by knowing ourselves.

All social life is therefore lived out against the material conditions which it inhabits as various traditions of knowledge are reworked according to the agent's interpretive understanding of an empirical reality. Our emphasis throughout this book, when dealing with the material conditions of archaeological data, has been to eschew questions concerning the 'meanings' these things may once have had. Meanings were never fixed in the thing itself, but were 'read' from the experiences and expectations gained from elsewhere. Meanings which were read into the material were also acted upon. Instead of an archaeology of meanings we have been concerned to develop an archaeology of agency, of past knowledgeable practices by which interpretive programmes were carried forward and transformed.

It follows from what has been said that theoretical categories do not represent free-floating, analytical devices which are innocent of historical content. Such categories are historical and they are transitory, they represent the ways we think ourselves into a reality which necessarily transform that reality in our eyes and thus transform our understanding of it. This entire argument draws us towards a position which some writers have routinely castigated as relativism. In other words, the pasts which are created in the present appear devoid of any external, objective measure by which assessment can be made of their 'validity' or 'truth'. It is as if no external reality, independent of interpretation, is being allowed to intervene in the construction of this 'relativistic' knowledge. This kind of criticism is misplaced. First, we are dealing with selections of material data without which no archaeological practice would be possible. Certainly our view of those data is necessarily prejudiced and interpretive, it is orientated by certain expectations and desires, but the data are not entirely malleable and different ways of seeing them will produce recognizable, objectified paths for future research. I would claim, for example, that the approaches which have been developed in this book deal with the data in a more detailed and 'fine-grained' manner than has been the case in other studies. I would suggest that this claim is recognizable and assessable by you, the reader. This 'fine-grained' analysis may be seen as a strength, it may not, but at least the issue can be discussed with reference to the interpretive programme itself. It can also be discussed with reference to the kinds of understandings which are available in this account of the period. Second, if history is created out of numerous and sometimes contradictory interpretive programmes of action, then there never existed a single and un-ambiguous reality. However, attempts to construct and impose such realities are always part of the processes by which a political hegemony is established. What is presenced in our material are, therefore, the conditions and the consequences of agencies which were able to act and to speak in the expectation of being understood and of being effective in achieving certain aims: in short, the ability to live in a socially recognizable way. If archaeology were to operate on the assumption that only one interpretive programme was presenced in our data, in other words that the data meant something (a truth to which they referred) and that the meaning is recoverable by us today (rather than material conditions having once given rise to a number of readings), then we would never grasp how history is created from multiple strands of human practice. Instead we would be recreating the violence of ideological authority; we would be having the last word. An interpretive archaeology tries to get close to understanding how other ways of seeing the world were once – and, one hopes, still remain – possible: nothing more.

NOTES

1   The literature of the 'New Archaeology' contains various analyses of the 'theory-laden' nature of observation. D. L. Clarke refers to the role of *controlling models* which determine that 'we observe what we believe and then believe in that which we have observed' (1972: 6). Binford has attempted to establish an experimental basis for the validation of obser-vational data through middle-range theory. It is the intention of his programme that such data should be given meaning independently of our ideas about the past (e.g. Binford 1977). For a critique of this position: Wylie 1989; Barrett 1990b.

2   This position is similar to that regarding historical writing outlined by Jenkins (1991).

3   Many aspects of traditional archaeology were far more refined than their characterizations make them appear in the critiques of the New Archaeology. Works such as Childe's *Piecing Together the Past* (1956), or G. Clark's *Archaeology and Society* (1960), both of which were normally ignored by Binford and D. L. Clarke, sound remarkably 'processualist' in their approaches.

4   Binford (1962) and D. L. Clarke (1968) established the basis for 'systems thinking' which has been developed by Renfrew (1984). Again, however, these ideas had been in use earlier than this (e.g. G. Clark 1960).

5   'Cross cultural comparisons concerning the organisational properties of some "system" obviously require a methodological procedure to define the totality of each system simply because system closure is analytically necessary to compare like with like' (Renfrew 1977: 89).

6   For the review of labour estimates: Startin and Bradley 1981. See also ch. 1.

7   Renfrew 1972. For the problems inherent in defining the 'totality': Shanks and Tilley 1987a: 119ff. and Shanks and Tilley 1987b: 28–60. For a discussion which parallels some of the argument which follows: Trigger 1990.

8   The strategy here is to interpret 'the past' through establishing a series of possible differences with the present. See also J. Thomas 1991 *passim*.

9   It could be claimed that post-processual archaeology has been somewhat slow in developing a self-critical stance. However, see the essays in Tilley (ed.) 1990.

10 Patrik (1985) attempts to distinguish between processual archaeology, which treats the archaeological record as an unambiguous and mechanical trace of the formation process (akin to the fossil record), and post-processual archaeology, which treats the archaeological record as a text which is ambiguously linked to the meanings which have been inscribed upon the record.

11 The appeal of the historical narrative is the appeal of a literature which 'symbolizes, through its own crises and resolutions, other kinds of crises and resolutions which we may have experienced in our lives, but without yet having properly comprehended. Such comprehension, when we have achieved it, will be likely to be less like the intellectual acquisition of a piece of knowledge and more like the emotional acquisition of a certain kind of disposition or habit' (Falck 1989: 109).

Bibliography

Abercrombie, N., Hill, S. and Turner, B. (1980): *The Dominant Ideology Thesis*. London: Allen and Unwin.

Abercromby, J. (1912): *A Study of the Bronze Age Pottery of Great Britain and Ireland and Its Associated Grave Goods* (2 vols). Oxford: Clarendon Press.

Anderson, P. (1980): *Arguments within English Marxism*. London: Verso.

Annable, F. K. and Simpson, D. D. A. (1964): *Guide Catalogue of the Neolithic and Bronze Age Collections in Devizes Museum*. Devizes: Wiltshire Archaeological and Natural History Society.

Asad, T. (1979): Anthropology and the analysis of ideology. *Man*, 14 (n.s.), 607–627.

—— (1987): On ritual and discipline in medieval Christian monasticism. *Economy and Society*, 16, 159–292.

Ashbee, P. (1960): *The Bronze Age Round Barrow in Britain*. London: Phoenix House.

—— (1978): Amesbury barrow 51: excavation 1960. *Wiltshire Archaeological and Natural History Magazine*, 70/71, 1–60.

—— (1981): Amesbury barrow 39: excavations 1960. *Wiltshire Archaeological and Natural History Magazine*, 74/75, 3–34.

—— (1985): The excavation of Amesbury barrows 58, 61a, 61, 72. *Wiltshire Archaeological and Natural History Magazine*, 79, 39–91.

Ashbee, P., Smith, I. F. and Evans, J. G. (1979): Excavation of three long barrows near Avebury, Wiltshire. *Proceedings of the Prehistoric Society*, 45, 207–300.

Atkinson, R. J. C. (1961): Neolithic engineering. *Antiquity*, 35, 259–262.

—— (1968): Silbury Hill, 1968. *Antiquity*, 42, 299.

—— (1969): The Date of Silbury Hill. *Antiquity*, 43, 216.

—— (1970): Silbury Hill, 1969–70. *Antiquity*, 44, 313–314.

—— (1971): The southern circle at Durrington Walls: a numerical investigation, in G. J. Wainwright and I. H. Longworth (eds) *Durrington Walls: Excavations 1966–1968*. London: Reports of the Research Committee of the Society of Antiquaries of London No. 29, 355–362.

—— (1979): *Stonehenge: Archaeology and Interpretation*. London: The Penguin Press.

Atkinson, R. J. C., Piggott, C. M. and Sanders, N. K. (1951): *Excavations at Dorchester, Oxon*. Oxford: Ashmolean Museum.

Barker, C. T. (1985): The long mounds of the Avebury region. *Wiltshire Archaeological and Natural History Magazine*, 79, 7–38.

Barker, G. and Webley, D. (1978): Causewayed camps and early neolithic economies in central southern England. *Proceedings of the Prehistoric Society*, 44, 161–186.

Barrett, J. C. (1985): Hoards and related metalwork, in D. V. Clarke, T. G. Cowie and A. Foxon (eds) *Symbols of Power at the Time of Stonehenge*. Edinburgh: HMSO, 95–106.

—— (1987): Contextual archaeology. *Antiquity*, 61, 468–473.

—— (1988a): Fields of discourse: reconstructing a social archaeology. *Critique of Anthropology*, 7, 5–16.

—— (1988b): The living, the dead and the ancestors: neolithic and early bronze age mortuary practices, in J. C. Barrett and I. A. Kinnes (eds) *The Archaeology of Context in the Neolithic and Bronze Age: Recent trends*. Sheffield: J. R. Collis, 30–41.

—— (1989a): Time and tradition: the rituals of everyday life, in H.-A. Nordstrom and A. Knape (eds) *Bronze Age Studies*. Stockholm: Statens Historiska Museum, 113–126.

—— (1989b): Food, gender and metal: questions of social reproduction, in M. L. Sørensen and R. Thomas (eds) *The Bronze Age–Iron Age Transitions in Europe: Aspects of continuity and change in European societies c.1200 to 500 BC* (2 vols). Oxford: British Archaeological Reports International Series 483, 304–320.

—— (1990a): The monumentality of death: the character of early bronze age mortuary mounds in southern Britain. *World Archaeology*, 22, 179–189.

—— (1990b): Sciencing archaeology: a reply to Lewis Binford, in F. Baker and J. Thomas (eds) *Writing the Past in the Present*. Lampeter: St David's University College, 42–48.

—— (1991): Towards an archaeology of ritual, in P. Garwood, D. Jennings, R. Skeates and J. Toms (eds) *Sacred and Profane*. Oxford: Oxford University Committee for Archaeology Monograph 32, 1–9.

Barrett, J. C., Bradley, R. and Green, M. (1991): *Landscape, Monuments and Society: The prehistory of Cranborne Chase*. Cambridge: Cambridge University Press.

Barrett, J. C. and Needham, S. P. (1988): Production, circulation and exchange, in J. C. Barrett and I. A. Kinnes (eds) *The Archaeology of Context in the Neolithic and Bronze Age: Recent trends*. Sheffield: J. R. Collis, 127–140.

Beck, C. and Shennan, S. (1991): *Amber in Prehistoric Britain*. Oxford: Oxbow Monograph 8.

Bell, M. (1983): Valley sediments as evidence of prehistoric land-use on the South Downs. *Proceedings of the Prehistoric Society*, 49, 119–150.

Bellamy, P. (1991): The excavation of Fordington Farm round barrow. *Proceedings of the Dorset Natural History and Archaeological Society*, 113, 107–132.

Bender, B. (1978): Gatherer-hunter to farmer: a social perspective. *World Archaeology*, 10, 203–222.

—— (1985): Prehistoric developments in the American midcontinent and in Brittany, Northwest France, in T. D. Price and J. A. Brown (eds) *Prehistoric Hunter-Gatherers: The emergence of cultural complexity*. London: Academic Press, 21–57.

Binford, L. R. (1962): Archaeology as anthropology. *American Antiquity*, 28, 217–225.

—— (1977): General Introduction, in L. R. Binford (ed.) *For Theory Building in Archaeology*. London: Academic Press, 1–10.

Bloch, M. (1977): The past and the present in the present. *Man*, 12 (n.s.), 178–292.

—— (1985): From cognition to ideology, in R. Fardon (ed.) *Power and Knowledge: Anthrological and sociological approaches*. Edinburgh: Scottish Academic Press, 21–48.

—— (1991): Language, anthropology and cognitive science. *Man*, 26 (n.s.), 183–198.

Boserup, E. (1965): *The Conditions of Agricultural Growth: The economics of agrarian change under population pressure*. New York: Aldine Publishing Company.

Bourdieu, P. (1977): *Outline of a Theory of Practice*. Cambridge: Cambridge University Press.

—— (1984): *Distinction: A social critique of the judgement of taste*. London: Routledge and Kegan Paul.

—— (1990): *The Logic of Practice*. Cambridge: Polity.

Bradley, R. (1976): Maumbury Rings, Dorchester: the excavations of 1908–1913. *Archaeologia*, 105, 1–97.

—— (1984): *The Social Foundations of Prehistoric Britain: Themes and variations in the archaeology of power*. Harlow: Longman.

—— (1985): *Consumption, Change and the Archaeological Record: The archaeology of monuments and the archaeology of deliberate deposits*. Edinburgh: University of Edinburgh, Department of Archaeology Occasional Paper 13.

—— (forthcoming): *Altering the Earth: The origins of monuments in Britain and continental Europe*. Edinburgh: Society of Antiquaries of Scotland.

Braithwaite, M. (1984): Ritual and prestige in the prehistory of Wessex *c*.2200–1400 BC: a new dimension to the archaeological evidence, in D. Miller and C. Tilley (eds) *Ideology, Power and Prehistory*. Cambridge: Cambridge University Press, 93–110.

Braudel, F. (1980): *On History*. London: Weidenfeld and Nicolson.

Briard, J. (1984): *Les Tumulus Amorique: l'age du bronze en France – 3*. Paris: Picard.

Britnell, W. J. and Savory, H. N. (1984): *Gwernvale and Penywyrlod: Two Neolithic long cairns in the Black Mountains of Brecknock*. Cardiff: Cambrian Archaeological Monographs 2.

Brothwell, D. R. (1961): Cannibalism in early Britain. *Antiquity*, 35, 304–307.

Burgess, C. (1979): The background of early metalworking in Ireland and Britain, in M. Ryan (ed.) *Proceedings of the Fifth Atlantic Colloquium*. Dublin: Stationery Office, 207–214.

—— (1980): *The Age of Stonehenge*. London: Dent.

Burl, A. (1976): *The Stone Circles of the British Isles*. London: Yale University Press.

—— (1988): Coves: structural enigmas of the neolithic. *Wiltshire Archaeological and Natural History Magazine*, 82, 1–18.

—— (1992): Two early plans of Avebury: a review article. *Wiltshire Archaeological and Natural History Magazine*, 85, 163–172.

Burstow, G. P. and Holleymen, G. A. (1957): Late Bronze Age settlement on Itford Hill, Sussex. *Proceedings of the Prehistoric Society*, 23, 167–212.

Case, H. (1969): Neolithic explanations. *Antiquity*, 43, 176–186.

—— (1973): A ritual site in north-east Ireland, in G. Daniel and P. Kjaerum (eds) *Megalithic Graves and Ritual*. Copenhagen: Jutland Archaeological Society (Proceedings of the 3rd Atlantic Colloquium, Moesgard 1969), 173–196.

—— (1977): The beaker culture in Britain and Ireland, in R. Mercer (ed.) *Beakers in Britain and Europe*. Oxford: British Archaeological Reports Supplementary Series 26, 71–101.

Chapman, R. (1981): The emergence of formal disposal areas and the 'problem' of megalithic tombs in prehistoric Europe, in R. Chapman, I. Kinnes and K. Randsborg (eds) *The Archaeology of Death*. Cambridge: Cambridge University Press, 71–81.

Cherry, J. (1978): Generalisation and the archaeology of the state, in D. Green, C. Haselgrove and M. Spriggs (eds) *Social Organisation and Settlement*. Oxford: British Archaeological Reports International Series 47, 411–437.

Childe, V. G. (1956): *Piecing Together the Past*. London: Routledge and Kegan Paul.

Christie, P. M. (1967): A barrow cemetery of the second millennium BC in Wiltshire,

England. *Proceedings of the Prehistoric Society*, 33, 336–366.

Clark, G. (1960): *Archaeology and Society: Reconstructing the prehistoric past* (3rd edn). London: Methuen.

Clarke, D. L. (1968): *Analytical Archaeology*. London: Methuen.

—— (1970): *Beaker Pottery of Great Britain and Ireland* (2 vols). Cambridge: Cambridge University Press.

—— (1972): Models and paradigms in contemporary archaeology, in D. L. Clarke (ed.) *Models in Archaeology*. London: Methuen.

—— (1976): The Beaker network – social and economic models, in J. N. Lanting and J. D. van der Waals (eds) *Glockenbechersymposium*, Obberied 1974. Haarlem: Bussum, 459–476.

Clastres, P. (1977): *Society Against the State*. Oxford: Basil Blackwell.

Conkey, M. W. and Gero, J. M. (1991): Tensions, pluralities and engendering archaeology: an introduction to women and prehistory, in J. M. Gero and M. W. Conkey (eds) *Engendering Archaeology*. London: Basil Blackwell, 3–30.

Corcoran, J. X. W. P. (1972): Multi-period construction and the origins of the chambered long cairn in western Britain and Ireland, in F. Lynch and C. Burgess (eds) *Prehistoric Man in Wales and the West: Essays in honour of Lily F. Chitty*. Bath: Adams and Dart, 31–63.

Cosgrove, D. E. (1984): *Social Formation and Symbolic Landscape*. London: Croom Helm.

Cunnington, M. E. (1929): *Woodhenge*. Devizes: George Simpson.

—— (1932): The 'Sanctuary' on Overton Hill, near Avebury. *Wiltshire Archaeological and Natural History Magazine*, 45, 300–335.

Daniel, G. (1963): *The Megalith Builders of Western Europe*. London: Pelican Books.

Davies, S. M., Stacey, L. C. and Woodward, P. J. (1985): Excavations at Alington Avenue, Fordington, Dorchester, 1984/5: Interim report. *Proceedings of the Dorset Natural History and Archaeological Society*, 107, 101–110.

Devereux, P. (1991): Three-dimensional aspects of apparent relationships between natural and artificial features within the topography of the Avebury complex. *Antiquity*, 65, 894–898.

Donaldson, P. (1977): The excavation of a multiple round barrow at Barnack, Cambridgeshire 1974–1976. *Antiquaries Journal*, 57, 197–231.

Drewett, P. (1982): Later bronze age downland economy and excavations at Black Patch, East Sussex. *Proceedings of the Prehistoric Society*, 48, 321–400.

Entwistle, R. (1989): Relativism and Interpretation in Prehistoric Archaeology: Some thoughts on the formulation of archaeological evidence with special reference to the use of palaeo-environmental data. Unpublished PhD thesis, Reading University.

Entwistle, R. and Grant, A. (1989): The evidence for cereal cultivation and animal husbandry in the southern British Neolithic and Bronze Age, in A. Milles, D. Williams and N. Gardner (eds) *The Beginnings of Agriculture*. Oxford: British Archaeological Reports International Series 496, 297–314.

Evans, C. (1988): Acts of enclosure: a consideration of concentrically-organised causewayed enclosures, in J. C. Barrett and I. A. Kinnes (eds) *The Archaeology of Context in the Neolithic and Bronze Age: Recent trends*. Sheffield: J. R. Collis, 85–96.

Evans, J. G. (1984): Stonehenge – the environment in the late neolithic and early bronze age and a beaker-age burial. *Wiltshire Archaeological and Natural History Magazine*, 78, 7–30.

Evans, J. G. and Wainwright, G. J. (1979): The Woodhenge excavations, in G. J. Wainwright (ed.) *Mount Pleasant, Dorset, Excavations 1970–1971*. London: Reports of the Research Committee of the Society of Antiquaries of London No. 37, 71–74.

Falck, C. (1989): *Myth, Truth and Literature: Towards a true post-modernism*. Cambridge: Cambridge University Press.

Fleming, A. (1971): Territorial patterns in Bronze Age Wessex. *Proceedings of the Prehistoric Society*, 37(i), 138–166.

—— (1972): Vision and design: approaches to ceremonial monument typology. *Man*, 7 (n.s.), 57–72.

—— (1973): Tombs for the living. *Man*, 8 (n.s.), 177–193.

—— (1988): *The Dartmoor Reaves*. London: Batsford.

Fletcher, R. (1984): Identifying spatial disorder: a case study of a Mongol Fort, in H. J. Hietala (ed.) *Intrasite Spatial Analysis in Archaeology*. Cambridge: Cambridge University Press, 196–223.

—— (1992): Time perspectivism, *Annales*, and the potential of archaeology, in A. B. Knapp (ed.) *Archaeology, Annales, and Ethnohistory*. Cambridge: Cambridge University Press, 35–49.

Foley, R. (1981): A model of regional archaeological structure. *Proceedings of the Prehistoric Society*, 47, 1–17.

Foucault, M. (1980): *Power/Knowledge: Selected interviews and other writings 1972–1977*. London : Harvester Wheatsheaf.

Friedman, J. and Rowlands, M. J. (1977): Notes towards an epigenetic model of the evolution of 'civilisation', in J. Friedman and M. J. Rowlands (eds) *The Evolution of Social Systems*. London: Duckworth, 201–276.

Gadamer, H.-G. (1975): *Truth and Method*. London: Sheed and Ward.

Garwood, P. (1991): Ritual tradition and the reconstruction of society, in P. Garwood, D. Jennings, R. Skeates and J. Toms (eds) *Sacred and Profane*. Oxford: Oxford University Committee for Archaeology Monograph 32, 10–32.

Gibson, A. M. (1982): *Beaker Domestic Sites*. Oxford: British Archaeological Reports British Series 107, 2 vols.

Giddens, A. (1979): *Central Problems in Social Theory*. London: Macmillan.

—— (1981): *A Contemporary Critique of Historical Materialism*. London: Macmillan.

—— (1984): *The Constitution of Society: Outline of the theory of structuration*. Cambridge: Polity.

—— (1985): *The Nation-State and Violence*. Cambridge: Cambridge University Press.

—— (1987): *Social Theory and Modern Sociology*. Cambridge: Polity.

Gillespie, R., Gowlett, J. A., Hall, E. T., Hedges, R. E. M. and Perry, C. (1985): Radiocarbon dates from the Oxford AMS system: archaeolometry datelist 2. *Archaeometry*, 27, 237–246.

Gingell, C. (1988): Twelve Wiltshire round barrows. Excavations in 1959 and 1961 by F. de M. and H. L. Vatcher. *Wiltshire Archaeological and Natural History Magazine*, 82, 19–76.

Goffman, E. (1971): *The Presentation of Self in Everyday Life*. London: The Penguin Press.

Goody, J. (1976): *Production and Reproduction: A comparative study of the domestic domain*. Cambridge: Cambridge University Press.

—— (1986): *The Logic of Writing and the Organization of Society*. Cambridge: Cambridge University Press.

Graves, C. P. (1989): Social space in the English medieval parish church. *Economy and Society*, 18 (3), 297–322.

Gray, H. St. G. (1935): The Avebury excavations 1908–1922. *Archaeologia*, 84, 99–162.

Green, C., Lynch, F. and White, H. (1982): The excavation of two round barrows on Launceston Down, Dorset (Long Crichel 5 and 7). *Proceedings of the Dorset Natural History and Archaeological Society*, 104, 39–58.

Green, C. and Rollo-Smith, S. (1984): The excavation of eighteen round barrows near Shrewton, Wiltshire. *Proceedings of the Prehistoric Society*, 50, 255–318.

Gregory, D. and Urry, J. (1985): *Social Relations and Spatial Structures*. London: Macmillan.

Grigson, C. (1982): Porridge and pannage: pig husbandry in neolithic England, in M. Bell and S. Limbrey (eds) *Archaeological Aspects of Woodland Ecology*. Oxford: British Archaeological Reports International Series 146, 297–314.

Grinsell, L. V. (1950): Shaving off the eyebrows as a sign of mourning. *Man*, 50, 144.

Harding, A. F. (1989): Interpreting the evidence for agricultural change in the late bronze age in northern Europe, in H.-A. Nordstrom and A. Knape (eds) *Bronze Age Studies*. Stockholm: Statens Historiska Museum, 173–181.

Harding, A. F. and Lee, G. E. (1987): *Henge Monuments and Related Sites of Great Britain*. Oxford: British Archaeological Reports 175.

Harrison, R. J. (1980): *The Beaker Folk: Copper age archaeology in western Europe*. London: Thames and Hudson.

Hawley, W. (1924): Fourth report on the excavations at Stonehenge. *Antiquaries Journal*, 4, 30–39.

—— (1925): Report on the excavations at Stonehenge during the season of 1923. *Antiquaries Journal*, 5, 21–50.

—— (1926): Report on the excavations at Stonehenge during the season of 1924. *Antiquaries Journal*, 6, 1–25.

—— (1928): Report on the excavations at Stonehenge during 1925 and 1926. *Antiquaries Journal*, 8, 149–176.

Heckman, S. (1986): *Hermeneutics and the Sociology of Knowledge*. Cambridge: Cambridge University Press.

Helms, M. W. (1988): *Ulysses' Sail*. Princeton: Princeton University Press.

Hertz, R. (1907): Contribution à une étude sur la représentation collective de la mort. *Année Sociologique*, 10, 48–137.

Hoare, R. C. (1810): *The Ancient History of Wiltshire*, vol. I: *South Wiltshire*. London: William Miller.

Hodder, I. (1984): Archaeology in 1984. *Antiquity*, 58, 25–32.

Hodder, I. (1985): Postprocessual archaeology. *Advances in Archaeological Method and Theory*, 8, 1–26.

—— (1989): This is not an article about material culture as text. *Journal of Anthropological Archaeology*, 8, 250–269.

—— (1990): *The Domestication of Europe*. Oxford: Basil Blackwell.

—— (1991): *Reading the Past* (2nd edn). Cambridge: Cambridge University Press.

Hughes, I. (1988): Megaliths: space, time and landscape – a view from the Clyde. *Scottish Archaeological Review*, 5, 41–56.

Huntington, R. and Metcalf, P. (1979): *Celebrations of Death: The anthropology of mortuary ritual*. Cambridge: Cambridge University Press.

Ingold, T. (1980): *Hunters, Pastoralists and Ranchers*. Cambridge: Cambridge University Press.

—— (1986): *The Appropriation of Nature: Essays on human ecology and social relations*. Manchester: Manchester University Press.

Jenkins, K. (1991): *Re-thinking History*. London: Routledge.

Johnson, D. E. (1980): The excavation of a Bell-Barrow at Sutten Veny, Wilts. *Wiltshire Archaeological and Natural History Magazine*, 72/73, 29–50.

Kinnes, I. (1975): Monumental function in British Neolithic burial practices. *World Archaeology*, 7, 16–29.

—— (1979): *Round Barrows and Ring-ditches in the British Neolithic*. London: British Museum

Occasional Paper No. 7.

—— (1981): Dialogues with death, in R. Chapman, I. Kinnes and K. Randsborg (eds) *The Archaeology of Death*. Cambridge: Cambridge University Press, 83–91.

—— (1985): *British Bronze Age Metalwork: Associated Finds Series* (A7-16 Beaker and Early Bronze Age grave groups). London: British Museum Publications.

—— (1992): *Non-Megalithic Long Barrows and Allied Structures in the British Neolithic*. London: British Museum Occasional Papers 52.

Kinnes, I., Gibson, A., Ambers, J., Bowman, S. and Boast, R. (1991): Radiocarbon dating and British beakers: The British Museum programme. *Scottish Archaeological Review*, 8, 35–68.

Kopytoff, I. (1986): The cultural biography of things: commoditization as process, in A. Appadurai (ed.) *The Social Life of Things*. Cambridge: Cambridge University Press, 64–91.

Kristiansen, K. (1978): The consumption of wealth in Bronze Age Denmark, in K. Kristiansen and C. Paludan-Muller (eds) *New Directions in Scandinavian Archaeology*. Copenhagen: National Museum of Denmark, 158–190.

Lanting, J. N. and van der Waals, J. D. (1972): British beakers as seen from the continent. *Helinium*, 12, 20–46.

Lawson, A. J. (1990): The prehistoric hinterland of Maiden Castle. *Antiquaries Journal*, 70, 271–287.

Layton, R. (1986): Political and territorial structures among hunter-gatherers. *Man*, 21 (n.s.), 18–33.

Leach, E. (1973): Concluding address, in C. Renfrew (ed.) *The Explanation of Culture Change: Models in prehistory*. London: Duckworth, 761–771.

Lévi-Strauss, C. (1972): *The Savage Mind*. London: Weidenfeld and Nicolson.

Lynch, F. (1973): The use of the passage in certain passage graves as a means of communication rather than access, in G. Daniel and P. Kjaerum (eds) *Megalithic Graves and Ritual*. Copenhagen: Jutland Archaeological Society (Proceedings of the 3rd Atlantic Colloquium, Moesgard 1969), 147–161.

MacKie, E. W. (1977): *Science and Society in Prehistoric Britain*. London: Paul Elek.

Malone, C. (1989): *Avebury*. London: Batsford and English Heritage.

Mann, M. (1986): *The Sources of Social Power*, vol. 1: *A History of Power from the Beginning to AD 1760*. Cambridge: Cambridge University Press.

Meillassoux, C. (1972): From reproduction to production. *Economy and Society*, 1, 93–105.

Mellars, P. (1976): Settlement patterns and industrial variability in the British mesolithic, in G. de G. Sieveking, I. H. Longworth and K. E. Wilson (eds) *Problems in Economic and Social Archaeology*. London: Duckworth, 375–399.

Mellars, P. and Reinhart, S. C. (1978): Patterns of mesolithic land-use in southern England: a geological perspective, in P. Mellars (ed.) *The Early Postglacial Settlement of Northern Europe: An ecological perspective*. London: Duckworth, 243–293.

Mercer, R. (ed.) (1977): *Beakers in Britain and Europe*. Oxford: British Archaeological Reports Supplementary Series 26.

Miller, D. and Tilley, C. (1984): Ideology, power and prehistory: an introduction, in D. Miller and C. Tilley (eds) *Ideology, Power and Prehistory*. Cambridge: Cambridge University Press 1–15.

Moore, H. L. (1986): *Space, Text and Gender: An anthropological study of the Marakwet of Kenya*. Cambridge: Cambridge University Press.

Musson, C. R. (1971): A study of possible building forms at Durrington Walls, Woodhenge and The Sanctuary, in G. J. Wainwright and I. H. Longworth (eds) *Durrington Walls:*

Excavations 1966–1968. London: Reports of the Research Committee of the Society of Antiquaries of London No. 29, 363–377.

Needham, S. P. (1988): Selective deposition in the British Early Bronze Age. *World Archaeology*, 20, 229–248.

Olsen, B. (1990): Roland Barthes: from sign to text, in C. Tilley (ed.) *Reading Material Culture*. Oxford: Basil Blackwell, 163–205.

O'Shea, J. M. (1984): *Mortuary Variability: An archaeological investigation*. London: Academic Press.

Pader, E.-J. (1982): *Symbolism, Social Relations and the Interpretation of Mortuary Remains*. Oxford: British Archaeological Reports International Series 130.

Parker Pearson, M. (1984): Economic and ideological change: cyclical growth in the pre-state societies of Jutland, in D. Miller and C. Tilley (eds) *Ideology, Power and Prehistory*. Cambridge: Cambridge University Press, 69–92.

Patrik, L. E. (1985): Is there an archaeological record? *Advances in Archaeological Method and Theory*, 8, 27–62.

Piggott, C. M. (1942): Five late bronze age enclosures in north Wiltshire. *Proceedings of the Prehistoric Society*, 8, 48–61.

Piggott, S. (1940): Timber circles: a re-examination. *Archaeological Journal*, 96, 193–222.

—— (1954): *The Neolithic Cultures of the British Isles*. Cambridge: Cambridge University Press.

—— (1962): *The West Kennet Long Barrow: Excavations 1955–56*. London: HMSO.

—— (1964): Excavations at Avebury, 1960. *Wiltshire Archaeological and Natural History Magazine*, 59, 28–29.

—— (1965): *Ancient Europe*. Edinburgh: Edinburgh University Press.

Pitt Rivers, A. L. F. (1898): *Excavations in Cranborne Chase*, vol. 4. Rushmore: privately published.

Pitts, M. W. (1982): On the road to Stonehenge: report on investigations beside the A344 in 1968, 1979 and 1980. *Proceedings of the Prehistoric Society*, 48, 75–132.

Pred, A. (1977): The choreography of existence: comments on Hagerstrand's time-geography and its usefulness. *Economic Geography*, 53, 207–221.

Proudfoot, E. V. W. (1963): Report on the excavation of a bell barrow in the parish of Edmondsham, Dorset, England 1959. *Proceedings of the Prehistoric Society*, 29, 395–425.

Ray, K. (1988): Context, Meaning and Metaphor in an Historical Archaeology: Igbo Ukwu, Eastern Nigeria. Unpublished PhD thesis, Cambridge University.

RCHME (1979): *Stonehenge and its Environs: Monuments and land use*. Edinburgh: Edinburgh University Press.

Renfrew, C. (1972): *The Emergence of Civilisation: The Cyclades and the Aegean in the third millennium BC*. London: Methuen.

—— (1973): Monuments, mobilization and social organization in neolithic Wessex, in C. Renfrew (ed.) *The Explanation of Culture Change: Models in prehistory*. London: Duckworth, 539–558.

—— (1976): Megaliths, territories and populations, in S. J. De Laet (ed.) *Acculturation and Continuity in Atlantic Europe*. Bruges: De Tempel, 198–220.

—— (1977): Space, time and polity, in J. Friedman and M. J. Rowlands (eds) *The Evolution of Social Systems*. London: Duckworth, 89–112.

—— (1979): Transformations, in C. Renfrew and K. L. Cooke (eds) *Transformations: Mathematical approaches to culture change*. London: Academic Press, 3–44.

—— (1982): Explanation revisited, in C. Renfrew, M. J. Rowlands and B. A. Seagrave (eds)

Theory and Explanation in Archaeology. London: Academic Press, 5–23.

—— (1984): *Approaches to Social Archaeology*. Edinburgh: Edinburgh University Press.

Richards, C. (1992): Doorways to another world: the Orkney-Cromarty chambered tombs, in N. Sharples and A. Sheridan (eds) *Vessels for the Ancestors*. Edinburgh: Edinburgh University Press, 62–76.

Richards, C. and Thomas, J. (1984): Ritual activity and structured deposition in later neolithic Wessex, in R. Bradley and J. Gardiner (eds) *Neolithic Studies: A review of some current research*. Oxford: British Archaeological Reports 133, 189–218.

Richards, J. (1990): *The Stonehenge Environs Project*. London: Historic Buildings and Monuments Commission for England, Archaeological Report No. 16.

Ricoeur, P. (1981): *Hermeneutics and the Human Sciences*. Cambridge: Cambridge University Press.

Robertson-MacKay, M. E. (1980): A 'head and hooves' burial beneath a round-barrow, with other neolithic and bronze age sites, on Hemp Knoll, near Avebury, Wiltshire. *Proceedings of the Prehistoric Society*, 46, 123–176.

Russel, A. D. (1990): Two beaker burials from Chilbolton, Hampshire. *Proceedings of the Prehistoric Society*, 56, 153–172.

Sahlins, M. (1987): *Islands of History*. London: Tavistock Publications.

Sangmeister, E. (1963): Exposé sur la civilisation du Vase Campaniforme. *Actes du Premiere Colloque Atlantique, Brest 1961*. Rennes, 25–55.

Shanks, M. and Tilley, C. (1987a): *Re-Constructing Archaeology: Theory and practice*. Cambridge: Cambridge University Press.

—— (1987b): *Social Theory and Archaeology*. Cambridge: Polity.

Sharples, N. M. (1991): *Maiden Castle: Excavations and field survey 1985–6*. London: Historic Buildings and Monuments Commission for England.

Shennan, S. J. (1978): Archaeological cultures: an empirical investigation, in I. Hodder (ed.) *The Spatial Organisation of Culture*. London: Duckworth, 114–139.

—— (1982): Ideology, change and the European Early Bronze Age, in I. Hodder (ed.) *Symbolic and Structural Archaeology*. Cambridge: Cambridge University Press, 155–161.

—— (1986): Interaction and change in third millennium BC western and central Europe, in C. Renfrew and J. F. Cherry (eds) *Peer Polity Interaction and Socio-Political Change*. Cambridge: Cambridge University Press, 137–148.

Sherratt, A. (1981): Plough and pastoralism: aspects of the secondary products revolution, in I. Hodder, G. Isaac and N. Hammond (eds) *Pattern of the Present: Studies in honour of David Clarke*. Cambridge: Cambridge University Press, 261–305.

—— (1986): The Radley 'earrings' revisited. *Oxford Journal of Archaeology*, 5, 61–66.

—— (1987): Cups that cheered, in W. H. Waldren and R. C. Kennard (eds) *Beakers in Britain and Europe*. Oxford: British Archaeological Reports International Series 331, 81–114.

Smith, I. F. (1965): *Windmill Hill and Avebury: Excavations by Alexander Keiller 1925–1939*. Oxford: Clarendon Press.

Smith, I. F. and Simpson, D. D. A. (1966): Excavation of a round barrow on Overton Hill, North Wiltshire. *Proceedings of the Prehistoric Society*, 32, 122–155.

Smith, M. A. (1955): The limitations of inference in archaeology. *The Archaeological News Letter*, 6, 3–7.

Smith, R. W. (1984): The ecology of neolithic farming systems as exemplified by the Avebury region of Wiltshire. *Proceedings of the Prehistoric Society*, 50, 99–120.

Startin, W. and Bradley, R. (1981): Some notes on work organisation and society in Neolithic

Wessex, in C. L. N. Ruggles and A. W. R. Whittle (eds) *Astronomy and Society in Britain during the Period 4000–1500 BC*. Oxford: British Archaeological Reports 88, 289–296.

Tainter, J. A. (1978): Mortuary practices and the study of prehistoric social systems. *Advances in Archaeological Method and Theory*, 1, 105–141.

Thomas, J. (1988a): The social significance of Cotswold-Severn burial practices. *Man*, 23 (n.s.), 540–559.

—— (1988b): Neolithic explanations revisited: the mesolithic–neolithic transition in Britain and southern Scandinavia. *Proceedings of the Prehistoric Society*, 54, 59–66.

—— (1991): *Rethinking the Neolithic*. Cambridge: Cambridge University Press.

Thomas, J. and Whittle, A. W. R. (1986): Anatomy of a tomb: West Kennet revisited. *Oxford Journal of Archaeology*, 5, 129–156.

Thomas, K. (1983): *Man and the Natural World: Changing attitudes in England 1500–1800*. London: Allen Lane.

Thompson, E. P. (1968): *The Making of the English Working Class*. London: Pelican.

Thorpe, I. J. and Richards, C. (1984): The decline of ritual authority and the introduction of beakers into Britain, in R. Bradley and J. Gardiner (eds) *Neolithic Studies: A review of some current research*. Oxford: British Archaeological Reports 133, 67–84.

Thurnam, J. (1869): On Ancient British barrows: Part 1, long barrows. *Archaeologia*, 42, 161–244.

—— (1871): On Ancient British barrows: Part 2, round barrows. *Archaeologia*, 43, 285–552.

Tilley, C. (ed.) (1990): *Reading Material Culture*. Oxford: Basil Blackwell.

Trigger, B. G. (1990): Maintaining economic equality in opposition to complexity: an Iroquoian case study, in S. Upham (ed.) *The Evolution of Political Systems: Sociopolitics in small-scale sedentary societies*. Cambridge: Cambridge University Press, 119–145.

Turner, V. (1967): *The Forest of Symbols: Aspects of Ndembu ritual*. London: Cornell University Press.

—— (1977): *The Ritual Process: Structure and anti-structure*. Ithaca, NY: Cornell University Press.

Ucko, P. J., Hunter, M., Clark, A. J. and David, A. (1991): *Avebury Reconsidered: From the 1660s to the 1990s* (2 vols). London: Unwin Hyman.

Van Gennep, A. (1960): *The Rites of Passage*. London: Routledge and Kegan Paul.

Vita-Finzi, C. and Higgs, E. S. (1970): Prehistoric economy in the Mount Carmel area of Palestine: site catchment analysis. *Proceedings of the Prehistoric Society*, 36, 1–37.

Wainwright, G. J. (1971): The excavation of a late neolithic enclosure at Marden, Wiltshire. *Antiquaries Journal*, 51, 177–239.

—— (1979): *Mount Pleasant, Dorset, Excavations 1970–1971*. London: Reports of the Research Committee of the Society of Antiquaries of London No. 37.

Wainwright, G. J. and Longworth, I. H. (eds) (1971): *Durrington Walls: Excavations 1966–1968*. London: Reports of the Research Committee of the Society of Antiquaries of London No. 29.

Waldren, W. H. and Kennard, R. C. (1987): *Beakers in Britain and Europe*. Oxford: British Archaeological Reports International Series 331.

Warnke, G. (1987): *Gadamer: Hermeneutics, tradition and reason*. Cambridge: Polity.

Wheatley, P. (1971): *The Pivot of the Four Quarters*. Edinburgh: Edinburgh University Press.

Wheeler, R. E. M. (1943): *Maiden Castle Dorset*. London: Reports of the Research Committee of the Society of Antiquaries of London No. 12.

Wheeler, M. (1956): *Archaeology from the Earth*. London: Penguin Books.

White, D. A. (1982): *The Bronze Age Cremation Cemeteries at Simons Ground, Dorset*. Dorchester: Dorset Natural History and Archaeological Society Monograph Series, No. 3.

Whittle, A. W. R. (1977): *The Earlier Neolithic of E. England and its Continental Background*. Oxford: British Archaeological Reports Supplementary Series 35.

—— (1981): Later neolithic society in Britain: a realignment, in C. L. N. Ruggles and A. W. R. Whittle (eds) *Astronomy and Society in Britain during the Period 4000–1500 BC*. Oxford: British Archaeological Reports 88, 297–342.

—— (1990a): A pre-enclosure burial at Windmill Hill, Wiltshire. *Oxford Journal of Archaeology*, 9, 25–28.

—— (1990b): A model for the mesolithic–neolithic transition in the Upper Kennet valley, north Wiltshire. *Proceedings of the Prehistoric Society*, 56, 101–110.

—— (1991): A late Neolithic complex at West Kennet, Wiltshire, England. *Antiquity*, 65, 256–262.

—— (forthcoming): Silbury Hill, Wiltshire: excavations in 1968–70 by R. J. C. Atkinson.

Woodburn, J. (1980): Hunters and gatherers today and reconstruction of the past, in E. Gellner (ed.) *Soviet and Western Anthropology*. London: Duckworth, 95–117.

Woodward, P. J. (1991): *The South Dorset Ridgeway: Survey and excavation 1977–84*. Dorchester: Dorset Natural History and Archaeological Society Monograph Series, No. 8.

Woodward, P. J., Davies, S. M. and Graham, A. H. (1984): Excavations on the Greyhound Yard Car Park, Dorchester, 1984. *Proceedings of the Dorset Natural History and Archaeological Society*, 106, 99–106.

Woodward, P. J. and Smith, R. J. C. (1987): Survey and excavation along the route of the southern Dorchester By-pass, 1986–1987 – An interim note. *Proceedings of the Dorset Natural History and Archaeological Society*, 109, 79–89.

Wylie, A. (1989): Matters of fact and matters of interest, in S. Shennan (ed.) *Archaeological Approaches to Cultural Identity*. London: Unwin Hyman, 94–109.

Yates, T. (1990): Archaeology through the Looking-Glass, in I. Bapty and T. Yates (eds) *Archaeology after Structuralism*. London: Routledge, 154–202.

Index